NARRATING THE CLOSET

Writing Lives
Ethnographic Narratives

SERIES EDITORS:

Arthur P. Bochner & Carolyn Ellis
University of South Florida

Writing Lives: Ethnographic Narratives publishes narrative representations of qualitative research projects. The series editors seek manuscripts that blur the boundaries between humanities and social
sciences. We encourage novel and evocative forms of expressing con-
crete lived experience, including autoethnographic, literary, poetic,
artistic, visual, performative, critical, multivoiced, conversational,
and co-constructed representations. We are interested in ethnographic narratives that depict local stories; employ literary modes of
scene setting, dialogue, character development, and unfolding action;
and include the author's critical reflections on the research and writing process, such as research ethics, alternative modes of inquiry and
representation, reflexivity, and evocative storytelling. Proposals and
manuscripts should be directed to abochner@cas.usf.edu
Volumes in this series:

Erotic Mentoring: Women's Transformations in the University, Janice
Hocker Rushing
*Intimate Colonialism: Head, Heart, and Body in West African Develop-
ment Work*, Laurie L. Charlés
Last Writes: A Daybook for a Dying Friend, Laurel Richardson
A Trickster in Tweed: The Quest for Quality in a Faculty Life, Thomas F.
Frentz
Guyana Diaries: Women's Lives Across Difference, Kimberly D. Nettles
*Writing Qualitative Inquiry: Selves, Stories and the New Politics of Aca-
demic Success*, H. L. Goodall, Jr.
Accidental Ethnography: An Inquiry into Family Secrecy, Christopher
N. Poulos
Revision: Autoethnographic Reflections on Life and Work, Carolyn Ellis
Leaning: A Poetics of Personal Relationships, Ronald J. Pelias
Narrating the Closet: An Autoethnography of Same-Sex Attraction, Tony
E. Adams

Narrating the Closet

An Autoethnography of Same-Sex Attraction

Tony E. Adams

Walnut Creek, California

Left Coast Press is committed to preserving ancient forests
and natural resources. We elected to print this title on 30% post
consumer recycled paper, processed chlorine free. As a result,
for this printing, we have saved:

2 Trees (40' tall and 6-8" diameter)
1 Million BTUs of Total Energy
179 Pounds of Greenhouse Gases
864 Gallons of Wastewater
52 Pounds of Solid Waste

Left Coast Press made this paper choice because our printer,
Thomson-Shore, Inc., is a member of Green Press Initiative,
a nonprofit program dedicated to supporting authors, publish-
ers, and suppliers in their efforts to reduce their use of fiber
obtained from endangered forests.

For more information, visit www.greenpressinitiative.org

Environmental impact estimates were made using the Environmental Defense
Paper Calculator. For more information visit: www.papercalculator.org.

LEFT COAST PRESS, INC.
1630 North Main Street, #400
Walnut Creek, CA 94596
http://www.LCoastPress.com

ISBN 978-1-59874-619-8 hardcover
ISBN 978-1-59874-620-4 paperback
ISBN 978-1-59874-621-1 electronic

Library of Congress Cataloging-in-Publication Data:

Adams, Tony E.
Narrating the closet : an autoethnography of same-sex attraction / Tony E.
Adams.
     p. cm.—(Writing lives : ethnographic narratives)
Includes bibliographical references and index.
ISBN 978-1-59874-619-8 (hardcover : alk. paper)—ISBN 978-1-59874-620-4
(pbk. : alk. paper)
1. Male homosexuality. 2. Gay couples. 3. Ethnology—Authorship. I. Title.
     GN484.35.A33 2011
     306.76'6—dc22

                              2010052550

Printed in the United States of America

∞™ The paper used in this publication meets the minimum requirements
of American National Standard for Information Sciences—Permanence of
Paper for Printed Library Materials, ANSI/NISO Z39.48–1992.

CONTENTS

PREFACE

When I came out to myself—when I realized that I found men attractive and began to think of myself as "gay"—I struggled immensely. I felt deviant, immoral, and ashamed for possessing such an attraction. I isolated myself from friends and family. I did not care much about life and engaged in numerous behaviors that endangered myself and others.

When I came out to others—when I told people that I found men attractive and that I identified as gay—more struggles emerged. Some friends said my attraction was "just a phase" and that I would "find a good woman" or "correct myself" soon. One family member no longer allowed me in her house, and another refused to speak to me for months. Some people accused me of hiding, lying, and being manipulative for not disclosing my attraction earlier. One person attempted to get me fired from teaching, and a few devoutly-Baptist folks tried to "save" me from my homosexual tendencies. Even though I simultaneously received unwavering support from many people, these instances of negativity never felt good.

I also know my struggles are not unique. Frequently I hear about young adults who have killed themselves because of shame, bullying, and people disparaging them for identifying as or being perceived to be lesbian, gay, bisexual, or queer (LGBQ). I regularly read reports of politicians calling homosexuality a disease, countries imprisoning or killing lesbians and gays because of their desire, and religious organizations condemning not only persons with same-sex attraction but also others who advocate for acceptance of and respect for these persons. I constantly hear about everyday struggles of sexuality from friends and acquaintances and, as a teacher, often encounter stories from LGBQ students about being physically harmed, kicked out of homes for coming out, and considered good for nothing by (former) friends and family.

I thus arrive at this book, a project that documents struggles of the closet, coming out, and same-sex attraction—struggles that, in my opinion, never end but rather continue over the course of a LGBQ person's life. In particular, I use autoethnography, interviews, life stories, and media and textual analyses to describe and analyze experiences of the closet—experiences of entering the closet, being closeted, and coming out—as well as discern paradoxical demands of the closet in everyday life. Throughout I illustrate how the closet functions as a perpetual, constitutive metaphor that prohibits a LGBQ person from living as an out person everywhere, all the time. I also show how the closet functions as a relational phenomenon, a construct for which *others* may hold a person accountable at a variety of times, in a variety of ways, and in a variety of places, and a construct that implicates persons of *all* sexualities.

And so I invite you on a journey of promise and pain. I invite you to consider the closet and coming out in nuanced ways. I invite you into a discussion that not only promotes compassion and understanding but may also make experiences of same-sex attraction more humane and tolerable. I invite you into a project that gives a voice to those afraid to speak or who have ended their lives for feeling less than human. I invite you into a work that encourages us all to acknowledge and appreciate one another more.

Acknowledgments

Every story I tell implicates others—friends and family, students and acquaintances, co-workers and colleagues. Here I want to recognize and thank some of these others, all of whom make, and have made, my life and my stories possible: Wendy Adams, Ric Ashcraft, Ahmet Atay, Nilanjana Bardhan, Marielana Bartesaghi, Korrie Bauman, Elizabeth Bell, Laura Bergeron, Christopher Birdsong, Derek Bolen, Robin Boylorn, Jay Brower, David Brunnell, Ken Cissna, Ann Copeland, Amy Darnell, Norm Denzin, Sara Dykins Callahan, Rachel Dubrofsky, Liz Edgecomb, Eric Eisenberg, Laura Ellingson, Patty English, Craig Engstrom, Elissa Foster, George Garrett, Ryan

Gildersleeve, Craig Gingrich-Philbrook, Bud Goodall, Jonny Gray, Charles Guignon, Scott Gust, Antoine Hardy, Andrew Herrmann, Stacy Holman Jones, Kathy Hytten, Travis Jameson, Richard Jones, Jane Jorgenson, Ashley Kincaid, Kim Kline, Yvonne Kline, Michael Levan, Linda Levitt, Wren Levitt, Cara Mackie, Jimmie Manning, Hilary Mathis, Kathy Mathis, Stephanie Mathis, Christy McIntyre, Chris McRae, Lucas Mehl, Sebastian Melo, Michaela Meyer, Derick Miller, Jeanine Minge, Ben Myers, Mark Neumann, Cheryl Nicholas, Mike Nicholas, David Payne, Ron Pelias, Sandy Pensoneau-Conway, Steve Phalen, Amy Pinney, Sheri Plummer, Chris Poulos, Carl Ratner, Craig Rich, Lori Roscoe, Leslie Rossman, Emily Ryalls, Patrick Santoro, Steve Schoen, Rachel Silverman, Jackie Smith, Larry Smith, Fred Steier, Nathan Stucky, Satoshi Toyosaki, Lane Thompson, Lisa Tillmann, Jillian Tullis, Chantal Varga, Adrienne Viramontes, Gina Warren, John Warren, Keysha Williams, Tim Willis, Jonathan Wyatt, Karen Wynn, Shawn Wynn, Wayne Wynn, Wayne Wynn, Jr., and Cameron Young.

I thank many of the students at Northeastern Illinois University, who remind me about the importance of education, particularly Jeremy Babcock, Matt Calabrese, Donna Goering, Nicole Kashian, Michalina Maliszewska, Dan Rippeteau, and Alexis Waters. I also express immense gratitude for my colleagues: Wilfredo Alvarez, Anna Antaramian, Karol Bayley, Katrina Bell-Jordan, John Bliss, Bernard Brommel, Melanie Bujan, Lisa Cantwell, Rodney Higginbotham, Kate Kane, Craig Kois, Cyndi Moran, Seung-Hwan Mun, Nanette Potee, Bob Ritesma, John Ross, Edie Rubinowitz, and Dan Wirth.

I thank Nicole Neuman for helping me write my first college paper; Brad Gangnon for helping me come out; Michael Connolly and Julie Wight for talking through drafts of this work; Stacey C. Sawyer for guiding me through the editing process; Michael Rome for unwavering support; Phil Adams for teaching me about resiliency; Marcy Chvasta for having faith in me and my work; and Lenore Langsdorf for showing me the joys of reading, writing, and revising.

I thank Brian Flowers for creating profound and engaging cover art.

I thank Keith Berry for making life so enjoyable.

I thank Brett Aldridge for his life; I miss you.

I thank Mitch Allen not only for granting me the honor to publish with Left Coast Press but also for making the publishing process seamless and meaningful.

I thank Carolyn Ellis and Art Bochner for never allowing me to fail, for pushing me to take risks, and for encouraging me to be the best person possible.

I thank Sharon Rome for teaching me about unconditional love.

And I thank Gerardo Moreno for having patience with long nights of drafting and editing. I hope I continue to make you happy for a very long time. I love you.

Tony Adams
January 2011

A Love Story Assembled from Primary Sources

A Hallmark card: two white dogs occupy the front, facing each other, trying to interlock jaws. A comic bubble emerges from one dog's mouth. The card reads, "I lick you. I mean, I LIKE you," followed by an inside inscription of "Okay, both" and a personal message: "Baby, have a happy end of the semester. I love you!! Phish kissee. ♥ Brett"

□

"Phish kissee": a term of endearment that Brett and I made after adopting a Beta fish named Alexander Prettifish. Brett and I would exchange fish kisses, an act modeled after what the two of us thought phish kissees would look and feel like.

□

A yellow Post-It note placed on my office desk: "Phish Kissee to a boy who has a thesis." I defended my Master's thesis that day. It included a dedication to Brett: "Thank you for your remarkable presence this past year. I hope that, at least in some form or another, you will always remain in my life. And thank you for understanding when it came to my school-related stuff. I may have been busy, but I thought of you often."

A. E. ADAMS (2003, p. ii)

11

☐

A dedication to me, from Brett, in his Master's thesis, a project completed one year after mine, one month after moving away from each other, 20 months before his death: "To Tony, my closest friend and unfailing support: who has taught me that love may adapt and evolve in disconcerting ways . . . but may also, from time to time, escape intact, if not quite unscathed."

A<small>LDRIDGE</small> (2004, p. iii)

☐

Another note: "Good morning and good morning. Fish kissee and fish kissee."

☐

A card for my 24th birthday. The front has an image of an ornately dressed woman of Asian descent surrounded by an array of flowers, the inside filled with a personal message:

> *Happy Birthday. I love you and hope you have a good day and year, you dirty old man!! I hope you'll let me take you out for a birthday dinner tonight or later this week.*
> *Have a happy, happy day.*
> *Happy Birthday to you!*
> *Happy Birthday to you!*
> *etc. etc.*
> *♥ Brett*

☐

A note posted on my desk: "Hello Tony. I am writing a paper and became afraid that my brain might explode so I thought I'd write you a little note. Here it is, Brett."
Another yellow Post-it: "Thank you darling!!"
And another: "Fish kissee."
And another: "Hello from Brett A. Fish kissee. Fish kissee. Fish kissee."
And another: "Darling, I went home. Call me there when you get here."

☐

A note with relational code: "Who is a pumpkin?" followed by "Who is?" followed by "Who?" followed by "♥." "Pumpkin" became our intimate term for each other, a term I'll never use on or around anyone ever again.

□

"Tony, I am in the Kleinau [theatre], or as the French call it, Le Kleinau," another note reads. "Come find me and we will have talking. ♥ B"

I can tell a lot about a person by the language she or he uses. Brett: Creative, energetic, and bursting with love, note after note after note.

A Love Story Culled from Memory

Brett's desk is behind mine. Backs facing each other, the two of us exchange comments about his first time teaching and his first time in graduate school and about my second year teaching and my second year in the same graduate program. I find Brett fun and attractive but never consider dating him because I'm insecure (and don't think he'd like me) and fear rejection (so I never express interest). Besides, a friend of mine likes him, and I don't want to interfere. I'm also interested in a different guy who's not interested in me, a man I often talk about with Brett, my back-faced colleague. Positioned in this way, I cannot see Brett's face, the face of a person I upset with my talk about the other man: Brett liked me but never said so; he was insecure and feared rejection, too. Besides, he knew I liked someone else and didn't want to interfere.

□

I arrange a dinner with the guy I like and his best friend, not a date just a friendly meeting. I tell Brett that he's welcome to come. He says he'd like to and that he'd drive. In his purple Pontiac Sunfire, I notice unwrapped needles strewn about the floor. "I'm diabetic," Brett says. "Cool," I say, not knowing what diabetes is or why diabetes has any relation to the needles.

□

"Brett slipped into a diabetic coma one night. . . . He had talked to some friends earlier that day and felt fine" (Joshua, 2006).[1]

□

At the restaurant I sit next to the guy I like who doesn't like me. Brett and the guy's best friend sit on the opposite side of the table. Everyone eats chips and salsa, rice and beans. I watch Brett pull out a needle, insert it into a bottle of clear liquid, and then into his upper arm. "I'm diabetic," he says as he wipes a drop of blood from the quickly pierced skin.

The dinner ends and nothing progresses with the guy I like. He refuses to date, even though I continuously probe him about dating. Brett and his friend pretend they do not hear me get rejected. Feeling foolish and insecure, I try to stay friends, believing that friendship is better than nothing, though I hope he'll change his mind and realize that the two of us would be good together. I say "bye" to the guy and his friend, get into the purple car and hope that Brett had an okay time, hope that he doesn't find me silly, hope that he won't quit talking with me.

□

The next day at the office Brett greets me with a nervous "Hi."

"Hope you had fun last night," I say.

He replies with a "Yes, I did" followed by "Would you go on a date with me?"

An ambivalent "sure" comes from my mouth, shocked that he would ask after the previous night's affair, shocked that he, a fun and attractive person would find me, Mr. Insecurity, attractive.

"I've wanted to ask you for the past month," Brett says, "but you always talked about the other guy and I didn't want to interfere. Being insecure, I didn't want to feel rejected."

□

A date at Garfield's. While looking at the menu, the two of us realize that we're both vegetarian and should've gone to a veggie-friendly place. We also realize that the two of us aren't there for the food. The meeting is about being and talking together, seeing if we are compatible, seeing if Brett is likable, seeing if he finds me likable, seeing if I can quit thinking about the other guy I like. When the food arrives, Brett takes out a needle, fills it with insulin, and inserts it into his upper thigh. This time the shot does not draw blood. I try to fathom how inserting a needle into the body feels.

The date goes well and ends with a brief kiss. At school the next day I ask if he'd like another date. He says "yes." So we go on another date and continue being together, often, for the next year and a half.

☐

"I had sex with another man," Brett says on entering our apartment. I look at him, quickly, and then laugh. I think, hope, he's kidding. "I promised that I'd always be honest with you," he continues. "It happened last week when you weren't home."

☐

I know Brett's home tonight in his room listening to Judy Garland, k. d. lang, or *The Mikado* soundtrack. At the gay bar across the street I'm on the prowl for an attractive man to make Brett jealous, to flaunt my guy-catching abilities. After a few drinks I spot a victim and invite him to stay the night. I lie by saying I live with a friend whom I've never been attracted to and with whom I've never been intimate. My prey agrees to stay. Entering the apartment the two of us move toward my room but are interrupted by Brett opening his bedroom door to apologize for hurting me and to wish me a good night. He sees my man and slams the door without saying anything. I've won, but still feel sad, ashamed, and immature. Some victory.

☐

"Brett slipped into a diabetic coma one night. . . . He had talked to some friends earlier that day and felt fine." (Joshua, 2006)

☐

Brett's the guy I lived with when I came out to my dad. Brett and I moved in together one month before my dad's memorable call.

"I heard a rumor about you," my dad says. I become nervous. "I heard that you're living with a guy. In fact, not just living with, but *fucking* this guy. Is this true?"

"Weeelllll," I stutter, "no, it's not true. Who would say something like that?"

"That doesn't matter. I'm just glad it ain't," he says.

"Yeah, me, too, father. That's silly. I'll talk to you soon." The conversation ends.

Before this conversation I had decided to never come out to my father. I planned to live my entire life without telling him that I am gay. I feared being disowned and hated and did not feel I could deal with his response.

"Call him back," Brett pleads. "This is your chance."

But here was Brett, a person who came into my life, loving me, teaching me the value of openness, giving me the strength to do what I never imagined doing before. I called dad back.

"Hello," he answers in an upbeat, much happier tone.

"Yeah, dad, it's me. I just wanted to tell you that it's true—I am living with a guy, my boyfriend in fact."

I hear nothing, so I decide to lie to try to make the situation better by telling him that his recently deceased mother (my grandmother), a person he loved immensely, knew about my attraction. "Grandma knew about my sexuality and my boyfriend, but she thought it would be best if I didn't tell you. She was fine with it but realized, as did I, that you would not accept it. Sorry if I'm a disappointment."

Silence, but soon a stuttered response: "Shheee knneww?"

"Yeah, she did father."

"Well," he utters more fluently, "I guess I'll call you soon."

"Bye, dad. Take care."

My dad didn't speak to me for six months (Adams, 2006).

□

After a year of living together, Brett decides to try to act on Broadway, and I decide to pursue my doctorate. We separate geographically but remain close emotionally.

□

"Ttt-ony?" I hear when I answer the phone.

"Yes?"

"It's Adrienne. I hate having to be the one to tell you. . . . I'm so sorry, but . . ."

"What's the matter?" I ask.

"Brett's dead," she says. "His sister just called me. You should call her."

Adrienne and I hang up, and I call Brett's sister.

"Hi, Sarah?" I ask, unsure of her name. "This is Tony Adams. I lived with Brett in Carbondale,"

"I've heard about you" she says through tears. "Brett died last night of diabetes. I've been calling people listed in his cell phone. I'm sorry. I didn't want to have to tell you this."

□

Brett's family—people I never met—told Adrienne and me that Brett died of juvenile diabetes, a condition he had since his early teens. During the next week two of Brett's friends told me that, on the weekend of his death, Brett told his dad that he was gay.

Brett was 29. Before our relationship, he lived with a man for four years. Because he lived near his parents, I *assumed* he had come out to his family, assumed he told them he was gay. But previous conversations with Brett replay in my head:

"Are you 'out' to your family?" I ask.

"They know," he responds.

and

"How do your parents feel about your sexuality?" I ask.

"We don't talk about it," he responds.

and

"I'd like to meet your family," I say.

"Maybe one day," he suggests.

Brett never told me he had *said* anything to his family about his sexuality. He only said "they know," nothing more. What did "they know" mean? I wonder.

□

Brett's absence leaves a void in my life. When I first learned he had died, I would call his cell phone and hear "Hi. This is Brett. Leave your name and number. I'll get back to you soon." Now when I call I hear "The number you have reached. . . ." His service has ended. Soon, someone else will have his number.

What caused Brett's death? The simple explanation is Brett died of diabetes. I don't want to believe his death had anything to do with coming out to his father, but the thought stays with me; Brett had not only diabetes but also a history of attempted suicide.

□

I search for evidence. I turn to memories of Brett's autobiographical performance, *Best Face Forward*, and his master's thesis describing the production of the performance. Putting on a production at the Kleinau Theatre at Southern Illinois University Carbondale is a noteworthy achievement, especially for a master's student. Brett's performance ran three nights—October 2, 3, and 4, 2003; it detailed his journey through personal narrative, identity, and performance. I remember the show having gay—*very* gay—content as it discussed hooking up, sexually, with men. I also remember that *none* of his family came to see it. Granted, they lived in Oklahoma and Brett in Illinois, but for such a noteworthy achievement, wouldn't they want to attend?

I turn to Brett's thesis on autobiographical performance—autoperformance. In 86 pages, he references sexuality three times. In the first reference Brett worries that audiences will call him a faggot (Aldridge, 2004, p. 50). In the second Brett refers to himself, in third-person voice, as homosexual (p. 56). In the third Brett asks the audience to join him for a Gay New Year's Eve (p. 79). One read suggests that Brett was out in his thesis (but this does not mean his family read the thesis, although they could if they knew it existed—it is a public document). Another read is that nowhere did Brett explicitly mention his same-sex attraction—it is always referenced tangentially: he worries about *others* calling him a faggot, refers to his homosexuality in third-person voice, and asks the audience to participate in a gay holiday celebration.

Maybe I'm reading too much into Brett's words. But I can't help it. I want to see "I came out to my family [insert time and place here]." I want a certainty I can't achieve.

□

Brett helped me overcome the most important disclosure of my life: telling my father that I am attracted to men, that I identify as gay. I envied Brett's apparent openness and ability to approach the world without regret, his courage and confidence about saying, knowing, *whom* he loved. A pillar of strength, he made me feel strong, too. To think that Brett may have killed himself after telling his father that he was gay makes me ill.

□

I will never know if Brett killed himself. His obituary says his was a diabetes-related death. I could contact his family and ask if diabetes really was the cause, but this could make for unnecessary, painful controversy. Even if they confirmed the diabetes story, I know an alternative story exists—a coming-out suicide story. Besides, why would they tell me?

□

Brett is dead and I miss him. Nothing will bring him back.

□

A year after Brett's death I have a dream. I see Minneapolis, San Francisco, and Carbondale, Illinois, familiar places all mixed together. I'm standing somewhere in a medium-sized, hilly downtown, the ground covered with snow. A man walks past. "Brett," I say, and he looks. I run toward him and he casually turns around. "I'm okay," he says, and then tells me that he's not really dead but that he had to change his name. I wake but force myself back to sleep. I dream again, the setting is the same but without snow and without Brett. "Have you seen Brett," I ask a stranger on the street, but she doesn't answer. "Brett!" I yell, and get no response. I wake.

CHAPTER ONE

Coming Out Matters

Brett's death motivates me to write about the closet, the metaphorical "origin of gay identity" (Urbach, 1996, p. 69; see also Betsky, 1997), and about coming out of the closet, the "most canonical expression of being gay" (Perez, 2005, p. 177; see also Kong, Mahoney, & Plummer, 2002). Gay identity—an identity constituted by same-sex attraction—is defined by the closet, a canonical, metaphorical construct that can become, for a person with same-sex attraction, a "fundamental feature of social life" (Sedgwick, 1990, p. 68; see also Brown, 2000), a construct the person might come to live by (Lakoff & Johnson, 1980).

Brett's death motivates me to write about aspects of the closet not often addressed by coming-out research, such as how a person enters a closet (in order to "come out" one must first somehow "go in"), the connection between timing and coming out, and the relational characteristics of same-sex attraction. Contrary to the opinion of writers who minimize the significance of the closet (for example, Hutson, 2010; Jolly, 2001; Seidman, 2002; Signorile, 2007), the closet still manifests itself in a variety of painful ways; consequences for coming out still exist.

Brett's death motivates me to "demystify" the workings of the closet, to make known the "scripts and storylines" the construct makes possible (Freeman, 2010, p. 139), and to call attention to harmful relational patterns tied to same-sex attraction. When these scripts, storylines, and patterns are made known, they can then be talked about, negotiated, and changed, "undone" and "loosened" (p. 139; see also Berlant, 1997; Bornstein, 1994; Garfinkel, 1967; Hacking, 1990).

Brett's death motivates me to write for the sake of relationships fractured by the disclosure of same-sex attraction, relationships that changed once a person discursively moved from one identity to another—that is, from heterosexual to lesbian, gay, bisexual, or queer (LGBQ)—a paradigm shift (Kuhn, 1962) that alters most "every aspect of [a] life narrative" (Couser, 1997, p. 64; see also Garrick, 1997) and that retroactively revises the past (Hacking, 1990, p. 249; see also Freeman, 2010). I write for persons ostracized because of such change; persons banned by peers and kicked out of homes; for people like Ricky, a high school student who, on arriving at a football game, hears "What the fuck is that fag doing here? That fag has no right to be here" and who is then bombarded with bottles, rocks, and ketchup (Pascoe, 2007, p. 68).

Brett's death motivates me to try to lessen the all-too-frequent suicides by same-sex desiring persons (Bornstein, 2006; Goltz, 2009; Russell & Bohan, 2006), to write for people who believe they are "truly good for nothing" (Lorde, 1984, p. 168); for people like Jonathan Reynolds, a 15-year-old boy regularly teased about possibly being gay who positioned himself on railroad tracks in the path of an oncoming train—a boy who, lying face-up against one rail with his feet against the other, held his cell phone above his head and text-messaged his family and friends to tell them that they are not to blame for his death. "Tell everyone that this is for anybody who eva [sic] said anything bad about me," he wrote.

> I do have feelings too. Blame the people who were horrible and injust [sic] 2 me. This is because of them, I am human just like them. . . . None of you blame urself [sic] mum, dad, Sam [his 14-year-old sister] and the rest of my family. This is not because of you. (cited in de Bruxelles, 2007)

I also write for families of victims of hate crimes such as N. J. Supel's son, who was "gay bashed" at the age of 17 and, at 25, lives with "steel rods in his back and is addicted to pain medications" (2008, p. 20), and for families like those described by James, a friend who quit going to his parents' house because of his mother's reaction to his same-sex attraction.

"I haven't been to my parents' house since 1990," he says in an interview (2003). "I came out to my mom in 1988 and she totally freaked out."

"Did she say you couldn't come to their house?" I ask.

"No, but the first few times I visited after coming out she made me use paper cups and paper plates and plastic silverware. She kept my food in a separate place in the kitchen, and I wasn't allowed to eat off of the regular dishes."

"Because you said you were gay?"

"Yeah. She equated being gay with having AIDS, and AIDS, she thought, was easily contagious. But the AIDS epidemic was strong at the time so I somewhat understood her reaction."

"Then you stopped visiting?"

"No, I stopped when she started following me into the bathroom to spray Lysol disinfectant on everything I touched. I felt contaminating."

Brett's death motivates me to write for the same-sex partners who told me that on their stop at the border of Canada and the United States they were accused of kidnapping their son, accused of trying to smuggle him across the border, of being pedophiles. I also write for the gay man who told his sister and her husband that he and his partner would gladly watch their kids, if needed, should they want to travel somewhere for their wedding anniversary. "If you think I'd let you two perverts look after my kids, you're sicker than I thought," the husband replied (Burnie, 2008). Same-sex partners and children: a potentially disgusting mix.

Brett's death motivates me to write for persons who come out after years of (heterosexual) marriage who must now negotiate not only their sexuality but also a spouse's feelings of betrayal (Cooper, 2010; Grever, 2001; Pearson, 1986). "The grief experience of straight spouses who learn of their husbands' or wives' homosexuality cannot be minimized," Duffey writes.

> Few marry without the hope of enjoying long-lasting, supportive, passionate love. Learning that a spouse is gay places the straight spouse in a difficult position. A person must consider which loss is more palatable: staying married to a spouse who may love you deeply but who ultimately feels attraction and romantic love toward others or undergoing the grief experience involved in divorcing and releasing all that comes with it. (2006, p. 90)

I also write for children who knew a parent as heterosexual but who must then negotiate the parent's newly revealed LGBQ identity. "I just found out my dad was gay," a former student writes in an email:

I was wondering if you have some time to talk. He was "outed" having an affair with a man. He's still married to my mother, but they have separated. A lot of people in my family do not know. I know he feels ashamed, scared, and worried. I want to help him know that it's okay. I hate that he feels he must hide his feelings. I understand his apprehension and will respect his privacy, but I am afraid the secrecy and shame will hurt him more. I know it hurts me.

Brett's death motivates me to write for a person unable to be at the bedside of a loved one because their relationship is unsanctioned by hospital authorities and state and federal laws, and for people like Mark, a person dying from HIV-related conditions, whose family abandoned him during the time of his illness. When they did see him on their once-a-year visits, Paula Jacquard, his home health care worker, says she found herself "saying 'gay' repeatedly in an effort to desensitize them" (Jacquard, 2007, p. 22). At his side near death, she called his mother and sister one last time.

"What should I say?" Mark's mother asked several times.

"He's your son," Paula replied. "Tell him that you love him, and anything else you need to say will come to you."

Paula wanted Mark to hear that the people he saw only once a year did care. But "by that time, I was all that Mark saw," she writes (p. 22). Those last few words, a forced telephone conversation, a last, embodied interaction tarnished by a person's claim of same-sex attraction and others' fear of the claim . . . and the person.

Brett's death motivates me to acknowledge distressing conversations tied to same-sex attraction, conversations such as the one I heard in a bar in which a distressed man spoke of coming out to his brother earlier that day and his brother responding by saying he must either change his attraction or leave the family; and conversations such as the one I heard at a church gathering in which a distressed man spoke of how his mother did not want him and his partner at the family reunion. The couple attended the reunion during the previous five years, but this year the mother said the family did not want them around; the family did not want to be forced to acknowledge or validate the same-sex relationship (see also Lim-Hing, 1990/91).

Brett's death motivates me to write against messages condoning hate and harmful acts, messages such as a comic strip that appeared in *The Observer*, the college paper of Notre Dame:

"What's the easiest way to turn a fruit into a vegetable?" one character asks.

"No idea," says the other.

"A baseball bat." (Glaadblog.org, 2010)

Or messages such as that received by John Ray, a Professor at Montana Tech (Butte), in response to a campus-wide email he sent criticizing the negative responses to the university's showing of the same-sex love film *Brokeback Mountain*:

> SHUT THE [FUCK] UP. . . . PLEASE STOP SENDING THESE STUPID EMAILS. GET A SHRINK IF YOU NEED SOMEONE TO COMMUNICATE WITH. WE DON'T CARE!!!!!!!!!!!!! I SWEAR TO GOD . . . I WILL FIND WHERE YOU LIVE AND BEAT YOU IF YOU KEEP SENDING THESE DUMB EMAILS OUT TO EVERYONE. (cited in Emeigh, 2006)

Brett's death motivates me to write against misogyny among gay men, the demeaning of women in gay male language (Jones, 2007), and gay men's obliviousness to all forms of oppression, not just oppression based on same-sex attraction (Tillmann, 2009a). I write against such exclusionary situations as when a (heterosexual) father and (heterosexual) daughter decide to visit a gay male bar, but the daughter is asked to leave, because the bar adheres to a men-only policy. "[I]f a homosexual was refused service," she says to a reporter, "[I] would be the first to stand up for his rights" (CBC News, 2007). Or the decision by the Peel Hotel in Melbourne, Australia, to exclude heterosexuals and lesbians from the venue in order to provide "gay men with an environment where they could freely express their sexuality;" apparently, there was a problem with heterosexuals and lesbians making gay men "feel like zoo exhibits." "It's a very sad day when two friends, regardless of their sexuality, can't go into a venue and dance together" (anonymous, cited in Miletic, 2007). I also write against a LGBQ person's fear or hatred of heterosexuals such as that illustrated by the "I hate straights" campaign:

> Don't be fooled, straight people own the world and the only reason you have been spared is you're smart, lucky, or a fighter. Straight people have a privilege that allows them to do whatever they please and fuck without fear. But not only do they live a life free of fear; they flaunt their freedom in my face. (Queers, p. 1; see also Berlant, 1997)

Brett's death motivates me to write for him, for me, for us. I recognize that I write with uncertainty: the closet may not have occupied a significant part of Brett's life, but I also recognize that I write from experience and that the closet does occupy a significant part of mine. I'm a gay man. I live in and out of the closet. I perpetually negotiate coming out, and, consequently, struggle with same-sex attraction.

Origins

I started this project unwittingly more than a decade ago when I began hating myself for liking men, for calling others faggots and dykes and sissies and fairies, for laughing at the boy in high school who hung himself for (possibly) being gay, for not being fazed by the religion teacher's son who suffocated himself inside the family car because, as some rumors suggested, he may have been gay, too. I recall other sources of guilt and shame as well.

I remember recording an episode of *Beverly Hills 90210* with Brian Austin Green in tight white boxer briefs and replaying the scene over and over again until the tape quit working.

I remember waking at 4:30 every weekday morning to watch a man on an exercise program who sometimes wore spandex that highlighted his bulge. I muted the sound on the television so my mother wouldn't hear. I felt depressed on weekends when the show wasn't on.

I remember going to Walgreen's with my grandmother and sneaking off to the magazine aisle, where I took an issue of *Men's Health* (a magazine with many shirtless men) and hid it inside *Sports Illustrated for Kids*. When my grandmother found me in the magazine aisle, she said she'd buy the *Sports Illustrated for Kids*. I adamantly refused, worrying that she'd find my *Men's Health* tucked between the pages.

I remember finding my mom's *Playgirl,* which she kept hidden under her bed, enjoying that I no longer had to look at underwear models in the JC Penney's catalog but making sure that each time I looked at the magazine I would do so slowly, turning each page with care, then replacing the magazine just as my mother had it—cover-side up, title toward headboard.

Formally, I started this project in 2001 when I allowed myself to embrace my attraction to men, when I began to identify as gay. This embrace altered every aspect of my life story and made new stories possible, stories that, for me, weren't available before being named, identified, and categorized (Hacking, 1990; Rosenhan, 1984). When I embraced the label "gay" my life changed in significant psychological, relational, material ways. I often woke to onslaughts of despair. I quit talking to members of my family. I isolated myself from close friends. I engaged in acts that put my health at risk. I acted carelessly and felt alienated.

The same year I started the master's program in Speech Communication at Southern Illinois University Carbondale. There I worked on projects outlining my struggles with identifying as gay and projects discerning relational characteristics of internalized homophobia, a self-inflicted fear and hatred made possible by a personal embrace of same-sex attraction (Adams, 2002, 2003a). In 2004 I began doctoral work at the University of South Florida, where I continued to research the ways in which LGBQ identities, same-sex attraction, and the closet emerged in and influenced social interaction (Adams, 2005, 2006, 2010; Adams & Holman Jones, 2008).

Eventually I came to this book as a necessary culmination not only of my previous research and experience but also of my love for Brett and my grief over his death, a loss that left me confused and a loss that revealed untidy questions about the closet, coming out, and same-sex attraction. In particular, I wondered:

> How is same-sex attraction discussed and lived?
> What does it mean to come out of—and, consequently, stay in—the closet?
> When and how does—and should—coming out happen?
> How does a person's same-sex attraction affect not only the self but also others?
> How can I work to make experiences of same-sex attraction and the closet more humane?

Method[1]

To investigate these questions I reflected on my experience of the closet and coming out, and I documented conversations that I had with others about same-sex attraction. Even though I foreground my experience throughout much of this book, I also tap into other sources for insight, particularly interviews I conducted with persons who identify as LGBQ and with mass-mediated representations of the closet and coming out.

I have self-identified as gay for a decade. I make my gay identity known most everywhere. Most of my family knows I find men attractive, and I openly discuss my intimate same-sex relationships with friends and acquaintances, colleagues, students, and strangers. Consequently I am frequently held accountable, by myself and others, for many of the assumptions about the closet, coming out, and same-sex attraction outlined in this book; they inform, emerge in, and are reinforced by my interactions.

I mention characteristics of my public embrace of gay identity, because there have been many situations in which persons who (struggle to) identify as LGBQ have asked me about my experiences with coming out. Consequently I have participated in many meaningful and serendipitous conversations about the closet, coming out, and same-sex attraction. For instance, there was the person interviewing me for a job who told me, during the interview, that he was gay, but no one at his workplace knew; he was scared it would tarnish his case for promotion. There was the high school acquaintance, who, after seeing on my Facebook.com webpage that I like men, emailed me for advice on getting out of reparative therapy, therapy that tried to change—"correct"—his same-sex attraction. There was the student who, the week after I came out to the class, wrote in a course paper that she likes women but refuses to talk about it with anyone, and the student who told me that his mother and father said he was "no longer their son" and kicked him out of their house. (As of this writing, four years later, not much has changed: the woman says she still has come out only to one other person, and the man has not seen or talked with his parents.) In classrooms and my office, on the street, in restaurants and bars, and at festivals and church, I never know when I will hear struggles with the closet, coming out, and same-sex attraction.

Such spontaneous and unsolicited disclosures offer insight into the closet that more intentionally structured efforts to gather information about this construct do not. But these experiences require me to use great care: ethically, I must protect the privacy of these persons by masking or altering identifying characteristics such as circumstance, topics discussed, and/or race, gender, and name. Persons with same-sex attraction encounter many personal and social pressures; consequently their identities need to be protected, especially if their experiences are being used in ways they never may want or know.

Since 2003 I have interviewed 15 friends and acquaintances—six lesbians and nine gay men—about their experiences with the closet, coming out, and same-sex attraction. I interviewed friends and acquaintances for two reasons. First, I wanted to make the interviews as comfortable as possible; knowing the people with whom I spoke facilitated such comfort. Second, I wanted to talk to people who trusted me. Although trust is always important in research, the need for trust is heightened, I believe, when a person speaks about experiences with same-sex attraction; because consequences for coming out still exist, and because what the person says may appear in a public, easily accessible document (for example, this book), trust in the researcher is important.

In addition to my experience and others' commentary, my data for this book also include mass-mediated representations of same-sex attraction, specifically memoirs of persons who possess same-sex attraction and televised, film, and audio representations of the closet and coming out. I found these representations to be important because they not only provide public, easily accessible insights into experiences of the closet and relational characteristics of same-sex attraction but also help to constitute an understanding of what coming out is, how the closet can feel, and what identifying as lesbian, gay, bisexual, and/or queer can mean.

In particular I examined eight memoirs—*Surviving Madness* (Berzon, 2002), *Gary in Your Pocket* (Sedgwick, 1996), *Body, Remember* (Fries, 2003 [1997]), *What Becomes of the Brokenhearted* (Harris, 2003), *Covering* (Yoshino, 2006), *Mean Little Deaf Queer* (Galloway, 2009), *Times Square Red, Times Square Blue* (Delany, 1999), and *Truth Serum* (Cooper, 1996)—and six anthologies—*Word Is Out* (Adair & Adair, 1978), *Boys Like Us* (Merla, 1996), *A Member of the Family* (Preston, 1992), *When I Knew* (Trachtenberg, 2005), *From Boys to Men* (Gideonse & Williams, 2006), and *Whistling in the Dark* (Rao & Sarma, 2009). I also examined coming-out interactions featured in sitcoms and films such as *Will & Grace*, *Sordid Lives*, *Were the World Mine*, *For the Bible Tells Me So*, and *A Single Man*, and in episodes of the *Savage Love Podcast*.

Notes on Terminology: Clarifying "Sex," "Gender," and "Sexuality"

"What does it mean to say, 'I am heterosexual?'" I often ask students.

"It means you're attracted to women," they respond.

"If I found men attractive, would I be heterosexual?" I ask.

"No," they typically say. "You could say you were heterosexual, but people might think you're gay or bisexual."

"Why?" I ask.

"Because you're a man," they respond.

"And . . ."

"A man who finds men attractive is gay. A man who finds women attractive is heterosexual. A man who is attracted to men and women is bisexual."

Although I do not want to simplify or dismiss the nuances of sexuality, identity, and attraction, I use this example to show why any discussion of sexuality is simultaneously a discussion about sex and gender; when we talk about hetero-, bi-, and homosexuality, we talk about men, women, and their attraction to other women and men.[2] Consequently, a book about sexuality—particularly about the closet and coming out, same-*sex* attraction, and the nuances of saying "I am LGBQ"—warrants a discussion of sex and gender.

Sex, gender, and sexuality are mutually constitutive, "intimately entangled axes of analysis" (Sedgwick, 1993, p. 72). As Seidman observes, "managing gender [and I add sex] has been and still is at the heart of managing sexual identity" (2002, p. 49). Jackson agrees, noting that "we recognize someone as male or female" before making "assumptions about heterosexuality or homosexuality" (2006, p. 113). The "homosexual/heterosexual distinction," she writes, "depends upon socially meaningful gender [and sex] categories, on being able to 'see' two men or two women as 'the same' and a man and a woman as 'different'" (p. 113; see also Edwards, 2005; Meyerowitz, 2002; Sedgwick, 1990; Stryker, 2008).

I use the term "sex" to refer to "*biological* criteria for classifying persons as females or males" (West & Zimmerman, 1987, p. 127, my emphasis; see also Davidson, 1985). Biological criteria include a person's internal chromosomes and reproductive organs as well as the person's genitalia. Usually genitalia significantly influence a person's sex classification, particularly because they are more visible than a person's chromosomes, hormones, and reproductive organs (Dreger, 2006; Garfinkel, 1967; Sullivan, 2008). However, once a person is classified according to genitalia, many people assume that the person's less visible sex characteristics align with the person's genitalia. For instance, if I had a penis and testicles—signs of male genitalia—untrained others (for example, nonmedical professionals)

Gender is performance (handwritten annotation)

may assume that I also possess male chromosomes, hormones, and reproductive organs.[3]

"Sex" is further complicated by gender. I use the term "gender" to refer to the enactment of criteria for classifying persons as male or female, man or woman, masculine or feminine (West & Zimmerman, 1987, p. 127). Gender is assumed to be "congruent with genital configuration" (Gagné, Tewksbury, & McGaughey, 1997, p. 479), what Sloop calls the "genitalia-equals-gender" equation (2004, p. 131). Gender is an ambiguous abstraction never physically or psychically actualized (Gelber, 1997; Gingrich-Philbrook, 1998), an "ephemeral, contextual, and complicated" identity (Hopkins, 1998, p. 54) "continually constituted and reconstituted" through mundane, embodied practices (Glenn, 2000, p. 5; see also Butler, 1990). If gender is performed badly, if it does not match a person's perceived and/or assigned sex, the person may evoke criticism, punishment, or physical harm from others (Garfinkel, 1967; Sloop, 2004).

A person's sex classification can influence a person's gender—for example, a person designated as male (sex) is usually encouraged to be masculine (gender). However, gender can also influence a person's sex—for instance, if I see a person acting like a "woman" (gender) walking on the street, I might perceive the person as "female" (sex). Furthermore, a person's identification with a gender may inspire the person to modify sex. For example, a person designated at birth as male (sex) but who feels like and identifies as a woman (gender) may choose to undergo *sex* reassignment surgery. (To my knowledge, surgeries for *gender* reassignment do not exist.)

I use the term "sexuality" to refer to one person's sex *and* the person's attraction to another person's sex (Butler, 2004; Ginsberg, 1974; Sedgwick, 1990, 1993; Somerville, 1994). Some authors define sexuality in terms of a person's attraction to others' gender (for example, Adam, 2000; Elizur & Ziv, 2001; Glave, 2005; Jackson, 2006; Padva, 2004; Stryker, 2008), but sexuality defined in terms of gender (performance) implies that a feminine man partnered with a masculine man would be a heterosexual couple. However, I argue that in many contexts, same-gender coupling does not indicate sexuality. For instance, throughout most of the United States, same-sex, different-gendered partners could not marry, because the law would typically classify them as a same-*sex* couple (and same-*sex* marriage is still illegal in many states).

Sex, gender, and sexuality intersect in multiple ways and, as I illustrate throughout this book, directly inform conceptualizations of "the closet" and "coming out"—a metaphor and event constituted by same-*sex* attraction and lesbian, gay, bisexual, and queer *sexualities*. Consider, for instance, an interview Howard Stern conducted with the bald, tattoo-covered, muscular, and mustached porn star Buck Angel (Stern, 2006). Buck identifies as a "man with a vagina," but Stern tries to invalidate Buck's claim to a "man" identity. "If you have a vagina you're a woman," he remarks, though Stern uses "he" to describe Buck during much of the interview. It is only when Stern thinks about Buck's vagina that he classifies Buck as a woman. Buck's male-gendered body conflicts with his female-sexed body, and while Buck argues that a vagina does not make a woman (gender), Stern argues that Buck's vagina (sex) trumps and disqualifies Buck's claim of being a man (gender).[4]

To complicate the situation, some of Stern's staff label Buck "gay" even though they never explain why. What makes Buck gay? If Buck is gay, how does the closet apply to his life? Is sexuality based on Buck's gender or sex? If sexuality rests on his (masculine) gender and he is physically (sexually) attracted to others who perform and identify as men (gender), then this same-gender coupling might mark Buck as gay—and thereby make him able to come out of the closet. If sexuality rests on Buck's (masculine) gender and his attraction to others who pass as female (gender), then Buck may be considered "straight"—and thereby make coming out not a concern for him. If sexuality rests on Buck's (female) sex *and* his attraction to others with female sex criteria, then Buck might be a lesbian—and thereby make it necessary for him to concern himself with coming out. However, if sexuality rests on Buck's (female) sex, particularly his vagina, and his attraction to others with male sex criteria, then this may mark Buck as straight—and, again, thereby make coming out an unnecessary concern for him. Interestingly, bisexuality is not discussed as a possibility. While I contend that same-sex attraction rests on sex more than gender, sexuality becomes more complex when a person's sex and gender conflict.

Or consider another example of how sex, gender, and sexuality interrelate. In 2007 the United States Air Force acknowledged that it tried to find a way to make a "chemical that would cause enemy soldiers to become gay" and thus "irresistibly attractive to one another," causing enemy military units to fail (Hammond, cited in Anonymous). Although Pentagon officials quickly dismissed the plan, this case illustrates a variety of assumptions about sex, gender, and sexuality. First, the plan assumed that enemy soldiers are of the same sex, most likely men. Second, by saying the chemical will increase same-sex attraction, the plan assumed that all the enemy soldiers are heterosexual.[5] Third, the plan assumed, or perpetuated the assumption, that persons with same-sex attraction will be unable to control themselves sexually; they will become irresistibly attracted-to-each-other sex-addicts.[6]

Luisa, a person who identifies as a "masculine woman" and a "lesbian," provided another example of how sex, gender, and sexuality intersect. She told me about a time she used a restroom in a bar in Racine, Wisconsin.

"I entered the women's restroom and noticed a lady primping herself in the mirror," Luisa said in an interview (2006). "She wore black boots, tight jeans, a black form-fitting shirt, and had a beautiful body, long dark hair, and green eyes. I glanced at her quickly, because I did not want her to know that I was looking. But I then saw her stop primping, tilt her head to the side, and look at me."

"Did you look back?" I asked.

"No. I walked into a stall, and heard her leave. I got a weird vibe from her, like she didn't know what gender I was. I felt that she wanted to ask if I was in the correct restroom. I exited the stall and went to wash my hands when the restroom door opened. I looked in the mirror and saw a guy standing behind me. I then saw the lady walk in behind him."

"I would've been nervous," I said.

"Yeah, it wasn't a good situation. I quickly grabbed paper towels, dried my hands, and reached for the door, but the guy grabbed my hand, swung me around, and slammed my head into the wall. That's all I remember. My friends came into the restroom after hearing the guy tell the owner that he didn't understand why 'dykes' were allowed in the bar. They found me in the stall with my head on the toilet and my hands covered in blood."

"And then what?" I ask.

"My friends took me to the hospital and called the police. An officer arrived and asked if I wanted to press charges. I said no. I wasn't ready for my family to find out about my sexuality. I was scared."

Based on her sex (female), Luisa decided to use the "woman's restroom." Once there, she noticed a woman suspiciously look at her as if she were in the wrong bathroom; her "masculine" gender seemed to conflict with the (female) sex she claimed, demonstrated by the act of

walking into a woman's restroom. At this point, Luisa's sex/gender ambiguity may have motivated discomfort. Based on gender, the woman in
the bathroom may have assumed that Luisa belonged in the men's restroom. However, when the man who assaulted Luisa left the restroom,
he said that he "didn't understand why 'dykes' were allowed in the bar."
Instead of being thought of as male, the man may have assumed Luisa
was a dyke—a (sometimes) derogatory term that describes a (usually
masculine) woman who is attracted to other women.

Same-sex attraction—and, consequently, coming out of the closet—
becomes further complicated when sex can be defined in two ways:
sex-at-birth and sex-after-sex-reassignment-surgery—for example, a
male (sex-at-birth) attracted to a female (sex-after-sex-reassignment-
surgery) may be considered heterosexual, whereas if the man was
attracted to the person before surgery, he may be classified as gay.[7]
Moreover, these definitions of sex can further influence meanings
and experiences of gender, sexuality, and the closet.[8]

Assembling the Book: Notes on Writing

Once I embraced my same-sex attraction, I encountered a significant
amount of relational turbulence. I isolated myself from friends and
family. Some people refused to speak to me. I began to feel as though
I was lying if I perpetuated heterosexual assumptions ascribed to my
body, lying if I didn't say something about my intimate and meaningful relationships with men. I wasn't sure how to make sense of my
life, my value, or my goals.

I structure this book in terms of these feelings, and represent,
textually, how same-sex attraction felt at particular times. For instance, the next three chapters—chapters stemming from my learning, embracing, and revealing of same-sex attraction—describe times
when I felt confused. I was uncertain about my life and came to learn
about myself through fragmented and fleeting flashes of same-sex attraction. In the last two chapters I document life as more secure and
calm. I felt, and continue to feel, increasingly satisfied, and, instead
of focusing on the confusion, uncertainty, and fragmentation, I write
about the ways the closet, coming out, and same-sex attraction inform
my everyday experience.

My training in communication also informs this work. I am interested in human *interaction*—how people relate, what happens when

different assumptions and perspectives about social life align and collide, and why conflict happens. I attend to ways people use language, construct and interpret messages, and engage in harmful relational practices. I fuse abstract theory with practical, lived circumstance. These interactional practices make particular features of the closet, coming out, and same-sex attraction more salient than others.

Thus, I situate my discussion in face-to-face interaction and within relationships. For instance, a lesbian who is married to a man and who has children has a variety of relational worries with which she must contend upon coming out. She must worry about her husband's and children's responses to her same-sex attraction. She must worry about whether legal authorities will take her kids. She must worry about whether her kids will be harassed or dismissed from school solely for having, or being affiliated with, a mother with same-sex attraction (Cooper, 2010; T. C. Fox, 2010; Tam & Heinz, 2010). I situate my discussion in these kinds of contexts. And even though I try to acknowledge ways that technology can influence coming out and same-sex attraction, I foreground embodied, face-to-face relations.

Some of the content of this book is graphic. One reviewer mentioned that I should be charged with child molestation for making unsolicited advancements on a young boy. The problem with such a charge is that the boy was the same age as I was—we were both 13 (Chapter 2). Another reviewer mentioned that I should remove a graphic sex scene and accounts of self-destructive behavior (Chapter 3). I contemplated deleting these scenes but believed that the deletion would take away from one purpose of this book—to describe ways in which same-sex attraction and struggles with this attraction can affect a person's life. Some of what I say and did wasn't pretty, but that doesn't mean I should keep my actions hidden or silent. There was a time in my life when I had little care for myself or others. I wasn't suicidal and did not want my life to end, but I wasn't concerned with the consequences of my actions. I am not proud of what I did, but I realize these experiences are part of who I was, who I am, and who I try not to be.

This book's primary goal is to provide a "thick description" (Geertz, 1973, p. 10) of the experience of the closet and coming out and, in so doing, present a contemporary, practical, and relational understanding of same-sex attraction. To accomplish this I use my experiences, others' experiences, mass-mediated representations, and extant research to create a collage of texts—a "layered account" (Ronai, 1992, 1995, 1996)—of these phenomena.

I also attempt to show how the closet, coming out, and same-sex attraction function as relational phenomena—phenomena for which *others* may hold a person accountable in a variety of ways, at a variety of times, and in a variety of places and phenomena that implicate persons of *all* sexualities. In so doing, I not only show how others can make meaning of and, consequently, evaluate a person in terms of the closet, but I also reframe the traditional view of coming out as a discrete and linear, strictly personal affair to one shared by all persons who know of or interact with others who possess same-sex attraction.

I do not claim that my observations will resonate with everyone or that I work to test predictions, control outcomes, or make generalizations about the closet or coming out (Poulos, 2008, p. 47). Rather, I document my journey through, and processing of, the closet and coming out with the purpose of making experiences of same-sex attraction more humane, tolerable, and meaningful for others.

Although Brett's death served as a significant motivation to write, another motivation is a desire to make amends; to work to be a more compassionate person; to recognize and accept my messiness; to atone for my past and help relationships that I've abandoned to heal; to apologize to people I've taken for granted and to those I wished harm; to learn better ways of coping with my "inner demons" (Freeman, 2010, p. 35). I write to make known and help to appease human suffering, to encourage us to appreciate one another more, and, like Harris, to let others "know that they don't have to live their lives in a permanent 'don't ask, don't tell' existence" (2003, p. 6). I write not just about the person I am and have been but also about the person I want to be.

In the next three chapters I discern characteristics of three formative, lived moments that a person with same-sex attraction may experience in relation to the closet: "Learning the Closet," the time when a person first becomes familiar with the space referred to as the closet, the metaphorical space she or he may soon come to live by (Chapter 2); "Living the Closet," the time when a person *privately* acknowledges same-sex attraction but *publicly* discounts this attraction by saying and acting *as if* it does not exist (Chapter 3); and "Leaving the Closet," the time when a person discloses same-sex attraction to others (Chapter 4). I then analyze the everyday paradoxes of the closet commonly experienced by a person with same-sex attraction—interactional dilemmas that form when the person cannot escape the metaphorical space (Chapter 5). I conclude by offering strategies a person can use to reframe and better navigate difficult closet-related experiences (Chapter 6).

Learning the Closet: The Time of "Coming In"

I know my past by knowing my scars.

KENNY FRIES, *Body, Remember* (2003)

□

The signs were there, but when you don't know where you're going . . . the signs don't mean anything.

RAYMONDE C. GREEN, "Signs" (2006)

The closet:

a "private room";

a "place of private devotion" and "secluded speculation";

a "private repository" of "curiosities";

as suggested by the phrase "skeleton in the closet": a "private or concealed trouble in one's house or circumstances, ever present, and ever liable to come into view";

a "hidden or secret place, retreat, recess"; a "den or lair of a wild beast" (*Oxford English Dictionary*, cited in Sedgwick, 1990, p. 65);

a "life-shaping condition" (Seidman, 2002, p. 8);

a "place for what is very much routinely useful (a broom, a favorite coat, the umbrella that still works) but not all-the-time enough to warrant regular display" (Phillips, 1996, p. 333);

a "site of *interior* exclusion for that which has been deemed dirty" (Urbach, 1996, p. 66).

"Coming out" of the closet:

an "observable and systematic life process" (Kus, 1985, p. 178);

an act "predicated on family laundry, dirty linen, skeletons" (Rodriguez, cited in Betsky, 1997, p. 16);

an "acknowledgment of one's homosexuality, either to *oneself* or *publicly*" (my emphasis, *Random House Unabridged Dictionary, cited on dictionary.com*);

the "processes whereby gay men, lesbians, or bisexuals inform others of their sexual identity" (Gagné, Tewksbury, & McGaughey, 1997, p. 478);

a "rite of passage" for lesbians and gay men (Gray, 2001, p. 181);

the "saying of words" (Gooch, 1996, p. 86) and the doing of acts (Crimp, 1993) with the purpose of "proclaiming" same-sex attraction (Plummer, 1995, p. 82);

a "lifelong process" (Herdt & Boxer, 1992, p. 7);

an "act of dangerous communication" that "infects its listener—immaculately—through the ear" (Butler, 1997, p. 116).

□

When a person is said to be "in the closet," she or he is thought to possess a wild-but-hidden, potentially troubling secret. When a person chooses or is forced to leave the closet—a private space concealing a taboo curiosity—the person makes a contextually deviant attraction known. When a person fathoms coming out she or he anticipates another's response to be that coming out is a communicative act implicating others (Butler, 1997; Chirrey, 2003; Garrick, 2001; Jandt & Darsey, 1981; Mosher, 2001). One can and does come out to oneself, but audiences occupy a significant presence in coming-out processes since a person might—and sometimes must—expose a skeleton or wild beast that others may condemn.

However, if a person is said to have come out of the closet, then it must be assumed that the person earlier went into the closet—one must go in before coming out. But how does a person enter the metaphorical space? Is a person birthed into the room? If a person has no idea of what same-sex attraction is or means, or has no familiarity with such terms as "lesbian," "gay," "bisexual," and/or "queer," would the person be able to describe her or his experience as precloseted? Does a closet form only via hindsight, a reconstructed looking-back? What conditions must be met before a closet can exist, before a person could ever fathom coming out? When the closet is framed as the *origin* of same-sex attraction—a framing best noted by Sedgwick's title *Epistemology of the Closet* (1990)—precloseted experiences and epistemologies are often disregarded.

In this chapter I describe and analyze seven interrelated conditions that make the closet and, consequently, coming out of the closet, possible. I work to show how same-sex attraction looks and feels before a closet forms, before a person could conceive of living in or leaving the secretive lair.

□

1986. I am 7. My mother and father erect a large, car-sized satellite in our yard. Living in the Illinois countryside 5 miles from town we no longer need "rabbit ear" antennas to receive TV. The satellite gives us more than two channels. There isn't static interference with *Sesame Street* or *Mr. Rogers*, and my mom can watch *Scarecrow and Mrs. King* without having to stand by the television and continually adjust the receptors.

The satellite also introduces content from previously foreign spaces: news from Nevada, prayer from Pennsylvania, and well-endowed-naked-White-dudes-from-I-don't-know-where. It is with the dudes I begin.

As an only child in a middle-class family I have the privilege of having my own bedroom. My parents rarely enter the space unless they need dirty laundry or want to inquire into whether I made a mess of my toys. And so I can shut my door without much worry of interruption. With the introduction of the new satellite, I acquire my own television and satellite receiver and thereby electronically expand my sphere of privacy.

One night I retreat to the bedroom to watch TV before sleep. "Goodnight," I say to dad and mom, then kiss mom on the cheek.

"Night," Dad responds.

"Love you," Mom replies.

I walk to the end of the hallway and enter my room. I climb into bed, click on the television with the box-sized remote, and surf the plethora of channels now occupying my personal space. Disney, MTV, TBS, and ESPN. I stop at HBO.

Eight guys stand in a row in a dimly lit black room with their dicks dangling—big dicks to a 7-year-old. With sculpted bodies from hours of gym work, all the men sport a six-pack of abs complemented by bulging biceps. I stare at the submissive, standing men who seem to be awaiting inspection.

As I recall, a clothed man approached each unclothed guy, fondled his cock-and-balls, and asked him to cough. Maybe I was watching a medical documentary. I remember each nude man becoming erect in response to the clothed fondler. Maybe this was a show on how to be a male doctor, on what men should do to other men so that they can heal and be well. But then the clothed man put each erect penis in his mouth, though not all at once. The men engaged in an eight-man orgy until every man ejaculated. I remember there was caressing, spanking, sucking, and fucking, but I am unsure of the details.

"What the fuck are you watching?" my father screams upon entering my room; I didn't hear him coming.

"Turn that shit off!" he screams again.

My father approaches the television and unplugs it. He begins to say something but stops and stares at me with large, angry eyes. He yells fuck-this and fuck-that, grabs my wrist, and drags me into the bathroom. Uncertain of how I should respond or why my father is reacting in this way, I begin to cry. I hope his tantrum and my terror will soon end.

In the bathroom my father removes his belt and pulls down my pajama pants. He uses the belt to spank my ass as hard as he can. I wail. He spanks again. I scream. He engages in rigorous same-sex discipline, but this intimate, same-sex contact has a different meaning than the contact I observed on the HBO show. My father isn't trying to be kinky or incestuous. He's showing me that I must learn from this beating, not take pleasure from it. My ass receives its first lesson about same-sex attraction.

The spanking ends, and my father doesn't apologize. My eyes burn from crying, my ass is sore, and my mouth feels dry. I return to bed and quickly fall asleep.

"Boys should not look at other boys," he says to me the next morning on the way to school. "Boys get pleasure from looking at girls, not boys." I nod and pretend to understand.

"You're still allowed to watch TV," he says thinking I will better monitor its content and better monitor myself. I never again stray from Disney, MTV, TBS, or ESPN.

□

Condition #1: For the closet to exist, a person must be aware of and have the ability to describe her or his sexual attraction as "same-sex attraction" or understand what it might mean to identify as "lesbian," "gay," "bisexual," and/or "queer."

In his memoir Kenny Fries describes the first time anyone used "gay" to describe his feelings. During spring break of his first year of college, he visited Helen, a family friend. Upon entering her apartment, she said: "'You're gay, right?'" Fries wondered why Helen asked about his gayness but recalls being "relieved by Helen uttering this word." "I don't know if I'm gay," he said, adding that he "might be in love with [a man]" (1997, p. 44).

E. Lynn Harris, in his memoir, says that he "felt different" as a boy but did not know why: "As a child I only knew that if it wasn't my color, then what could it be?" (2003, p. 4).

Thomas Waugh (2009) recalls knowing about his same-sex attraction as a child but was unable to describe himself as "homosexual" until puberty, and Terry Galloway describes being "finally able to put a name" to her attraction after looking up "homosexuality" in the dictionary (2009, p. 90).

I identified as male, White, and Catholic long before I identified as gay. I did not learn the meaning of gay until my mid- to late teens. My same-sex attraction existed before I knew the term, but I could not describe this attraction as same-sex attraction or identify *as* gay (Gambone, 1996; Meyer, 1995). As Samuel Delany (1999) observes,

> anyone who self-identifies as gay must have been interpellated, at some point, as gay by some individual or social speech or text to which he or she responded, "he/she/it/they must mean me." That is the door opening. Without it, nobody can say proudly, "I *am* gay!" Without it, nobody can think guiltily and in horror, "Oh my God, I'm gay!" Without it, one cannot remember idly or in passing, "Well, I'm gay." (1999, p. 191)[1]

Stephen McCauley makes a similar observation:

> For a good while you'd been wondering why you didn't want to fuck your girlfriend, didn't want to go to the prom, actually liked gym class (or at least the locker room part of it). Now you had

the answers to these and other questions, all in one tidy three-letter word ["gay"]. (1996, p. 187)

When a person is immersed in hetero-normative contexts—contexts that privilege different-sexed attraction and frame persons as heterosexual until proven otherwise—then people often do not learn about same-sex attraction and/or LGBQ identities until later in life (Elizur & Ziv, 2001; Hayes, 1976; Kielwasser & Wolf, 1992; Meyer & Dean, 1998; Padva, 2004). "Our first crushes, first infatuations, and first broken hearts," Rob Williams and Ted Gideonse write, "are among the most profound moments of our adolescences, because they are often frustratingly silent and solitary experiences" (2006, p. ix).

If coming out of the closet is predicated on *disclosing* same-sex attraction and/or a LGBQ identity, then a person who does not know what this attraction is or what these identities are cannot come out. A person may begin to recognize that she or he is attracted to others of the same sex, but this does not mean the person will know how to or why a need exists to acknowledge this attraction or say "I am LGBQ." A person must thus be aware of and have the ability to describe attraction as "same-sex attraction" and, consequently, to understand what the closet and coming out might mean.

[handwritten marginal note: This is cruel.]

□

1991. I am 12. I take four Bud Lights from the refrigerator and put them in my backpack. I don't know what beer tastes like, but I know it makes people feel funny. I also know that feeling funny can induce impairment, a condition where a funny person can lose control.

"Can I stay the night at Aaron's?" I ask Mom.

"I suppose," she replies. "Need a ride?"

"No, I can walk."

I arrive at Aaron's and take my backpack into his room. We play Nintendo and Frisbee with his dog and then listen to the most recent *New Kids on the Block* album. I wait until his parents go to sleep before telling him about the beer.

"You want a Bud Light?" I ask.

"You have beer?" he replies.

"Yeah, I stole it from my parents."

I open a beer, take a taste, and find it warm, bitter, and disgusting. I take another sip.

"This is horrible," I say. "I'm not drinking anymore."

"I'll take it," Aaron replies.

I hand him the can. He finishes it in a matter of seconds.

"Can I have another?" he asks.

"Sure," I say. "Impressive," I think.

Aaron chugs beer two, downs the third, then the fourth.

"Let's get naked," Aaron suggests.

"Ummm, okay," I reply. "Then what?"

"Nothing, but we'll be more comfortable without clothes."

Aaron quickly removes his battered T-shirt, jeans, and boxers. I remove my running shorts, T-shirt, and white briefs. Aaron approaches me and takes my penis in his hand. I grab his, and we get hard together. He begins to suck. I reciprocate. He tells me not to tell. I tell him not to tell. We climb into bed and continue to touch each other's body. "This feels good," I think as I dose off to sleep.

□

Condition #2: The closet begins to form when a person recognizes that same-sex attraction—attraction often constituted or manifest by a LGBQ identity—possesses a marginal social status in that it is not practiced or validated by the majority of a population.

Even though an identity is marginal does not suggest that it is unworthy or bad. Examples of marginal identities could include persons with hobbies (such as a bowler, dancer, or gardener), nondominant but still respected religious sects in the United States (for example, Mormonism, Judaism), and persons in wheelchairs, particularly since many spaces try to accommodate but do not privilege wheelchair use. Furthermore, marginality is contextual: same-sex attraction and LGBQ identities may be accepted at some times and in some places but not at or in others.

With a few exceptions I do not remember people saying, "You're heterosexual, Tony." Rather, I remember people asking "if I had a girlfriend" and if I found a particular woman attractive. I remember learning what passes as love by observing (heterosexual) relationships in movies, books, and on television. I remember Catholic school health class where I learned how penises and vaginas fit together, each being the (only) complement to the other, the essence of manhood being the possession of a penis able to "adequately penetrate" a vagina (Bloom, 2002; Bryant, 2005; Greenberg, 2002; Padva,

2004), a genital interconnection that Fausto-Sterling calls the "true mark of heterosexuality" (1995, p. 132). Although I do not remember hearing rampant, explicit disregard for same-sex attraction, I remember priests saying that a man should "not waste his seed," a mantra condemning sex outside of marriage and nonprocreative acts such as masturbation and (male) same-sex intimacy. With time I learned that same-sex attraction is an attraction relegated to the margins of social life.

☐

1992. Often, Ben stays the night. Even though we are both 13, I'm jealous that Ben's approaching puberty faster than I am. He has a goatee, underarm hair, and a deep voice and has had numerous escapades with girls.

When Ben stays the night, we sleep in the same bed, a closeness I appreciate. When I think he's asleep, I'll lift his T-shirt to stare at his emergent belly hair, and his trim and toned stomach. I'm always cautious, because I don't want to wake him with my touch. If he flinches or wakes, I pretend I'm asleep. When I expose his belly, I consider my work a success.

I try to disassemble Ben's belt, then his jeans, slowly raising the latching button ever so slightly, trying to subtly remove the peg from its corresponding cloth notch. When I finish opening his jeans and expose his underwear, I consider my work a success.

While it's easy to unbutton and unzip Ben's jeans—he typically wears a size bigger than his waist—maneuvering his underwear is more difficult. Unbutton, unzip, spread jeans open, wait a minute before touching briefs.

I pull out a mini-flashlight and shine it on his crotch. Through his white underwear I see the outline of a half-erect penis, one bigger than mine. I then steer the penis through the opening of the briefs by widening the opening slowly and nudging it through the hole. My prodding often erects the penis fully, thus making it easier to slide through the slip. When I expose his penis, I consider my work a success.

I shine the light on Ben's face. He's smiling, but acts as if he's immersed in deep sleep. I stroke his penis, making it big and hard. I enjoy looking at it, touching it. I get erect, too. I arrive at a point where I'm unsure of what to do with my penis or with his, so I go to sleep. I decide against reassembling his clothes and allow him to do so the next morning. Ben and I quit sleeping together after a few of these excursions. We quit speaking, too.

□

Condition #3: The closet begins to form when a person recognizes that same-sex attraction—attraction often constituted or manifest by a LGBQ identity—might possess a stigmatized, devalued status in that it is condemned by many members of a population.

In *They Stand Apart*, Tudor Rees and Harley Usill call homosexuality a "'cancer of the soul,' a 'twist in the mind,' a 'bodily affliction,' or a commixture of them all" (1955, p. xi). In the same book Viscount Hailsham frames "homosexual practices" as "contagious" and "unnatural" (p. 24), compares same-sex attraction to heroin addiction, and believes homosexuality should be eligible for "criminal and social sanctions" (p. 31). Although these sentiments may sound dated, the belief in the "cancerous" and "unnatural" nature of homosexuality still manifests itself in explicit and insidious ways.

In a letter to the editor of *Tampa Bay Times*, Jerre Norton refers to the gay "lifestyle" as a "growing cancer" in the United States (2008, p. 17).

A BBC News reporter reports that some people living in Iraq fear being killed for being gay. "I don't want to be gay anymore," an interviewee says. "When I go out to buy bread, I'm afraid. When the doorbell rings, I think that they have come for me" (McDonough, 2006).

In anticipation of the 2006 World Pride Parade in Jerusalem, religious groups distribute flyers promising NIS (Israeli New Shekel) 20,000 (about $5,000) to "anyone who brings about the death of one of the residents of Sodom and Gomorrah" (Sela, 2006). Unlike gay killers in Iraq, Jerusalem gay killers earn money for killing gays. Parade officials cancel the parade.

In Idaho, a Post Falls business owner uses a marquee for social justice: "Ped[ophiles] queers fags your [*sic*] in Idaho now . . ." (cited in Brodwater, 2006). Jim Valentine doesn't want queers and fags in his community and makes his desire known to passing drivers.

In Oklahoma, State Representative Sally Kern calls homosexuality a "bigger threat" to the security of the United States than "terrorism" (Michels, 2008).

Reverend Albert Mohler, President of the Southern Baptist Theological Seminary, argues that it is "biblically justified" to biologically alter fetuses to cure nonheterosexual sexualities (Lindenberger, 2007); German Sterligov, a Russian billionaire, argues that the killing of lesbians and gays is biblically justified (Advocate.com, 2010).

Former professional basketball player, public figure, and role model Tim Hardaway expresses his dislike of gay people. "I hate gay people," he says, "so I let it be known. I don't like gay people and I don't like to be around gay people. I am homophobic. I don't like [gay]. It shouldn't be in the world or in the United States" (cited in Winderman, 2007). National Basketball Association (NBA) officials quickly distance themselves from Hardaway's comments, condemn his language, and ban him from NBA-related appearances. A few days later Hardaway tries to retract his comments, saying he doesn't "hate gay people," is "good hearted," and believes "hate" was a bad word to use (Associated Press, 2007). But one is reminded of a capital-T Truth of communication: utterances are irreversible.

"I grew up plagued by the knowledge that I liked boys," Lane Thompson writes on his blog.

I hated it and I wanted to be normal so badly. I was convinced there was something very wrong with me and I could not imagine disappointing my family so terribly. How could I be so vile? Everything I ever heard about gay people was foul and loathsome. How could these people be so despicable and dare show their faces? I have been trying to accept myself ever since. (2007)

Michael recalls learning that gay people were "drastically unusual people like circus freaks, curiosities, and oddly human-like. I got this sense about how these people were considered," he says in an interview (2008). "And I didn't want to do or say anything that would put myself in the category of circus freak."

"I told people I was gay in the 5th grade," Jackie says in an interview (2006). "And I remember being ridiculed. I remember students making fun of me at lunch and at recess. I also remember getting kicked out of a summer school program for saying I was gay. My teacher kicked me out for causing trouble."

"Because the other kids made fun of you?" I ask.

"Yes," she says. "The teacher said that I was the one causing trouble, because I was telling people that I was gay. I also remember being sent to the main office. Until then, the secretary was always nice to me. Now she stared at me with disgust. I felt like I was sick. I felt like something was wrong with me. I was only 11."

Harris remembers first learning about negative responses to same-sex attraction after having sex with another man in the back of a car. "When we finished," he writes,

> I felt excited, but Donald wore a look of disgust. I asked him if everything was alright. He looked at me and shouted, "You god-damn faggot." then he started beating me unmercifully with his large fists. Every time I tried to escape his car, his fists pounded my face. . . . Suddenly this psycho stopped beating me, spit in my face, and then leaned over me, opened the door, and kicked me with the heel of his shoe out of his car into the cold rain. On the graveled alley I saw blood on my hands. My nose was bleeding. But I didn't think about the pain of his fists. All I could think about was Donald spitting in my face. It was devastating. No one had ever done that to me. It was like he was saying to me, "You don't deserve to be a human being. You're lower than low. You ain't shit." (2003, pp. 88–89)

Bernard Cooper recalls asking his mother what a fag was. He says she turned from the stove, flew at him, and grabbed him by the shoulders, asking "Did someone call you that?" "Not me," he responded. "Oh," she replied, loosening her grip. Cooper says his mother was "visibly relieved" but still did not tell him about fags (1996, p. 6).

In her memoir Galloway remembers trying to mention homosexuality at a family dinner but didn't "have time to finish the word. It was like I'd shot off a gun and stampeded cattle," she says. "The commotion it caused left me with the strong impression" that homosexuality was wrong (2009, p. 90).

Raymonde Green, a contributor to *From Boys to Men*, remembers "faggot" being "not just a harsh word but a status associated with so much negativity . . . that it was something that I just knew there was no possibility of me being" (2006, p. 60).

When an attraction or identity is devalued, it is considered unworthy or bad. A person who aligns with the attraction or identity may thus feel shameful, different, and guilty (Ellis, 1998; Goffman, 1963; Solis, 2007). And, as Burgess observes, "an identity that requires outing" is one "typically thought to be undesirable, or aberrant" (2005, p. 128).

◻

1994. I am 15. I have a friend named Chad. He's a fellow classmate and golfing peer. He can grow a beard overnight and is often considered one of the sexiest men in high school.

"Want to stay the night Friday?" I ask Chad during a round of golf. "I have some beer."

"Sounds cool," he says.

I can't believe he agreed. We're not close friends, only golf acquaintances. I find him attractive, but I'm unsure what my attraction is, what it means, or how I can explain it to others.

"How about I come over after golf practice?" he asks.

"Cool," I reply.

On Friday we arrive at my house. We watch television, talk about our upcoming homecoming dates, and wait for my mom to go to bed. When we think she's asleep, I pull out my hidden collection of warm beer. We climb out my bedroom window and begin to drink.

I force myself to drink two cans. Chad drinks three quickly. When we finish the drinks, we return to my room and climb into bed.

"Let's play a game of truth or dare," he says.

"Fine," I respond, unsure of how to play.

"Truth or dare," he asks.

"Dare," I reply.

"I dare you . . . to take off your clothes, everything except your underwear."

"I, um, can't do that," I say.

"You must," he demands. "It's a dare."

I climb out of bed and strip to my briefs. I climb into bed again.

"Your turn," I say. "Truth or dare?"

"Dare."

"I dare you . . . to do five naked jumping jacks."

Without hesitation, Chad climbs out of bed. He removes his shirt, revealing patches of hair, and unbuttons his belt. He simultaneously pulls off his jeans and briefs, revealing a semi-erect penis, and begins to jump up and down.

"One," he whispers, up and down.

"Two."

"Three."

"Four."

"Five."

"Your turn," he says without reaching for his clothes. "Truth or dare?"

"Dare," I say.

"I dare you . . . to let me suck your dick."

I hesitate to respond.

"You must," he demands. "It's a dare."

"Sure," I say while removing my briefs. "But I've never . . ."

"Shhhh . . ." he interrupts.

Chad climbs into bed, tells me to roll on my back, and places his arms on my chest near my shoulders. He looks at my face, dick, face, and then dick again. He slowly caresses my now-erect penis. It feels good in his mouth. I feel comfortable with him, with us.

But Chad only teases my dick. He licks it for a minute or two, and then says he's tired. He climbs out of bed, puts on his briefs, and climbs next to me. The next day, Saturday, we wake without mentioning the night before. My mom drives him home.

"Faggot!" Chad says to me in the hallway at school. It is Monday morning, two days after our now-silenced rendezvous. Unsure of what's happening, I see him approach me.

"What?"

"You're nothing but a cocksucker," he says in passing.

"What are you talking about?"

"Shut the fuck up, queer," he responds, and quickly departs. A small audience stares at me. Nothing more about us is ever said.

□

*Condition #4: The closet begins to form when a person realizes that a marginal and devalued attraction or identity may encounter negative criticism from others **if discussed**.*

"Can you think of an example of when you first learned about the taboo-ness of same-sex attraction?" I ask Dave in an interview (2007).

"I remember watching a [heterosexual] sex scene on HBO," he replies. "I was 5 or 6. My mom said: 'Don't look at her breasts, don't look at her breasts.' But the entire time I was looking at the guy's chest. By her telling me not to look, I somehow knew that I should've been looking. But I didn't care to. I liked the guy's chest."

"But wait—she told you to *not* look at the woman's breasts," I say. "This seems to make heterosexuality taboo, not same-sex attraction."

"Yes, but she didn't think of homosexuality," he says. "Everyone was heterosexual to her. So she assumed I was heterosexual, but because of my age (she) didn't think I should look at breasts. Ironically, what she didn't want me to look at was what she wanted me to look at."

"What if she asked if you were looking at his chest?"

"I would have lied. It felt dirty. It felt like I shouldn't be looking at him. It wasn't right."

"I knew that my attraction to guys was something I didn't want to talk about with anybody," Michael says in an interview (2008). "I had to keep it hidden."

Philip Bockman describes first noticing his different, same-sex attraction after viewing the film *Tarzan*. Upon leaving the theater, Joey, his close friend, said: "Gee, that Jane is really sexy, isn't she?" Bockman realized that while "Joey had been focusing on Jane," he "had waited breathlessly for every glimpse of Tarzan's glistening muscles. I was alone," Bockman writes, "my feelings unacceptable. And I knew instinctively that *I could never reveal them*, not even to Joey. I felt condemned as I spoke the required words: 'Yeah, I thought Jane was sexy, too'" (1996, p. 76, my emphasis).

At 12 years old "I was disgusted viewing half-naked women in *Debonair* magazine, over whom my classmates used to drool," Bindumadhav Khire recalls in an interview. "But I had to pretend that I was just like them, as I was afraid of being ragged" (2009, p. 257).

In the documentary *For the Bible Tells Me So*, Episcopalian Bishop Gene Robinson describes a similar fear of speaking about his attraction:

> I think it was about 7th grade. And some friends somehow got a hold of a *Playboy* magazine. And I realized that these pictures were apparently doing things for these other guys that they weren't doing for me. And the second thing that I realized was that I *better not show or say* that these weren't doing anything for me. (Karslake, 2007, my emphasis)

These comments illustrate not only the marginal and devalued status of same-sex attraction but also how *speaking about* the attraction can be taboo. Thus a person may learn to stay silent about this attraction; there is a recognized need to hide (in the closet).

□

Sarah, 20. Tony, 19. Acquaintances. 1998.

Sarah, Jehovah's Witness. Tony, Catholic.

"Will you be my date for the company Christmas party?" she asks.

"You don't celebrate Christmas," he responds.

"I want to this year. I'll pay for everything."

"I suppose," he replies.

"We'll make it romantic," she suggests. He pretends not to hear.

Sarah RSVPs for the party and makes hotel reservations. Tony finds a fake I.D.

Sarah buys a size-6 dress, black heels, and a fake pearl necklace. Sarah buys Tony a black sport coat, matching pants, a yellow shirt, goldenrod tie, pair of black loafers, and a belt. Tony enjoys the free clothes. "Souvenirs," he thinks.

Before and during dinner Sarah and Tony drink double-shot Strawberry Daiquiris. After dinner they switch to beer. Sarah becomes comfortable with Tony. Tony knows he should please Sarah. Hands slide along each other's body. Fingers move into spaces taboo in public places. Sarah touches out of pleasure, Tony obligation. They decide to leave the party early, both knowing the touching will continue at the hotel with Sarah trying to restrain herself, and Tony hoping she will pass out.

The couple enters the room and moves toward the bed. The oversized comforter is quickly removed as they slide onto the unscented, starched-white sheets. Making out begins, slobbery, sloppy kisses shared by both. Tony is drunk, Sarah drunker.

"I wann-you innn me," Sarah slurs.

"Now?" Tony asks, worrying about the impossibility of an erection. "Are you sure?"

"Yeah, I'm surrre. I wann-you innn me!" she demands.

The kissing continues as each prepares for a more intimate connection. Tony removes Sarah's daisy-yellow dress, then his belt, pants, and button-up shirt. Sarah removes her bra and underwear, and then pulls Tony's boxers down to his knees. She grabs his limp penis.

"Whatzzz the matterrr?" Sarah asks.

"Nothing," Tony responds. "Nervous and drunk."

Tony finishes removing his underwear and grabs the condom from the nightstand. He's unsure of how it arrived there—he didn't bring protection. He climbs on top of Sarah, sits up and on the top of his feet. He hovers over Sarah and stares at her naked, drunk, stimulated body. He then looks to his smooth chest and belly and wonders how he will slide the protective sleeve over the unaroused penis.

"Whatzzz the matterrr?" Sarah asks.

"Nothing!" Tony responds. "I'm getting ready. Be patient!"

"I wann-you in me!" she replies.

Tony places the condom wrapper between his teeth. He tries to open it while simultaneously steering clear of touching and licking spermicide. He unfolds the condom and tries to slide it onto his still-limp penis. He stares at Sarah who is much calmer compared to a few minutes ago.

"She's hot," he tells himself, trying to get aroused.

"I want to be inside her now!" Nothing.

"I want to fuck her. She wants it, and so do I."

Minutes pass. The penis doesn't move.

"Whatzzz the matterrr?" Sarah asks. "Doan-you think-I'm prrretty?"

"Of course I do," he responds.

Minutes pass. The penis—still.

"Sarah is a man I want to fuck," Tony thinks. "Like John Stamos or Mario Lopez or Jason Priestly. Mark Wahlberg in his tight and bulging Calvin Klein's."

An erection begins.

"This man is hot," he continues to fantasize, "and he's hot for me."

An erection continues.

"I'm straddling this man's dick and it feels good, tight. He knows how to move and he likes it rough. He wants my dick in him now!"

An erection, hard and steady.

"Are you ready!" Tony asks Sarah. "I want to fuck you, now!"

"Yea-Iwanyou . . ." she mumbles in a single phrase.

Tony inserts his cock between her legs. "It's in," he tells himself and begins to slowly thrust. "Mmmmm . . ." Sarah whispers, nearly passed out from the alcohol. Tony hears and immediately pulls out. "Mmmmm . . ." she whispers again. He sees she's falling asleep and decides not to continue.

Tony slowly climbs out of bed, not wanting to wake Sarah. He rinses off his penis in the sink, disposes of the condom, and puts on his boxers. He climbs into bed, snuggles against Sarah's back, and drapes his arm across her breasts and stomach.

The next morning Sarah wakes Tony as she climbs out of bed. She smiles at him, says she has a headache, tells him they must check out by 11. He gets up, showers, and packs. Sarah and Tony talk little on the way home, neither of them discussing the night before or realizing that this will be the last time they speak.

☐

Condition #5: For the closet to exist, same-sex attraction and/or a LGBQ identity cannot be accessed easily.

I described how Dave hid his fascination with a bare-chested man from his mother. Michael mentioned that his "attraction to guys" was something he could hide. Bockman (1996) described how he refrained from revealing his same-sex attraction to his best friend. Khire (2009) and Robinson (cited in Karslake, 2007) realized they had to pretend to like looking at images of naked women, at least around their friends; like others, they had to keep their lack of heterosexual attraction a secret.

The *Oxford English Dictionary* defines a secret as something "kept or meant to be kept private, unknown, or hidden," a "thing known only to a few," something "concealed" and "classified," "confidential" and "undercover" (2001, p. 753). If a secret was known, then it wouldn't be a secret; the definition of secrecy rests on an assumption of inaccessibility (Simmel, 1964).

When a person realizes that she or he has something unknown to others, the person realizes that she or he harbors a secret. If coming out is predicated on *revealing* same-sex attraction and/or a LGBQ identity, then a person must recognize that this attraction and/or identity are not easily accessible—recognize that the attraction and identity are secret (to others).

☐

Amy has bubbling energy, a bright smile, and, based on the oversized brown backpack, seems dedicated to school. Like me, she's in her first semester at Southern Illinois University Carbondale and has completed two years at a community college. It is 1999.

During the first weeks of the semester, Amy and I arrive early to class, each awaiting the other. Always, we converse until the professor approaches the podium. Expectantly, we leave together, each speaking of forthcoming days, exchanging phone numbers, making plans.

"I just ended a three-year relationship," Amy says, suggesting a potential date. I think she likes me, but I'm not sure. Maybe her flirting is an act of politeness, not interest. She hasn't asked me out and hasn't mentioned any interest in a romantic affair.

"Want to go to dinner?" I eventually ask, feeling confident but fearing rejection.

"Sounds fun," she says. I gleam.

I find Amy smart, attractive, and motivated, and I think we'd make a great couple. "I should date her," I tell myself. "It's what I'd like to do to feel okay and normal."

We dine at Lonestar Steakhouse. In a few days we dine again at Applebee's and then at Quatro's Pizzeria. In a few weeks we try to watch *Shakespeare in Love*, but during the film we exchange our first kiss, a kiss that, for me, feels meaningless.

"Will you stay the night?" she asks. I refuse.

"I can't. I have class in the morning."

"Will you stay the night?" she asks in class the next day.

"I can't. I have to work."

"Will you stay the night?" she asks a few days later.

"I can't. I'm going out with friends."

We repeat our dining cycle one more time: Lonestar, Applebee's, Quatro's. We kiss before and after each meal, but are never together alone again.

□

Condition #6: The closet makes sense only if a person acknowledges that same-sex attraction will continue for an indeterminate amount of time, perhaps forever, or will, at the very least, take a significant amount of work to change.

The majority of Bernard Cooper's *Truth Serum* portrays his attempt to change same-sex attraction. "I became the scientist of my own desire, plotting ways to change my yearning for boys into a yearning for girls," he writes. "What I needed to do, I figured, was kiss a girl and learn to like it" (1996, pp. 6–7). He "had gotten to the point where I would try almost anything in order to change, from praying to giving up masturbation" (p. 54).

Harris refers to his gayness as the "one thing about me that I prayed constantly that God would change" (2003, p. 4). Galloway remembers acknowledging that lesbianism was "more than a passing thing" (2009, p. 133). Mike McGinty remembers realizing, at the age of 16, that his same-sex attraction was "never going away" (2006, p. 284), and Gareth Thomas says he once prayed to God to "change him" and "make him normal" (cited in Smith, 2010, p. 59).

"I realized that my [same-sex] urges were getting stronger," Todd Pozycki, a contributor to *From Boys to Men*, writes:

> [S]o I found the phone number of a ministry that claimed they could help people stop being homosexual. I was assigned a counselor who would meet and pray with me once a week until I became heterosexual, which I hoped would take no more than a month or two. (2006, p. 95)

When I first recognized my same-sex attraction, I believed it would change if I could get aroused by women. However, when I realized the relative stability of this attraction—that if I wanted to change it I might have to undergo years of repression and therapy—I started to embrace the attraction and its corresponding LGBQ labels. An acknowledgment of the stability of my attraction did not push me into the closet, but it did serve as a condition for its possibility.

When a person acknowledges that same-sex attraction may exist for a substantial amount of time or take a significant amount of work to change, when same-sex tendencies become more than one-time, fleeting feelings, when same-sex attraction feels as though it will endure rather than disappear, and when saying "I am LGBQ" or "I like persons of the same sex" are conceived of as statements of *being* (Cornell, 2007), then the closet begins to form. As Foucault writes: "Homosexuality appeared as one of the forms of sexuality when it was transposed from the practice of sodomy into a kind of interior androgyny. The sodomite had been a *temporary aberration;* the homosexual was now a *species*" (1978, p. 43, my emphasis; see also McIntosh, 1968; Meyer, 1995). Fuss agrees, noting that it is the transposition from a *temporary* aberration to a (more stable, enduring) species that "marks the moment of the homosexual's disappearance—*into the closet*" (1991, p. 4, my emphasis). If a perception of stability did not exist, then a person could allow time to pass, knowing that the marginal and devalued attraction may change—for (a perceived better) heterosexual desire.

□

"Another pitcher of Bud Light please," I say. The bartender fills my container. As I wait I see a woman staring my way. Our eyes connect and we exchange smiles.

"Four dollars," the bartender says. I give him a five, take the pitcher, and return to my friends on the other side of the bar. From the corner of my eye I see the woman watch my return.

When I finish my beer, I notice the woman still looking at me. I decide to approach her.

"Hi, I'm Tony."

"Beth. Nice to meet you."

"We've been exchanging glances all night," I say. "Thought I should introduce myself."

"Glad you did," she replies.

Beth separates from her friends, I separate from mine. We get another pitcher of beer and our own table. We exchange stories, finish the pitcher, and then get another. We flirt, touch, and prepare for the next move: an outside-of-bar date, one-night sleepover, or both. We decide on a sleepover at my apartment, a place within walking distance of the bar.

The alcohol allows me to think I can intimately perform for Beth. "She is attractive," I tell myself. "Who wouldn't be attracted to her?"

When we arrive at my room, we climb into bed. Beth's skin smells like beer; her hair, stale cigarette. We sloppily kiss and cuddle. I remove her shirt; she removes mine. Pants follow. I begin touching her breasts unsure of what I am supposed to do to or with them. She places her hand in my boxers and begins touching, and stroking my penis. No response.

"I guess I've had too much to drink," I say.

"That's okay," she replies. "We'll wait until morning."

The next morning I hope she forgets the "let's wait until morning" comment. She seems to forget, and I'm thankful.

Beth and I date for six months but spend most of our time together drunk. On most occasions alcohol allows me to think I can sexually perform for Beth. "She's attractive," I would tell myself. "I know I can be attracted to her." But I also knew the buzz could also serve as an excuse for not being able to perform.

"I guess I've had too much to drink," I'd say most every night.

"That's okay," she'd reply. "We'll wait until morning."

□

Condition #7: The closet makes sense only if a person embraces same-sex attraction and/or self-identifies as LGBQ.

A person who engages in same-sex sexual acts and/or who has same-sex attraction may not identify as LGBQ or feel that she or he should identify as such (Adam, 2000; Johnson, 2004). For example, some men may identify as gay only if they assume a passive, penetrated, "feminine" role in sex (La Pastina, 2006; Labi, 2007; Meyer, 1995; Phellas, 2005; Rao & Sarma, 2009; Ross, 2005). Other people—such as those working in the porn industry (Escoffier, 2003; Seidman, Meeks, & Traschen, 1999)—may not self-identify as LGBQ at all, regardless of sex-role played; an influence such as money may motivate same-sex sexual experiences to happen, not feelings of same-sex attraction or the need to identify as LGBQ. "I detest thinking of myself as gay," Ankleshwaria says in an interview, "except during sex" (2009, p. 205).

The metaphor of the closet—a metaphor descriptive of and made possible by same-sex attraction—can thus make sense only if and when a person identifies as having such attraction and/or as LGBQ. The closet does not apply to persons who do not consider themselves LGBQ or who *others* identify as LGBQ (but who may not self-identify in such a way). I could say "Barack Obama is gay," but my claim would not push Obama into the closet. I may think Obama is gay, or may identify as gay someday, or is lying to himself and others, but if Obama does not identify as gay, then he cannot come out of the closet; coming out is defined in relation to and predicated on the disclosure of a (self-acknowledged) same-sex attraction and/or LGBQ identity. For a person who does not have such attraction or identity, the closet has little relevance.

□

In this chapter I proposed seven conditions necessary for the closet—and, consequently, coming out of the closet—to exist. A person must (1) have the language of same-sex attraction and/or LGBQ identity, and recognize that same-sex attraction and/or LGBQ identity are contextually (2) *marginal* and (3) *devalued*; (4) realize that same-sex attraction may encounter criticism from others *if discussed*; (5) know that she or he harbors a secret, that same-sex attraction and/or LGBQ identity are not easily accessible; (6) recognize that same-sex attraction will not go away easily or on demand; and (7) *self*-identify as having same-sex attraction and/or as LGBQ. When these conditions are met, a person may discover the existence of the closet, a space where a door can be closed or opened, a space where coming out becomes possible.

□

2001. I am 22. Christina is my best friend of seven years and is seven years my senior. Our relationship begins in January. It ends in May. During our time together my same-sex attraction emerges, solidifies, and hurts.

"We should date," Christina suggests. "We have fun together."

"Sounds nice," I say, "but we live three hours apart."

"I'll come to see you every weekend," she replies.

"You'd do that?" I ask. "Convenient," I think.

"For you I would," she says.

We begin to identify as a couple. As planned, Christina visits every weekend. During our time together we relax and watch television, go to dinner, and occasionally see a movie. Beyond the casual kiss, we're never intimate. I'm not attracted to her but feel as though I should be.

"Why haven't we had sex yet?" she asks after a few months.

"I've been too busy," I reply. "And I'd like to wait until we're married."

"We could be more intimate."

"I suppose, but I think we're fine."

I do want to be intimate, but she doesn't excite me.

Two months into the relationship I begin to embrace my attraction to men. But I do not have LGBQ friends. The few people I think of as LGB or Q are people I've learned to ridicule, people whom I call fairies, queers, faggots, dykes, and disgusting human beings. I think of them as deficient creatures unable to get married, have kids, live meaningful lives, or stay free of sexually transmitted disease. I think of them as nothing more than scum of the earth, immoral creatures not worthy of life, beings destined for hell. The people I think of as LGBQ are people I despise—and am beginning to resemble.

Five months into the relationship, I think about ways of ending "us." I think about the possibility of making our relationship work, of getting married and having kids with Christina, while privately envisioning my love, lust, and attraction to men. I think about talking with Christina about my same-sex attraction but then wonder how she could understand something that even I don't understand. My attraction feels too new, weird, and disappointing.

"I don't like you," I tell Christina on the phone. "I'm not attracted to you, either."

"What? Why are you saying this?" she asks.

"I don't like you. You're boring. You're ugly. You're mean."

She remains silent, and I think I hear her cry.

"We're not compatible," I demand.

"Whhyy are you saying this!" she yells. "I love you, Tony!"

"But I don't love you. Never have, never will. Don't call me, either."

She hangs up the phone. I do not call her back. I feel guilty and relieved.

Christina is the last woman I try to date. Immediately after our breakup and, I believe, motivated by uncertainty, confusion, and despair, I retreat to Wyoming to bartend at a resort without a phone, email, or contact with family and friends. I retreat into alcohol, a medium for suppressing my same-sex attraction, a substance that will allow me to continually suppress my feelings throughout the day and in sleep, night until morning. I retreat into what I soon come to know and feel as the closet.

CHAPTER THREE

Living (in) the Closet: The Time of "Being Closeted"

Closets are a place of death.

MEL WHITE, in Karslake, *For the Bible Tells Me So* (2007)

□

Hello darkness, my old friend.

SIMON & GARFUNKEL, *The Sound of Silence* (song, 1964)

□

"Today's my last day," you say to your boss. "I'm leaving for Wyoming tomorrow. Sorry if this puts you in a bind. I need to leave."

"Why didn't you tell me earlier?" she asks.

"I didn't know earlier."

A retreat to a Wyoming resort made possible by completing an on-line application one Thursday afternoon, passing a phone interview on Friday, and telling friends and family on Saturday of the newly acquired bartending job—an abrupt decision to move more than 1,500 miles, a reckless and sudden separation from others without much concern for their feelings.

"Here's the rent for three months," you say to your roommate, handing him cash. "I'm leaving for Wyoming."

"Why?" he asks, seemingly amazed by the money and intrigued with your plans.

"Because I want to. Don't ask stupid questions."

□

The resort is located two miles east of the east entrance of Yellowstone National Park. There is a restaurant, gift shop, bar, horse stable, and gas station on the property along with a house once occupied by Buffalo Bill Cody, approximately 30 guest houses, and employee living quarters. You share a room with four guys, occupying the bottom of a two-tiered bunk. There is one shower, cleaned not too often, and your peers—other employees—prepare breakfast, lunch, and dinner every day. Most of the workers have made careers at the resort, many having been there for 10, 15, and sometimes 20 years. They treat you as an invasive stranger, as summer help who will soon leave.

These others also distrust you. Many used to live on the street and had to work to secure lodging and food. Then they see you, someone who has never lived on the street or has ever worried about sleeping and eating arrangements. You're an outsider, they believe, or a temporary insider, you believe, who will try to become, seem, and act as a permanent, sincere, and serious worker who cares about them. This is accomplished by saying that you'll stay in contact if and when you leave, but you know, secretly and silently, that when you're gone and when you refuse contact that their bitterness toward outsiders will increase. Their bitterness is justified, you think, but you care only about yourself.

□

Michael described a time between acknowledging same-sex attraction and disclosing this attraction to others. "By my freshman year of high school I knew I was attracted to men," he says in an interview.

> But I didn't admit my attraction until much later. It was admitting to someone else that I was gay that I believed was a big deal. My sexuality was my private lot to deal with, and so I never explicitly said I was gay until much later. (2008)

Harris also recalls recognizing that his "infatuations with men" might cause "major problems" (2003, p. 105) and, consequently, found it beneficial to date girls.

In this chapter I describe the time of living (in) the closet—the time between entering the closet and coming out to others, between *privately* acknowledging same-sex attraction but *publicly* disconfirming this attraction by saying and acting as if it doesn't exist, between coming out to oneself but not necessarily or intentionally to others (Chirrey, 2003; Downs, 2005; Gross, 1991; Rasmussen, 2004; Shakespeare, 1999). I illustrate not only ways that same-sex attraction becomes personally meaningful and the relational experiences of being closeted but also the potentially shameful and secretive practices that a person may use to (try to) stay in the metaphorical closet(ed) space.

□

A heroin addict shares your room, a man who says he's 35 but is easily mistaken for 50, a man who has worked at the resort for 12 years, a man whose veins burst through the skin of his nostrils and whose rotting teeth fall out. He says he'll get fake teeth if possible, teeth that will serve as insignia of a drug habit you pretend to understand but don't. He often asks for rides to town to buy Pabst Blue Ribbon, pornography, and heroin. You usually comply. You don't really care about him or his life. Let him enjoy himself, you think, but you that know his body will soon fail, unable to sustain the drug habit that controls him, an addiction you enable.

"Why won't you speak to me?" Christina, an ex-girlfriend, asks in a letter. "What did I do to hurt you?" she continues. "Why won't you call?" You trash the note and prepare for work.

A co-worker gives you a gift, a small bottle an inch-and-a-half in diameter with a small ship inside. The ship-in-the-bottle appeals to you; it speaks to your isolation, uncertainty, enclosing suffocation. He gives you the bottle because you engage him; you listen, react, and exude concern. Others disregard him, because they're tired of hearing him reminisce about a failed 30-year marriage and despair about estranged kids. However, your attention is superficial, and you feel guilty about taking the ship-in-the-bottle, one of his few possessions, because you know you won't talk to him after you leave. But you take it anyway.

□

You receive an envelope in need of a signature, the corner marked with $18.00 of postage. "I'm not sure what happened to us," Christina, the ex-girlfriend, writes in a letter. "I'm not sure why we've grown distant. I apologize if I scared you. Will you please call? I miss and love you. I only want the best for you and us." You quit reading and throw it away. You miss her and know you hurt her. But you're not ready to reveal or discuss same-sex attraction.

Your boss is a gay man. Being the first self-identified gay person you've ever met, you wonder why he's lived at the resort for eight years. You begin to embrace a familiar stereotype: He must be "sick" with HIV or AIDS (at this time in your life these are the same). He has retreated to Wyoming to die an isolated death away from his New Orleans family and friends, away from anyone who knew him before he came out as gay, before he became sick. Throughout the summer this stereotyped sickness becomes your reality as you worry he's contagious and wonder what to do if he touches, kisses, and tries to fuck you while you sleep, because you've heard gay men sometimes fuck sleeping men. (Or maybe that is what you'd like to do to sleeping men.) You'll worry more about your boss if he says you're cute, and asks you to stay the night, a gesture you perceive as gay code for wanting to fuck. A few weeks later, he does. In a drunken haze you politely refuse, but he asks again. You react abrasively, saying that you aren't gay and don't identify with that word and have no desire for relations with men—lies of course. You'd like to amplify this abrasiveness by telling him that even if you were gay you wouldn't touch his sick body, because he's a gross human being who did a wonderful thing by choosing to live isolated in Wyoming and thereby not disgrace his family and friends.

□

Elena, an interviewee, describes how the normalization of heterosexuality might motivate self-dislike:

> There are people who identify as heterosexual because that's who you're supposed to be. You're not supposed to be gay. You're not supposed to deviate from the idea of having 2.5 kids, a dog named Spot, a house and a husband. People can internalize these

ideas and live in a fairy tale world, a world that says you have to be straight in order to make it. Such ideas don't legitimize homosexuality. (2006)

"I find that a lot of people internally battle with being gay," Tyler, another interviewee, says. "They tell themselves, 'I want to live a normal life. I want the house with the picket fence and the dog and the family and I want people to wave at me when I walk down the streets. I want that life that has been painted for me, but I can't [have it]'" (2007). Tyler adds that people with same-sex attraction often feel "disenfranchised." Downs agrees, arguing that gay men, in particular, are "emotionally disabled by an environment that taught us we were unacceptable, not 'real' men and therefore, shameful" (2005, p. 21), men who, perhaps in the words of Lorde, absorb "loathing as a natural state" (1984, p. 156).

Living (in) the closet is a time when a person with same-sex attraction may "join a hostile conversation" about, or choose to avoid people with, same-sex attraction (Cory, 1951, p. 247; Harris, 2003); a time when "shame, denial, and self-hatred" are felt and lived most severely (Phellas, 2005, p. 79); a time when the "fear of revealing one's sexual identity becomes a focus in the life" of a LGBQ person (Clatterbaugh, 1997, p. 142); a time when LGBQ persons "wreak havoc on themselves and everyone around them" (Wright, cited in Shelburne, 2010); a time of what Freeman calls "existential frustration" (2010, p. 189); and a time characterized by inhibited interactions, intentional and intense use of hiding practices, acts of omission, lies, extreme bouts of selfishness, and risky and reckless sexual activities.

□

You begin to miss family and friends but know you can't speak about missing them, because you're one of the few employees who has others to miss, others who care and shower you with love. Feeling confused and alone you decide to leave the resort forever one random Monday morning at 2 A.M., after finishing work, after securing the evening's cash and locking the bar, after gathering clothes from the room shared with four guys.

The bottled-ship gift man stops you at the door. He asks if you've "had a good night" to which you reply "yes" and that you're "getting something in your car" to which he replies, compassionately, "watch out for the bison, bears, and moose," because they'll "charge, hit, and kill people during the dark hours of morning." "Thanks," you say, but say nothing of leaving or that you'll never see him again. It's easy to end relationships this way—by avoidance—which concerns you, but you act as if you don't care. When you arrive at the car, you still see the man sitting on the front step of the building. You enter the vehicle, turn on its headlights, and drive away without ever saying bye. You never want to be contacted by anyone at the resort, or by friends and family you've successfully managed to avoid these last few months.

You struggle in your relationships. You don't want to be lonely but fear speaking about same-sex attraction. You're unsure of how to embrace gay identity and dwell in confusion. You hate your abrasiveness with others but do not know how to act differently.

□

"I'd like to move to New York," Maria says. "But if I do, Susan would move with me. And this means that I'd probably have to tell my parents about us."

"You haven't told them?" I ask.

"No."

"But the two of you have been together for three years," I say.

"I know, but we tell a lot of people that we're only friends. I'm scared of how my parents would react. I don't want to be kicked out of the house. I don't want them to cut me off financially. I don't want them to hate me."

"Then why do you have to tell them? Why not keep the relationship a secret?"

"They'd think it's weird if Susan and I moved to New York together, and it's difficult knowing that those I love do not know who I love. What happens if I die? What if I am remembered to have never dated, never loved? What would Susan do? Come to my funeral and tell others that she was just a good friend? I've already had to face my death once. I can't think about my life and death without Susan."

I met Maria in one of my classes. She is someone I consider a "pillar of strength," a person who withstands significant turmoil but exudes self-confidence. When Maria was 25, she was diagnosed with cancer. She underwent chemotherapy; the cancer is in remission.

"That's something many 25-year-olds don't experience," I say.

"I know," she responds. "I had to plan my funeral. I had to think about dying. And now I'm scared to tell my parents that I'm dating a woman." A tear runs down her cheek.

"I could die on the way home," she continues. "The cancer could return. My funeral would happen, and people would never know of my love for Susan, our love for each other."

Seth, a friend, also describes being secret about same-sex attraction. "My first boyfriend was Nicholas," he says. "We met in school when we were 14. But this was a secret. You could never tell anyone at that age. It was taboo. At the time I also dated girls in order to hide. But this was a mistake. I ended up hurting Nicholas and causing myself more pain."

"I use the word *hiding* in its fullest sense," Dennis Hunter says. "It was never simply not telling my father my secret. It was hiding my dirty magazines, screening my phone calls, and, most of all, sneaking my boyfriend into my room after my father had gone to sleep" (1996, p. 290).

"I can't, to this day, imagine what childhood would have been like without the need for secrecy, and the constant vigilance secrecy requires," Bernard Cooper writes.

> The elaborate strategies, psychic acrobatics. . . . Every day you await disgrace. You look for an ally and do not find one, because to find one would mean you had told. You pretend to be a person you are not, then worry that your pretense is obvious, as vulnerable to taunts as the secret itself. In a desperate attempt at self-protection, you shrink yourself down to nearly nothing, and still you are there, as closed as stone. (1996, p. 70)

A scene from the short story *Brokeback Mountain*: Alma, Ennis's wife, asks Ennis to use rubbers during sex, because she dreads another pregnancy. Ennis refuses, saying he'd happily leave her alone if she didn't want any more of his kids. Elma responds, under her breath, with "I'd have 'em if you'd support 'em" and under the breath of that breath, with "what you like to do don't make too many babies" (Proulx, 1999, p. 269). Elma has suspicions that Ennis is attracted to and having sex with a man; however, at this time in the story, Ennis continues to aggressively hide this attraction. Shitole recalls a similar experience: "To deflect suspicion [of my same-sex attraction] . . . I have sex with my wife whenever she demands it. There are really very few times when I want to have sex with her. I do it just to please her and keep her happy" (2009, p. 77). Veils of secrecy—relationally manifest.

These situations illustrate not only how the time of living (in) the closet is a time of "deception and duplicity," a time when a person hides "homosexuality in the most important areas of life" (Seidman, 2002, p. 25), but also how such secrecy can affect a person and the person's close others (Simmel, 1964). Maria's inability to speak of her relationship with Susan not only makes life difficult for Maria and Susan but also keeps their relationship shrouded in secrecy. With his secrecy, Seth seemed to hurt not only himself by not speaking of his relationship with Nicholas but also Nicholas and the girls he pretend-ed to date (especially if the girls took the dates seriously). Hunter's hiding practices influenced his relationship with his father. Cooper's stonelike feelings also worked to keep close others at a distance, and Ennis's and Shitole's secrecy affected not only the relationship be-tween them and their wives but also relationships with their children.

Because of a desire to protect and, ironically, not to hurt others by disclosing same-sex attraction, living (in) the closet can make a per-son persistently vulnerable, especially if she or he vigilantly engages in hiding practices, omits information, and tells a surplus of lies in order to keep (not easily accessed) same-sex attraction and/or LGBQ identity secret.

□

"Watch me pee," a female acquaintance demands. You are 22.

"Okay," you say. You're drunk at a party and easily oblige but don't have any desire to watch.

When finished, she makes another request: "Now I want to watch you."

"Okay." You oblige since you're at a party, drunk, but you don't have any desire to watch her watch you pee.

"Drive me to the liquor store," she says when you finish.

"Okay," you say, believing you aren't too drunk to drive as long as someone else thinks you can drive well.

"Whadd'ya like?" she abruptly asks in the car. "Boys or girls?"

"Girls," you say after a slight pause. On the 10-minute trip, she asks about likes and dislikes, attractions and turn-offs, desires and disgusts, and, instinctively, you realize you should, figuratively, take a few steps back, assemble relational walls, deploy dishonest comments. You don't want her to think you're interested in an intimate relationship, and you lie and dodge questions and make up answers about seeing someone, a girlfriend who couldn't attend the party.

"Want to suck on my breasts?" she asks on the drive back. "I just got them pierced."

"Okay," you reply, drunk and obliging.

She reveals large, pale breasts and puts a hand on the back of your head, moves it through your hair, and then pulls you toward an exposed nipple. You lick and suck, unsure of what to do, disliking what's happening, enjoying that you're making a story to tell heterosexual friends about the woman who demanded that you lick and suck her pierced breasts. Your desire to remain secret about your attraction creates what Lawrence calls a "mockery of pleasure" (1914, p. 9), allowing you to participate in an undesirable, intimate affair that, upon ending, will immerse you in an agony of irritation, because you engaged in an intimate act that you didn't like or want to do; an agony of torment, because you engaged in an act that may have suggested a like of this person in an intimate kind of way; an agony of misery, because you still refuse to speak of same-sex attraction and so take advantage of this person only to make a story to tell friends whom you don't really want to impress by talking about an attraction you do not have.

After a few moans she pushes your head toward the other breast, and you continue to lick and suck, pretending you enjoy it, attempting to pass as straight, trying to garner pleasure from watching her receive pleasure from your tongue, mouth, and teeth. After a few minutes, she removes the hand from the back of your head, a gesture that implies you can stop.

□

"In high school I was always mean to kids I perceived as gay, calling them names like 'faggot' and 'queer,'" Tim says in an interview.

> I was also the kid who secretly had affairs with men. To this day, there are still 2–3 people I know that I used to call names. And they're now good friends. They haven't been mean to me, though they should be. They should call me a lot of things now. (2003)

Consider how Tyler renames himself for two kinds of people, those he perceives as friendly and those about whom he's uncertain:

> My first name is Tyler, and my middle name is James. When I meet people that may have a problem with my sexuality, I introduce myself as Tyler. When I meet people that I don't think will have a problem with my sexuality, I introduce myself as James. If someone says "Hey James!" I know they're friendly. If someone says "Tyler," I'm not sure. (2007)

Delany writes of a similar experience: "By my last year of high school, my friends were divided into two categories: those who knew I was 'queer' . . . and those who didn't" (1996, p. 12).

Or consider how Seth self-monitored his body in order to try to achieve a masculine-and-thus-often-assumed-heterosexual male identity:

> In high school, I remember how important it was to learn the correct way to hold my hands and to talk. I wanted to seem straight, not gay. I would watch how other students would hold their hands and how they would talk. I would try to keep my hands still and grasp a deep voice. But I felt mechanical. Nothing came out natural. I soon said, "Fuck! This is killing me! I hate having to act a certain way to be accepted and so people wouldn't doubt my sexuality." This imitating still haunts me. (2007)

Tim describes ridiculing gay peers while simultaneously having secret affairs with men. Tyler describes trying to regulate who might know of his gay identity by altering his name. Delany divided his social interactions by sexuality, and Seth describes engaging in particular nonverbal behaviors to avoid being marked as gay. These descriptions illustrate not only how life in the closet can make it difficult for a person to maintain a "consistent account" of her- or himself (Rust, 1993, p. 55)—to be the "self-same" person across multiple audiences (Garfinkel, 1967)—but also how a person may monitor "speech, emotional expression, and behavior in order to avoid unwanted suspicion" (Seidman, 2002, pp. 30–31). Furthermore, the hiding practices and alterations of information in which a (closeted) person may engage can haunt the person at a later time—that is, if same-sex attraction should happen to leak, others may hold Tim accountable for being mean or hypocritical, mark Tyler and Delany as manipulative, and Seth as insecure.

□

"I lied about not only my sexuality but about almost everything else as well," Harris says about a time before publicly embracing same-sex attraction. "I told so many mistruths that it became hard to remember what I'd said originally" (2003, p. 100). He recalls telling a friend that he was "going to Jamaica" with "Maria" and not "Mario" (p. 181) and telling his aunt about being in a relationship with Andre but saying "Andre was female" (p. 142).

Jeffrey, a participant in Downs's project on same-sex attraction in the United States, makes a similar observation. "I've been lying to everyone for most of my life," he recalls.

> I lied to Tom, my best friend in high school, when he asked me if I was queer. I lied to every girlfriend whom I used to prove to myself that I wasn't gay. I lied to my parents about who I was dating, what my life was really like, or even when I would get married. I've lied to my employers, my doctor, and even the priest at my parents' church by playing like I was straight. I've lied to every lover I've had about being monogamous when I wasn't. I guess I sound like some kind of monster, but I'm really not. (2005, p. 127)

George, a participant in Phellas's study of gay men in Cyprus, says that telling his parents "white lies" about his sexuality was a way of "keeping them happy and keeping [himself] happy" (2005, p. 71).

Sometimes a person with same-sex attraction may not tell explicit lies but rather omit information. "I would lie to my mom when she asked about having a girlfriend by saying 'I'm not seeing anyone,'" Dave says in an interview (2008). "I guess I wasn't lying but rather omitting a truth."

For a closeted person, lies and/or omissions of information can accumulate quickly; as Mahohar Shitole says: "If you lie once, you have to lie a hundred times to cover up the first lie" (2009, p. 77). These lies and omissions not only might be viewed as harmful and immoral, but they also may resurface at a later time. For instance, the people whom Harris, Jeffrey, George, and Dave lied to or omitted information from may hold Harris, Jeffrey, George, and Dave accountable for these lies and omissions. Furthermore, when others learn about such secrecy, they might also consider Harris, Jeffrey, George, and Dave liars, regardless of intention or need to lie, an ascription that might tarnish each person's character and mark him as untrustworthy.

□

A drive to meet Charles, a person who finds you attractive and asks you to spend the night, a man whom you drive two hours to see for eleven hours. He's a person with whom you can maintain local anonymity, because you haven't discussed your same-sex attraction with anyone. A drive to meet, eat, and drink at Houlihan's restaurant and then go to a club to drink and dance and talk about things not too significant. Although it's not explicit, the two of you know you're there for a one-time affair, not to embark on a future together. You leave the bar and drive to his apartment, both drunk and unsure of what will happen next. There you kiss, but when he tries to engage you sexually by first placing his hand and then his mouth on your semi-erect penis, you get nervous and lose your erection. You blame it on alcohol and ask to reserve intimate acts until morning. Feeling sick from drinking too much you wake before him, use the bathroom, and leave without saying "goodbye," or "thanks," or "talk to you later."

□

"I'll be back in the morning," you say to your roommate. "I'm staying with a friend."

"Okay," he says without question.

You make trips to Alex's three times a week for two months, trips no others know about, trips to see an 18-year-old runaway you met online, a man who lives with one of his friends he met on the Internet. Alex doesn't have a driver's license or a car or a job and spends most days in chat rooms or walking around the 300-person town where he lives. In a few months Alex secretly runs away again. Rumors say he moved back to his parents' home in Alaska, his name wasn't Alex, and he was younger than 18.

A typical trip to Alex's consists of arriving at his house at 9 P.M. and leaving early the next day to teach an 8 A.M. class. Most of the time is spent lying on a queen-sized bed in a musty room, a time of touching and talking and listening to alternative music. You find sleeping next to Alex comfortable but sometimes wake restlessly to watch his white tanked-top body and young-but-worn, slightly-bearded face sleep.

The onset of mononucleosis (a.k.a. mono) prohibits you from seeing Alex for a few weeks. When your health improves, he'll have moved someplace else with someone else he met online, and he'll disconnect all his Internet chat accounts and email addresses. You can't discuss your grief about Alex's sudden disappearance with anyone, because you don't have any close LGBQ friends, and your closest straight friends do not know about him or these trips.

□

Smith describes Gareth Thomas's closet-life as fluctuating between nights of "diving headfirst onto a pub table covered with pints" and then vanishing from friends, for days and weeks, without explanation; nights of drinking 12 shots and "materializing in the deejay's booth wearing sunglasses and a headband with two metal springs from it like antennae, scratching records like a street rapper, getting the whole joint jumping" and then, for days and weeks, being "unreachable, stonewalling everyone's texts and calls" (2010, p. 58).

Harris believes he had "no interest in being friends with someone" who was like him, because he did not like himself and didn't think he could like other gays (2003, p. 111).

Before I came out "I tried to stay away from gay people," Mike, an interviewee in Phellas's project, says. "For a while I dated a woman to convince myself and the people around me that I was heterosexual. If I was with friends and homosexuality was brought up I would be the first one to criticize gay people" (2005, p. 72).

As these experiences suggest, closeted people might isolate themselves from and cease contact with meaningful, significant others (for example, parents, friends) in order to keep same-sex attraction hidden and, simultaneously, to encourage these others to continue to remember them in "positive" (read: heterosexual) ways (Bell & Valentine, 1995; Cooper, 2010; Liang, 1997). By choosing the "safety of solitude" rather than the "danger of social encounters" (Goffman, 1967, p. 39), an LGBQ person might try to "restrict the tendency of others to build up a personal identification" (Goffman, 1963, p. 39). Garfinkel makes a similar observation about shame: "A prominent function of shame is that of preserving the ego from further onslaughts by withdrawing entirely its contact with the outside" (1956, p. 421). I consider suicide an extreme form of isolation, precipitated when a person chooses to "face and accept destruction" rather than face "anxiety and the loss of self-esteem" (Leary, 1957, p. 15).

A LGBQ person may also steer clear of other LGBQ persons out of a fear that others, by association, might cast her or him as LGBQ (see Boyd, 2006; Cory, 1951; Garfinkel, 1967). As Lee argues, "if a young homosexual became aware of others like himself through the medium of heterosexual culture"—a culture that views homosexuals as repulsive—then the homosexual may work to "deny" his "commonality" with homosexuals, thus making a "continued separation from the gay community" possible (1979, p. 193).

Again I return to the issue of accountability: isolation is an act that may strain a relationship but also one that others might criticize at a later time; the LGBQ person may be held accountable for being selfish and narcissistic and/or self-hating and politically irresponsible for such retreat.

□

"Stay in bed," he says. "I'll be back in a few hours." You like sleeping in his bed and enjoy being around him but find him too comfortable with men, too gay. When he returns he takes you to an isolated waterfall, a place where the two of you kiss. With the exception of skin-tight white boxer briefs, he removes his clothes and asks to remove yours, a request adamantly refused after looking at and admiring his smooth, toned body. You know the work he does to maintain it and wish you had such discipline but then feel uncomfortable looking lustfully at a man, a man who likes you, who cares, whose heart you'll soon break. In a few weeks you'll meet another man you like, or think you like, and tell this beautiful, caring man that you don't want to see him anymore, because he's too openly gay and likes to please you too much and doesn't worry about what others think about men dating and loving men.

□

"When kids in high school learned I was gay, they started threatening me," Dave says in an interview (2008). "I had one semester left. I stayed as long as I could but soon couldn't handle the threats."

"What type of threats?" I ask.

"The most significant was at the beginning of my last semester," he says, "three days after we returned from winter break. A bunch of football players pulled a gun on me."

"A gun?"

"Yeah. After school they surrounded me and held the gun to my forehead. They said 'You need to get out of this school or you're going to go in a body bag.' I also couldn't go to the police, because I would've been outed to everyone in my family. And I couldn't do that."

"But you were already outed at school. . . ."

"Yeah, but I did not want my extended family and my grandparents to be ridiculed about my sexuality. I knew it could happen. I didn't want them to start getting hate mail."

"So how did you respond to the gun incident?" I ask.

"I went to the guidance counselor to see if I could transfer schools. I had one semester left. Academically, I was in the top 20 of my 1,200-person class. And I didn't care if I graduated with my friends, because many weren't my friends anymore."

"How did the counselor respond?"

"She said, 'Dave you're being dramatic.' She said you've one semester left. I said, 'I will be dead. Let somebody stick a gun to your head.' Then she said I could go to the police, which, again, wasn't an option."

"This is intimidating," I say, "especially for being . . . 18?"

"Yeah, I just turned 18. I wasn't thinking of anyone but my family. I left the counselor's office thinking that I didn't have the support necessary to transfer schools, and so I went to the administrative office and asked for a withdrawal form. I quit school. But this made for an additional problem. My family was so proud of me for being in the top 20 of my class and that I was going to be the first to go to college. I had a full ride to a private university. But now all they knew was that I had a semester of high school left and I quit. What a disappointment. Many of them even said, 'I'm so disappointed in you, why couldn't you finish?' My parents didn't tell my relatives that they already kicked me out of the house for being gay or that I had a gun pulled on me. All my family knew was that I quit just because."

"Do they still talk about this?"

"Yeah, and it's been more than a decade. I was going to be the one to go to college and to make something of myself and do something that wasn't manual labor or something that wasn't a job just for paying bills. When they thought I was no longer the one who would do this, the focus shifted to my younger brother. He became the person—and still the only one—to have graduated from college. I was happy to see him graduate high school and college, but it was supposed to be me. I have a difficult time talking about this with anyone."

"I can't believe this entire situation rests on a disclosure of sexuality," I say.

"I know. This is why I believe that once we, as gay people, get comfortable with our sexuality, we become selfish," he says. "When we're not comfortable, we accommodate everyone else. This was me being selfless again, never telling anyone the reason why I had to quit school. I couldn't. Talking about the gun incident would mean talking about being gay. For many years, my relationship with my family all but died, because I couldn't be honest. Even if I came out to them, I still think that being gay would've been my fault. I'd rather be a disappointment for not finishing school."

☐

Never talking to people close to you about whom you like and whom you love—this is selfless behavior, to never speak of same-sex attraction out of concern for these people (Cooper, 2010; Feigenbaum, 2007; Glave, 2005; Van Gelder, 1998 [1984]). But soon you dislike being selfless and make your attraction a topic of talk. "That's fine with me," a friend says, "but I can't speak to you anymore." You realize the more you talk about "it," the more you may hear the latter part of the sentence. A solution devised: become selfless again and tell the newly estranged friend that you've "changed your mind" and were going through a "phase." Though you know these comments are lies, you want to improve the relationship, an improvement made possible by discursively making visible one type of attraction and making invisible another. Living (in) the closet—a time of conflict between "love and respect for another" and "love and respect of yourself" (Fries, 2003 [1997], p. 93).

☐

You create a picture-free personal ad on Yahoo.com. Sex: male. Age: 22. Race: White. Height: 5'6". Weight: 160 lbs. Attracted to: women and men. Best attributes: personality, smile, ability to drink alcohol.

"Nick," a 24-year-old, 5'8", 160 lbs., White, "heterosexual," employed-by-the-Navy male whose best attributes include his body, eyes, and sense of humor, responds by asking if you'd like to meet. Excited that a man takes an interest in your profile, you agree to meet that night.

"Thanks for contacting me," you say upon meeting Nick. "I like your apartment" comes next followed by, "Will my beer fit in your fridge?" He seems nice and safe. He's attractive, too.

The two of you sit on separate sides of the worn leather couch and prepare to watch an Austin Powers film. "Can I get you a beer?" he asks. "Sure," you respond. You match each other beer for beer: If Nick drinks one, you do, too; if you drink one, so does he.

"Want to stay the night?" he asks after 10 beers. You know he knows your response, knows you cannot drive, knows you've been staring at him all night.

"Yeah," you say.

"Want to sleep in my bed?" he asks. You know he knows your response, knows you will say the bed is better than the couch, knows that you want to touch him.

"Yeah," you say.

In the bedroom you move in and out of a drunken haze, forgetting where you are, realizing that you're going to touch and get touched by Nick, worrying about the hangover you'll have tomorrow. The next morning you still feel intoxicated, shifting in and out of pleasure and disgust, in and out of confusion and comfort, in and out of worry and excitement. You wake realizing that you've stayed with and are lying next to a stranger you first call Nate and who asks if you want to get "fucked again." The "again" makes you nervous, because it implies that someone fucked you once already, but you say "sure," because you can't remember being fucked and want to remember how being fucked feels.

You climb out of bed, put on clothes, take some aspirin, wander through the apartment and notice the amount of beer consumed, worry about the lack of sexual protection used in fucking, and overcome this dissonance by telling yourself that Nick is safe, because he is a nice guy and would not want to transmit disease. "I'll chat with you soon" you say, to which he replies "okay," but the two of you never meet again.

□

Wednesdays and Sundays: ritual visits to the town's gay bar, a disregard of Thursday and Monday obligations. You drink to get drunk, because drunkenness makes confident flirting possible. Drinks of choice: triple-shot screwdrivers (three shots of vodka with remainder of glass filled with orange juice) and Long Island Iced Teas (usually one shot each of tequila, vodka, rum, and gin with remainder filled with Coca-Cola).

A goal most evenings, never spoken of, often assumed, explicitly denied: find an attractive man with whom to spend the night, never at your place, always at his. Depending on the amount of alcohol consumed, standards of attractiveness vary, standards not often realized until the next morning. In the morning, if you find the man next to you unattractive, you make the waking encounter the last interaction. If he mentions the possibility of a relationship you say, abruptly, that it was nice meeting and you must go to work. He gives his phone number, but you refuse to give yours. You leave by saying that you might see him at the bar on a Wednesday or a Sunday, passively implying that sleeping together will never happen again.

But if in the morning the sleep-mate is found attractive, you ask to see him later that day and evening and the next day and the next day's evening, too. There is hope that a relationship might develop, but he'll say it was nice meeting and that he must go to work. He never offers a phone number, but you aggressively give yours, and he says that he may see you again on a Wednesday or a Sunday night, indirectly implying that a sleep-together will not happen again.

□

Reckless acts made possible by life in the closet: the many nights of driving home drunk, falsely believing in sobriety, swerving over the middle, yellow-dotted highway line, putting other drivers at risk, avoiding construction cones and frightened deer, hitting and destroying a stop sign with the car and leaving the scene of the collision only to have the police call you the next day to say that your license plate was found at the previously stop-signed intersection.

Reckless acts: going home with someone whose name you don't know but who you think likes you, believing your intimate interaction is promising and will progress into something more than just a one-time affair but then waking the next day, to a person who, if found unattractive, will be avoided in the coming days and weeks, making an other's feelings of inadequacy possible.

Reckless acts: not responding to letters and calls from family and friends, not because you're scared to tell them that you're gay (you assume they may have speculated) or because you're scared to talk about your current same-sex relationship (you assume they won't care), but because you feel like never wanting to talk to them again.

Reckless acts: not showing up to a college class you're teaching, because you've decided to spend the night with a stranger, or arriving to teach unprepared, because you woke 15 minutes before class begins.

Reckless acts: having sex in a bathtub in the room next to where your roommate sleeps, a person you disregard by selfishly choosing to have sex with two others, a person to whom you came out to only the previous week, a person who, before you, did not know any gay people. But you still decide to occupy the bathroom, with the men and without much care, until 4 A.M., the next morning apologizing to your roommate when the three of you greet him in the kitchen. "No problem," he says, but you sense he is uncomfortable and angry and regrets living with a gay man.

Reckless acts: refusing to visit a doctor to see if you've contracted any STDs; refusing to acknowledge that you've had unprotected anal sex once (maybe twice) without regret (it felt good!); refusing to believe you've had protected anal sex 5 (maybe 10) times, and refusing to talk about the 10 (maybe 20) blow jobs you've given. Reckless is not sharing this history with the guy you meet tonight, the guy who adds to the oral sex count. Since he's nice and since you find him attractive, he adds to the anal sex count, too, and, depending on the level of intoxication, you may allow the sex to go unprotected.

□

Living (in) the closet: a time when support masked as unconditional love is questioned, support based on others knowing you as or wanting you to be a particular kind of (heterosexual) person, support garnered from regularly appearing and professing a nonexistent attraction, support that allows you to feel hesitantly and temporarily secure.

Living (in) the closet: a time when you retreat from friends and family out of fear; a time when same-sex attraction is kept secret, and different-sexed others are asked on dates—a planting of intimate and meaningful relational seeds in a person whom you may never desire, intimately, regardless of how nice or attractive the other is or how much you lie and try; and a time when isolation teases, when you refuse to treat someone of the same sex with respect even though you still kiss and fuck the person and then abruptly, without reason, end contact, motivating him to cry, scream, and say the "go fuck yourself" line. You understand the other's hurt but take care of yourself so that you aren't the person that has to tell another to go fuck himself.

Living (in) the closet: a time when same-sex attraction is privately embraced, a time when a LGBQ identity begins to take hold on a person, a time when despair, uncertainty, and sadness about this attraction and identity are most prone to be lived, evidenced by a person's excessive and intentional use of hiding practices, acts of omission, and lies, extreme moments of selfishness, and risky or reckless activities. Although these practices, acts, lies, and moments may be necessary for protection, they also put a LGBQ person at risk: if and when the person discloses same-sex attraction—comes out—the person may be accountable for these self-protecting practices, acts, lies, and moments, thus making possible complicated, relational situations as well as assessments of manipulation and deceit.

□

Thanksgiving morning, 7 A.M. Your cell phone rings. You scramble through the comforter on the foreign bed and try to locate the buzzing device. The guy next to you moans a moan that suggests he's angry and wants to return to sleep.

"Hello," you say in a quiet, raspy voice.

"What time are you coming home?" the woman, your mother, asks.

"I'm not," you reply, and then continue with a lie. "I have too much work."

"Where are you?" she asks.

"At home, sleeping."

"Why aren't you coming home?" she continues. "I haven't seen you in months."

"I have to work," you say, but know you'll spend the day with your boyfriend.

"But you've never missed Thanksgiving."

"I know, but I have too much work."

"Are you gay?" she asks; you become nervous.

"Ummm . . . no. Why?"

"Have you ever tried to be gay?" she continues.

"Ummm . . . no! Why are you asking these questions?"

"Just wondering. You've been distant the last few months. I miss you."

"I'm busy mom, that's all. I'm not gay. I promise."

Not prepared to talk about your attraction to men you retreat comfortably, knowingly, into promise after promise, lie after lie.

CHAPTER FOUR

Leaving the Closet: The Time of "Coming Out"

"What are we toasting?" Gareth Thomas asks his mother in response to his coming out.
"The start of the rest of your life," she replies.

GARY SMITH (2010, p. 62)

Much research on same-sex attraction addresses the time of leaving —"coming out" of—the closet, the time a person speaks *to others* about same-sex attraction and/or a lesbian, gay, bisexual, or queer (LGBQ) identity; the time when a person often undergoes, for self and others, a "paradigm shift" (Kuhn, 1962) by discursively transitioning from one group—heterosexual—to another—LGBQ (Garrick, 1997; Yoshino, 2006); a time that can drastically reshape life (Plummer, 1995). In this chapter I discern 12 interrelated premises of coming out and, when relevant, illustrate how these premises are situated in, and made possible by, social interaction.

□

Premise #1: Same-sex attraction is inextricably tied to the metaphor of the closet.

As illustrated, same-sex attraction and the closet are mutually constitutive (Betsky, 1997; Brown, 2000; Sedgwick, 1990; Urbach, 1996). This relationship is best exemplified by the phrase "coming out of the closet," the act whereby a person discloses same-sex attraction and/or a LGBQ identity to another (Butler, 1997; Fuss, 1991; Gross, 1991). Coming out is the "most canonical expression of being gay" (Perez, 2005, p. 177), a "central narrative of a positive gay experience" (Plummer, 1995, p. 84), a metaphor by which a person with same-sex attraction often comes to live (Lakoff & Johnson, 1980).

□

Premise #2: Coming out makes sense only in relation to hetero-normative contexts.

Hetero-normative contexts frame heterosexuality and different-sex attraction as better than homosexuality and same-sex attraction (Butler, 1993, 1999; Foster, 2008; Yep, 2003). These contexts also frame a person as straight until proven otherwise, thus making the act of identifying as heterosexual unnecessary but simultaneously require a person to come out—that is, confirm same-sex attraction through discourse or action (for example, saying "I am gay," intimately kissing someone of the same sex; see Butler, 1991; Garrick, 2001; Shallenberger, 1991; Solis, 2007). "The closet is not a function of homosexuality in our culture," Douglas Crimp writes,

> but of compulsory and presumptive heterosexuality. I may be publicly identified as gay, but in order for that identity to be acknowledged, I have to declare it on each new occasion. By "occasion," I mean something as simple as asking a cab driver to take me to a [gay] bar like the Spike, or kissing my friend Jeff goodbye on a crowded subway when he gets off two stops before me on our way home from the gym. Fearing for my safety, I might choose not to kiss Jeff, thereby hiding behind our fellow riders' presumption that we're straight. (1993, p. 305)

Conversely, such homo-normative contexts as LGBQ bars, bathhouses, and pride parades make coming out irrelevant; a person's same-sex attraction is often assumed until she or he is proven straight.

□

March 2003. Amy, my first girlfriend, the one I met four years earlier in college, finds my email address on the Internet.

Hi Tony! This is Amy—it's been a long time. How are you?
I'm married to a wonderful man. We're getting ready to have our first child.
Are you married? Seeing anyone? Children?
I can't wait to hear from you!

I am glad to hear from Amy and decide to write back.

Hi Amy! Thanks for writing! That's great about the marriage and the child. I'm in school finishing my master's. I'm not married and I don't have children, but I am seeing a great guy. (Yes, a guy.) His name is Brett. Where do you live? We should try to meet. I'd like to meet your family.
Write back soon, Tony

Sometimes, after coming out to another person, I worry about how the person will react and how our relationship might change.
A week passes without response, and I send Amy another message:

Hi Amy! I hope you're well. I'm wondering if you received my previous email.
Take care, Tony

I do not hear from Amy and begin to doubt the possibility of a friendship. Did I say something offensive? Did she receive any of my emails? Maybe she is shocked that I am dating a guy. Maybe she thinks I am immoral. Maybe this wasn't the right time to come out. Maybe she feels betrayed by me—did she feel used? I send one more message.

Hi Amy. I'm wondering about your lack of response.
Did I offend you? I hope not. I apologize if I did.

I never receive a reply.

□

Premise #3: Coming out is necessary when same-sex attraction is not easily accessible.
In Chapter 2 I mentioned that one condition of the closet entails the recognition that same-sex attraction is secret from and/or not

easily known *by others*. It is this characteristic of same-sex attraction that makes coming out—the revealing of this attraction and/or a LGBQ identity—necessary and possible.

LGBQ identities—identities tied to same-sex attraction—lack definitive and permanent characteristics. Consequently, they are "discreditable" identities that must be confirmed, repeatedly, through discourse and action (Foucault, 1978; Goffman, 1963; Yoshino, 2006). If LGBQ identities and/or same-sex attraction were visible, coming out would be unnecessary as others would know of a person's identity and/or attraction based on how the person sounds or looks; a person would never have to say or do anything, never have to come out. "For it is one of the misfortunes and pleasures of gay life," Scott writes "that the imposed invisibility of homosexuality creates an obsession with identifying who is and who isn't, a practice engaged in to finer and finer degrees of exactness" (1994, p. 302). Notwithstanding the existence of legendary "gaydar"—the "totally unscientific sixth sense that many people rely on to tell if [someone] is gay or straight" (Colman, 2005, p. 91; see also Burgess, 2005; Nicholas, 2004)—knowledge of others' same-sex attraction is uncertain and fraught with unreliability and error (Bennett, 2006).

In addition, as I mentioned in Chapter 1, gender inversion is often used, erroneously as indicative of same-sex attraction (whereas gender conformity—the aligning of a person's sex and gender—is often indicative of heterosexuality; see Bloom, 2002; Escoffier, 2003; Hutson, 2010; Johnson, 2004; La Pastina, 2006; Meyer, 1995; Perry & Ballard-Reisch, 2004). Consider, for instance, how the lyrics of the song "Cowboys Are Secretly Frequently (Fond of Each Other)" (Sublette, 1981) equate gender inversion with (mostly male) same-sex attraction: "inside every man there's a feminine," "inside every lady there's a deep manly voice loud and clear," "inside every cowboy there's a lady who'd love to slip out," and "when you talk to a cowboy don't treat him like he was a sister."

Or consider comments about gender inversion and gay men made by Matt Hunt, a blogger on Myspace.com:

> i [sic] wish it would be realized that being gay does not automatically mean being feminine. it'd be nice to see less of the flamboyant, asshole, drag queens prancing around, and more men that actually act like men. keep the pitch of your voice down,

and stop walking like you're bowlegged—its pissing society off. (Hunt, 2007)

Matt disdains gay (sexuality) men (sex) who do not act masculine (gender) and directs his disdain toward feminine gay men. Attributions of same-sex attraction stemming from gender inversion also perpetuate the myth that gay men are women trapped in male (sexed) bodies and lesbians are men trapped in female (sexed) bodies (Hunter, 1992; Rüling, 2006 [1904]; Solis, 2007; Stein, 2010; Ulrichs, 2006 [1862]).

Furthermore, like all discourse and action, gender inversion is contextual: perceptions of, and expectations for, sex, gender, and sexuality change with time, place, and circumstance. A heterosexual (sexuality) woman (sex) who dresses masculine or acts like a man (gender) for a "highly ceremonialized occasion" (Garfinkel, 1967) such as Halloween, a costume party, or a theater production may be allowed, by self and others, to engage in this "inversion" with less possibility of being viewed as having same-sex attraction; her (perceived) heterosexuality is safe as she inverts sex and gender in legitimate, gender-transgressing contexts. But once Halloween, the costume party, or the theater production ends she may be encouraged, by self and others, to "return" to a more acceptable sex and gender alignment, a return to sex and gender conformity. If the woman continues to engage in gender inversion beyond legitimate, gender-transgressing contexts, others might begin to consider her LGBQ.

By engaging in gender inversion, has this woman come out (Hutson, 2010)? I do not think so. The woman's (self-claimed) heterosexuality may be questioned, but this does not mean she has "come out." The woman comes out only when she confirms same-sex attraction and/or a LGBQ identity discursively (for example, by saying "I am a lesbian").

I also believe that *any* manipulation of sex and gender can mark a person as LGBQ even if gender inversion does not occur. For instance, if a person believes her or his sex does not match her or his gender—a feeling that says nothing about the person's sexual attraction *to others*—the person may identify or be marked as transsexual or transgender. However, transidentities are often conflated with categories tied to same-sex attraction (for instance, lesbian, gay, bisexual, queer) *not* with categories of sex and gender (for example, female and male, woman and man, masculine and feminine), a conflation best noted by the use of LGBQT. Transidentities are not necessarily identities constituted by same-sex attraction but are often understood as or equated with same-sex attraction (Meyerowitz, 2002; Murphy, 2007).[1] Furthermore, any manipulation of sex and gender might motivate others to mark a person as having same-sex attraction or as LGBQ whether or not the person wants such ascription.

The "harassment and the discrimination" of lesbians and gay men, Matt Kailey writes, is often based on "*perceived* sexual orientation—perceived through that person's gender presentation" (2005, p. 94). Whereas attributing a person's (not easily accessible) attraction to her or his (visible) gendered body is an attempt to make surveillance and regulation of sexuality possible (Foucault, 1978; Hacking, 1990; Walker, 1993), attraction is much more complex, hidden, and inaccessible than appearance-based, gender inverted attributions suggest. These characteristics of same-sex attraction make some people uncomfortable: lacking definitive, permanent aural and visible characteristics, it must be pinned down and negotiated through discourse and action; I can say I am queer today, straight tomorrow, and bisexual the next, and there will be no (visible) trace of my transition.

□

Premise #4: Coming out happens only when same-sex attraction and/or a LGBQ identity is disclosed through discourse and action.

The death of my ex-boyfriend Brett—a possible suicide—may have been motivated by his father's negative response to his coming out. But what makes this possibility difficult to prove was that Brett possessed many stereotypically gay characteristics. He enjoyed theater, was infatuated with Judy Garland, and had a flamboyant and sarcastic demeanor. He was out to most everyone at the school where we met, dated many men, and lived with one for four years. I assumed that Brett's family assumed that he was (or could be) gay. However, even though Brett may have been graceful, flamboyant, and sarcastic he may not have come out—or been out—to his family; I am not sure he ever disclosed—confirmed—his same-sex attraction for them.

Dave shared a similar account of confirmation when coming out to his mother (2008). Dave's mother worked overnight shifts in a factory. One evening, unexpectedly, she came home and found an unfamiliar man, Dave's boyfriend, staying the night. Shirtless upon hearing her arrival, Dave quickly put on the nearest shirt. But he accidentally put the shirt on inside out, the tag facing outward on the front. Based on her later response, he believed his mom noticed the tag and thus assumed his shirt had been off before her arrival. This mistake, Dave believes, motivated his mom to *ask* about his gay identity two days later when she called and asked him to pick her up from a bar.

"But mom," he said, "I have school in the morning. Can't you just stay the night with a friend and come home tomorrow?"

"What's the matter?" she replied. "Got somebody there?"

"I'll be right there," he responded.

Even though his mom may have found it weird that Dave had his shirt off around an unfamiliar man at their house, this did not confirm, for her, that Dave was gay; it only suggested that he might be. It was not until Dave said something—came out explicitly—in response to her ascription of same-sex attraction that her suspicious could be confirmed.

"Tell me it's not true," she said, upon entering the car.

When Dave didn't respond to the question, his silence served as an act of confirmation, a moment of coming out that motivated her to scream and kick the windshield and, later that evening, beat him up enough to send him to the hospital with a concussion.

After coming home from work that one time, Dave's mother may have thought that Dave was gay, but she did not react to him as gay until *he* confirmed the possibility two days later. Why didn't his mother get angry when she first noticed his shirt and the boyfriend? Why did she *ask* about Dave's sexuality initially? Confirmation of his same-sex attraction in action (silence) was necessary.

Or consider a scene in the film *Sordid Lives* (Shores, 2000). A mother describes attending a gay-themed theater production in which her son was an actor. As viewers, we get a glimpse of the production she describes, a performance of six naked men on a stage who come together to form three couples. Each man gently caresses the other, and we see the mother squirm in her seat. But, for the mother, the son's participation in this production—and her witnessing of it—does not mark his body as gay or imply, to her, that he has same-sex attraction. Throughout the remaining film she denies others' attributions of her son's gayness and discusses the son's gay identity *only when he says something* about it. Until he says so—until he confirms it in discourse—he has not come out to her.

A conversation on an episode of the *Savage Love* sex-advice Podcast speaks to the necessity of confirming same-sex attraction for coming out as well. Dan Savage, the host, receives a call from a man who thinks his mother may be a lesbian.

> "How is it that you know your mother is a lesbian?" Dan asks.
>
> "I had actually known the woman she's seeing before she did," the caller responds. "I came from a very small town and there is a small gay clique. And she was one of them I met through another friend. You know, you kind of just pick up on things. I would walk down to the basement and there they would be, not doing 'that,' but not doing what friends do."
>
> "And this has been going on all of your life?" Dan continues.
>
> "I've mostly known for the last five or six years," the caller replies.
>
> "Are you and your mother honest with each about the fact that she's a lesbian?" Dan asks. "Does she acknowledge that she is a lesbian? *Has she outed herself to you?*"
>
> "No," says the caller. "She admitted once that she had an affair, but [said] she was kind of drunk and stoned at the time."
>
> "It's not like your mother has *said* 'Hey, I'm a lesbian. I'm with this woman, but don't tell your father?'" Dan asks again.
>
> "Yeah," the caller replies.
>
> "So this is all you reading into this situation," Dan says. "And you may be reading it exactly right."
>
> The caller responds with "I want mom to *come out* and say 'Look! I'm gay. And I'm going to go live with this woman I love!'" (Savage, 2007, my emphasis)

Dan implies that the caller's mom will come out only when something is *said*—put into discourse—not necessarily when she engages in a particular act (for example, a one-time, drunk and stoned, same-sex love affair).

Or consider professional rugby player Gareth Thomas's "coming out" conversation with Johnno, a former team manager who confronted Thomas about his reckless behaviors.

> "Look, it's one of two things," said Johnno. "Do you want me to make it easier on you, Alf [Thomas's nickname]. Do you want me to *say it for you?*"
>
> Alf nodded. "Either you cheated on Jemma [Thomas's wife] with another woman, which I don't think you have . . ."

Silence.

"Does it have something to do with your sexuality, mate?"

Tears filled Alf's eyes. "You knew all the time," he said. (cited in Smith, 2010, p. 61)

Even though Johnno may have speculated about Thomas's same-sex attraction, his speculation did not mean that Thomas came *out* to him. For Thomas to have come out to Johnno, Thomas had to confirm his attraction discursively—in this situation, by tearing up and replying "you knew" to a direct question, posed by Johnno, about his sexuality.

Similarly, Darius Ankleshwaria says that even though people may perceive him as gay or have heard through "hearsay" that he is gay, he maintains safety and protection by *not* talking about his sexual orientation—that is, by not putting it into "words"—because, if he did, he believes that he could not "retract" the "statement" at a later time (2009, p. 204).

The Don't Ask, Don't Tell discharge policy of the United States military also illustrates the relationship between same-sex attraction ("homosexuality") and the need to confirm this attraction in discourse or action:

> Sexual orientation will not be a bar to service unless manifested by homosexual conduct. The military will discharge members *who engage in homosexual conduct,* which is defined as a homosexual act, a *statement* that the member is homosexual or bisexual, or a marriage or attempted marriage to someone of the same gender. (Pentagon, cited in Anonymous, 1993, p. A16, my emphasis)

A person with same-sex attraction and/or who identifies as LGBQ can serve in the military but cannot act on or speak of this attraction or these identities; she or he cannot come out. Although exceptions exist, a person can get discharged legally only by speaking of same-sex attraction or by saying "I am LGBQ."

And so, for coming out to happen, same-sex attraction and/or a LGBQ identity *must be confirmed* through discourse (for example, by saying "I am a lesbian") or action (for instance, intimately kissing someone of the same sex). For instance, if I say Barack Obama is gay, this does not mean that Barack is gay or has come out. I need *his* confirmation of *my* claim for the closet to matter, for coming out to happen; he must say or do something to mark same-sex attraction.

I recognize that others can influence and sometimes force a person to come out, but I want to make clear that a person must confirm charges of same-sex attraction through discourse or action. Liang further suggests that coming out does not happen if others do not "apprehend the significance" of this discourse or action (1997, p. 292). For instance, if others do not hear the words "I am LGBQ" or apprehend the significance of a person wearing an "earring on the right ear lobe" (p. 292), displaying a particular color of handkerchief (Bornstein, 1994), showing a symbol affiliated with a LGBQ cause or organization (Brouwer, 1998), or perceiving a couple holding hands as family or close friends, then coming out by these persons to such un-apprehending others has not yet happened.

As I mentioned, inferences about same-sex attraction and/or LGBQ identities may also stem from gender inversion—the idea that a person's gender (embodied performances of masculinity and femininity) differs from her or his sex (biological criteria)—or gender nonconformity—a person enacting gender in unique, radical ways (Hutson, 2010). However, a person who engages in gender inversion or nonconformity has not come out (Bloom, 2002; Perry & Ballard-Reisch, 2004). For instance, I might consider a man who dresses and acts like a woman to be gay, but does this mean that he has come out (to me)? No—the man's confirmation of same-sex attraction and/or gay identity is necessary.

Or consider discourse about Elena Kagan, Barack Obama's appointee to the United States Supreme Court. The *Wall Street Journal* published an image showing Kagan with short hair playing softball. During the confirmation hearings and motivated by gender inversion, people found Kagan, a (assumed) female, too masculine. Consequently, they began questioning her heterosexuality; they asked, wanted, and needed confirmation *from her* that she was not a lesbian.[2] Kagan could not have come out by the publication of the image. She could have come out only if she had said "I find women attractive" or "I am a lesbian" (which she did not do).

Coming out is also not necessarily relevant for people who engage in same-sex sexual acts. For instance, a man may consider himself gay only if he engages in a passive, penetrated, "bottoming" role in a same-sex sex acts (La Pastina, 2006; Meyer, 1995; Phellas, 2005; Rao & Sarma, 2009; Shakespeare, 1999). A man who actively penetrates—a man who "tops" another man—need not identify as gay and, consequently, may not worry about coming out.

But even bottoming may not encourage a man to identify as gay or suggest that he has same-sex attraction. As Escoffier (2003) observes, a majority of men who have sex with men in the pornography industry identify as heterosexual even though they engage in penetrative acts. In the context of porn, same-sex sexual acts may not indicate a person's sexuality; men may be penetrated for financial reasons, not because of a gay identity or same-sex attraction. Thus, coming out as gay may have little relevance for these men.

Furthermore, when I say "a person comes out," I am saying that she or he makes a claim about same-*sex* attraction and attraction for others with similar *genitalia*. In most cases coming out is neither a claim about same-*gender* attraction—attraction to masculine or feminine others—nor a claim about an attraction to a person with similar chromosomes and reproductive organs. When I, a man (sex), say "I am gay," I am saying "I am sexually attracted to someone with similar genitalia" (a criterion of sex). I am not saying "I am attracted to someone with similar reproductive organs and chromosomes" (also sex criteria), and I am also not expressing an attraction to masculine, feminine, and/or androgynous persons, characteristics tied to gender not sex. I conceive of coming out as a disclosure of same-*sex* attraction, an attraction to same-sex genital relations.[3]

I am not saying that other people do not influence a person's outing process, or that if a person is not out others will assume the person is straight, or that rumors about a person's same-sex attraction are irrelevant or invalid. But coming out is an act of disclosing same-sex attraction and/or a LGBQ identity; the attraction and/or identity is self-claimed, confessed, and personally made public (Shugart, 2005). As Foucault says, sexuality is "elusive by nature; its energy and its mechanism escaped observation, and its causal power was partly clandestine;" sexuality must thus appear "through the labor of a confession" (1978, p. 66). Coming out is a "linguistic act that offers up the promise of a transparent revelation of sexuality" (Butler, 1991, p. 15), an act that puts one "inside the realm of the visible, the speakable, the culturally intelligible" (Fuss, 1991, p. 4) and an act based on the condition that "'speaking' one's identity is the most appropriate form of 'knowing' it" (Minson, 1981, p. 21).

□

June 2003. I see Beth, my second girlfriend, the one I met at a bar three years previously; the woman with whom I spent most of my time drunk. She's working in a Gap clothing store in Springfield, Illinois. I'm looking at the clearance rack in the back of the store when I notice her in the front, folding women's polo shirts, not being too attentive to clientele. I hesitate, unsure of how to proceed: Do I approach her? Does she hate me? Do I tell her that I like men? Does she think she's unattractive because I wasn't attracted to her? I decide to leave and avoid possible conflict, but just then our eyes connect. I sense confusion. I wonder if she recognizes me, wonder if she thinks that I want to meet with her, wonder if she wonders why I am invading her space. She doesn't smile or frown or wave or quit folding. I exit the store but glance back at her through the storefront glass. She continues to work, uninterrupted, never looking outside, never acknowledging that our paths ever crossed.

□

Premise #5: Same-sex attraction is (contextually) stigmatized and contentious.

As illustrated throughout much of this book, persons who possess same-sex attraction can be targets of harassment and physical violence solely for claiming this attraction or being perceived to be LGBQ (Kimmel & Mahler, 2003; Pascoe, 2007). In the United States, same-sex partnerships are not recognized as a legitimate kind of coupling in a variety of contexts (for example, national and some state governments, hospitals, families), and institutions such as the military (Brouwer, 2004; Butler, 1997) and the educational system (Gust & Warren, 2008; Kirk, 2008; McIntosh, 2007; Meyer, 2005) require a person to vigilantly regulate or remain silent about LGBQ identities. Same-sex relations are often absent from or disregarded in mundane conversation (Feigenbaum, 2007; Foster, 2008; Glave, 2005), and a variety of religions position the "homosexual lifestyle" as inappropriate, immoral, and in need of change (Bennett, 2003; Chávez, 2004; Cobb, 2006; Stewart, 2005).

□

Premise #6: Because same-sex attraction can be contentious and stigmatized, and can arouse hatred, disclosing same-sex attraction—coming out—can be dangerous.

Coming out is a time that can consist of "contempt, tolerance, and fear of loss of approval" (Burgess, 2005, p. 129), a time of "sacrifice and danger" that can promote "hostility, rejection, and even violence from family, friends, and total strangers" (Gross, 1991, p. 374). "I don't enjoy flaunting my homosexuality," Gary Fisher writes in his diary (1981), "not because I'm ashamed of it but because it draws attention from people who misunderstand. I can do without the funny looks and the whispers" (cited in Sedgwick, 1996, p. 149).

The hostility, rejection, and violence that a person may experience on coming out typically occur for three reasons. First, people might consider same-sex attraction and/or a LGBQ identity inappropriate and/or immoral. I believe that this is the common, often-reported worry a person has about coming out: others may disparage the person for claiming to possess an inappropriate and/or immoral attraction.

Second, as I discussed in Chapter 3, when a person comes out, the person reveals—and, consequently, can be held accountable for—a history of hiding practices, lies, omissions of information, moments of selfishness, and/or reckless acts—all of which may have occurred when the person was closeted and all of which the person found necessary to protect her- or himself from hostility, rejection, and violence. "I don't think I have ever lied when asked a direct question [about my sexuality]," Steven Saylor writes in a letter to his mother. "But I am guilty of being secretive and closed with you" (1992, p. 64). By coming out, he continues, "the burden of evasion was off me; there was no longer a secret about *why* I was secretive" (p. 67). Saylor echoes Simmel's observation that a secret "contains a tension that is dissolved in the moment of its revelation" (1964, p. 333); however, new tensions can emerge when a person comes out, particularly when others hold the person accountable for closeted, pre-coming-out acts.

A third reason a person may experience hostility, rejection, and violence upon coming out could be because the person did not come out at the right time: others may feel as though the person's same-sex attraction was hidden too long or not long enough, or the disclosure was inappropriate for the context (for example, family reunion, celebration, holiday gathering, public setting). For instance, in response to professional rugby player Gareth Thomas's coming out, two players put a hand on his back, said his attraction was "no big deal," and then asked "Why didn't you tell us before?" (Smith, 2010, p. 61)

And, as I discuss again in Chapter 5, I have received complaints for coming out too soon in a college class and complaints for not coming out soon enough or at all; others might hold me accountable for any action I take (silence or disclosure) in relation to the classroom context. Furthermore, such complaints are not directed at my attraction or closeted, pre-coming-out acts but at the amount of time I hid my attraction—the "duration" of my secret (Brown-Smith, 1998, p. 26).

☐

September 2003. I try to contact Christina, my third girlfriend, the woman I went out with when I began to embrace my same-sex attraction, the person I regretfully called boring, ugly, and mean. Before we, or I, ended the relationship, we had been close friends for seven years. I still have her email address and assume that she hasn't changed it in the two years since breaking up.

> Hi Christina. You may be shocked that I'm writing. You also may be shocked by the content of this email. I had to write it. I wish I wrote sooner.
>
> I'm gay. I have been attracted to men for a while but never accepted my attraction. I tried to wish it away but realized it wasn't that easy. I'm telling you this because I want you to know that you did nothing to break us up. My frustrations about us stemmed from my confusion. You're a wonderful, loving, intelligent, and attractive person who I cherish and miss. I apologize for any hurt I've caused.

I know this could be the last contact I have with Christina especially if she is angered by my writing or upset about my sexuality. Based on my previous experience with Amy, I write knowing this and thus try to control the possibility of no response.

> I realize that you may not respond to this letter. I realize that you might hate me. I understand any response you have. I just want you to know that you're a great person. I'm sorry for my actions. I'm sorry for not writing.

A prompt reply from Christina:

Tony, I could never hate you. Even if we haven't talked in a few years, you're still one of my best friends. I'm glad you wrote. During and after our relationship I was hurt. I'd be lying if I said I wasn't. But after a few months, I began thinking about how you turned into a different person, a monster of sorts. I didn't know you the last few months. You'd get mad at everything. You forgot how to laugh.

She concludes with "I miss you." Our friendship resumes.

□

Premise #7: Because coming out can be dangerous, a person with same-sex attraction may feel a need to try to find the right time to disclose this attraction.

"Coming out under any circumstances is an uncertain business," Jacqueline Taylor says. "No matter who you're coming out to and no matter what you already know about them, there is no way to predict how anyone will respond to this disclosure" (2000, pp. 69–70).

"There's always a right time to come out, and you have to feel the environment for when that right time is," Tyler says in an interview (2007). "You have to get a sixth sense about who is going to take it better than others."

"As a teacher, I'm uncomfortable with students knowing that I am gay in the first week of class," Michael says (2008). "But halfway through a semester, I don't care if they know. There's a certain amount of calculation and prediction every time you come out."

"A critical component of coming out is all in the timing," Vince Falconi, a reporter for *The Daily Mississippian,* writes.

While the Thanksgiving turkey is being carved, for example, may not be the best time to blurt out "Mom, Dad, I'm gay!" as you reach for the cranberry sauce. Awkward! Rather, choosing just the right time and setting to discuss your sexual orientation with those most important to you is crucial in feeling secure in getting out of the closet. (2006)

Stemming from a perceived need to balance openness and honesty with safety and protection (Bochner, 1984; Rawlins, 1983), a person may metaphorically "test" the "relational waters" before coming out

(McLean, 2007, p. 161); she or he may feel a need to try to predict the right time to disclose, try to create ideal relational conditions, and try to control the timing of the coming-out event (Alexander & Losh, 2010).

However, should a person try to better time the disclosure of same-sex attraction, should the person stay in the closet in relation to others, then she or he simultaneously perpetuates and builds on a history of hiding practices, lies, omissions of information, moments of selfishness, and a participation in reckless acts—a history that, as mentioned previously, may come to haunt the person when and if she or he ever decides to come out to these people.

□

You planned to come out at dinner, but that didn't happen.

"Can we go for a walk," you ask.

"Sure," she says.

After a few minutes fear hasn't diminished, but you know you must act. You don't want her, a good friend, to hear from someone else.

"I have to tell you something." She stops.

You lean toward her ear, nervously gesturing that it's a secret, unable to say the "I am gay" words loud and proud. They still sound disgusting so you whisper "I am gay."

She smiles.

"Why didn't you tell me sooner?" she asks.

"I was scared."

The walk continues, and you're relieved. A burden, released. "Why didn't you tell me sooner?" she'll ask again. "You knew I'd be fine."

"I didn't know that."

□

Premise #8: The act of coming out and others' immediate reactions to this act—those immediate seconds, minutes, hours, and days—are significant, often-scarring moments in a person's life, moments perpetually remembered and narrated.

A scene from the television sitcom *Will & Grace* portrays the coming-out experience of Jack, a main character, to his mother. As audiences, we see him say, "Mom, I'm gay" and witness her initial sadness to the disclosure. I find this interaction profound for one significant reason: in eight years of *Will & Grace*—186 episodes—this is the *only* episode where Jack's mother appears. From a production standpoint, this suggests that Jack's coming out and the reaction to his coming out are *the* defining moments in the (gay) son-mother relationship.

"One night my dad and I were watching a comedian on TV," Dave says in an interview, recalling the time he came out to his father.

> The comedian made a gay joke and started laughing. My dad started laughing, too. I looked at him and said, "You know that's not funny," and he said, "Yeah it was," and I said, "No it's not. Your son's gay." He looked at me and said, "Are you sure?" and I said, "Yeah, I'm sure," and he said, "I'm okay with it. I still love you." (2008)

Although his father supported him initially, a few days later the support changed. "I thought all was fine as he became only a little distant for a couple of days," Dave says.

> But three days later, when I returned home from school, I found my stuff on his front porch. He met me at the front door and said "I'm sorry but I'm not okay with you being gay. God made Adam and Eve and not Adam and Steve and I can't have you in my life anymore." And then he slammed the door.

"Barefoot Ron," a contributor to the Parents and Friends of Lesbians and Gays (PFLAG) website, offers "gentle wisdom" for parents responding to a child's coming out:

> PARENTS: Don't underestimate for a minute how important it is for you to be supportive to your gay/lesbian child especially, in the *first few minutes* AFTER they come out to you. Yes, those *first few minutes* are very important and will always be remembered. (Barefoot Ron, n.d., my emphasis)

Suzanne Westenhoefer makes a similar observation, calling the *"first five* minutes" after coming out "really the hardest" (cited in Human Rights Campaign, 2005, p. 23, my emphasis). Those immediate moments post-disclosure: sometimes awkward and often scarring, moments remembered and narrated, time after time.

□

"Mom, I'm gay."

Silence. One one-thousand, two one-thousand, three one-thousand . . .

An expressionless face faces you; a mild frown forms.

Those first few minutes...

"It's just a phase," she replies. "I was also confused at 22."

"I don't think so, Mom."

One one-thousand, two one-thousand, three . . .

"You're too young to know," she says.

"I don't think so, Mom."

One one-thousand, two . . .

"Mom?"

Those first few minutes, important they are.

□

A call from Dad.

"I heard a rumor about you," he says. You become nervous. "I heard that you're living with a guy. In fact, not just living with, but fucking this guy. Is this true?"

One one-thousand, two one-thousand . . .

"Weeelllll," you stutter, "no, it's not true. Who would say something like that?"

"That doesn't matter," he abruptly suggests. "I'm just glad it ain't."

"Yeah, me too father. That's silly. I'll talk to you soon." The conversation ends.

One one-thousand . . .

Five one-thousand . . .

Ten one-thousand . . .

You call Dad back.

"Hello," he answers in an upbeat, much happier tone.

"Yeah, Dad, it's me. I just wanted to tell you that it's true—I am living with a guy, my boyfriend in fact."

A few seconds of talk to end the conversation; a silence the next six months (Adams, 2006). These reactionary seconds and months: awkward and scarring.

□

"I planned to come out to my father at dinner," Michael says in an interview (2008). "I wasn't going to come out to my father at my work, because I wasn't out at work. I thought dinner would be more relaxed. I also knew that we would be in public so he couldn't freak out."

"What happened?" I ask.

"Dinner moved along, and I realized that I couldn't do it. So I then decided to come out at desert. But the pie arrives and we eat the pie and I still don't come out to him."

"Because you were nervous?"

"Yes, but also, ironically, it felt weird being in public surrounded by strangers. I decided then that I had to say something to my father when we were alone."

"So when did you say something?"

"After dinner, in the car, as we headed to my house. I knew that John, my partner, was going to be there, and I vowed to tell my father before we arrived. We were about 10 minutes away, and I had to say something."

"Dad, there's something I need to tell you," Michael says, reenacting the interaction. "I need to tell you that I'm gay."

Silence.

"Well, I don't take that as good," he said.

Silence.

"I needed to tell you, because when we get to the house John's going to be there. He's my partner. We live together. I know this is springing a lot on you all of a sudden. If you're uncomfortable and need to stay at a motel, if you need to get out of the situation, I understand."

"No, no, no," he said. "I'll be fine."

"Okay," I replied.

Silence.

"Just don't tell your mother," he said. "It'll kill her."

"Okay," I replied.

"This car is front-wheel drive, isn't it?" he added, a non sequitur.

"Yeah, it is," I replied.

□

"I'm attracted to men," you say.

"It's just a phase," someone remarks.

"What a waste," says another; you've not felt like waste before.

"Have you tried sex with a woman?" someone asks.

□

At a bar predominantly occupied by gay men, I see Scott, a former student who I knew identified as heterosexual a few years ago.

"Scott!" I yell. We meet and exchange hugs. I then look at his face, and, with my eyes, try to ask, nonverbally, "Why are you here?" He interprets my implied question accurately.

"A lot has changed since you last saw me," he says. "A lot."

"Everything all right?" I ask.

"Yeah, sort of. I broke up with my girlfriend. And . . . today I came out to my parents. They told me that I could no longer live with them. They kicked me out of the house."

I offer condolences and support, and tell him to give them time.

I see Scott again in a few weeks and ask, "How are the parents?"

"We haven't talked," he says. "I tried to go to their house, but they wouldn't let me in."

I offer condolences and support, but sense his hope has started to fade.

"They just need more time," I reply.

□

Premise #9: Coming out is considered necessary, important, and politically responsible.

"Disclosing one's sexual orientation is thought to be [a] ubiquitously positive experience that creates self-acceptance and confidence through repeated practice," writes Phellas.

> In fact, for gay men and lesbians, not making public pronouncements about their sexual orientation is presumed to be negative and less than healthy psychologically and is characterised by negative terms, such as living double lives, hiding, being in the closet, and being closeted. Living double lives or being closeted is presumed to indicate shame, denial, and self-hatred. (2005, p. 79)

"The idealization of coming out," McLean says, "constructs a binary of disclosure that positions coming out as 'good,' as it enables the healthy development of sexual identity, and positions nondisclosure as 'bad'" (2007, p. 154). Rasmussen (2004) agrees, noting that persons with same-sex attraction who "fail in their duty to come out may be marked as lacking" or as "somehow ashamed of their inherent gayness" (pp. 145–146).

Coming out is often framed as healthy (Cole et al., 1996; Downs, 2005; McLean, 2007; Seidman, 2002), mature (Rust, 1993), moral (Mohr, 1992), honest (Smith, 2010), and politically responsible (Burgess, 2005; Corrigan & Matthews, 2003; Gross, 1991; Signorile, 1990, 2007). Consequently, not disclosing—not coming out—can frame a person as unhealthy, immature, immoral, dishonest, and politically irresponsible; she or he engages in an act of silence indicative of unhappiness, shame, and self-hatred (Hopcke, 1993; Meyer & Dean, 1998; Seidman, Meeks, & Traschen, 1999). There is an "attitude of contempt for people who are closeted," says Chee (2006, p. 114), as staying in is considered an act of "betrayal" (Delany, 1996, p. 1).

□

Premise #10: Coming out is considered unimportant, inappropriate, and selfish.

I had a professor whom I considered to be supportive of same-sex attraction but who questioned the importance of or reason for LGBQ pride parades. "I don't walk around saying 'I am straight' or showing pride for my heterosexuality," he said in a conversation about my research. "Attraction is something private and for which pride is irrelevant."[4]

Kenji Yoshino recalls being called "selfish," "hedonistic," "narcissistic," and "oversexed" on coming out (2006, p. 71; see also Cooper, 2010; Glave, 2005; Van Gelder, 1998).

Some people—even those who possess same-sex attraction— consider same-sex attraction a "purely a personal matter" (Panikkar, 2009, p. 241), a "strictly private affair" (Ankleshwaria, 2009, p. 200), and a person's "own business" (Gupta, 2009, p. 174).

One of the arguments against the repeal of the Don't Ask, Don't Tell policy of the United States military is that public declarations of same-sex attraction—declarations that would allow service personnel to come out—will hurt the morale of personnel, particularly heterosexuals (Dao, 2010; Donnelly, 2009).

And, as I have indicated throughout this book, some people find same-sex attraction socially inappropriate and/or immoral.

Given these assumptions and potential responses, a person who comes out may be perceived—by self and others—as unimportant, selfish, inappropriate, and offensive. Consequently, staying in the closet—staying silent about same-sex attraction—may demonstrate care and respect—for others.

□

Premise #11: Coming out is sometimes conceived of as a finite, linear process with a definite—and ideal—end.

Some authors suggest that coming out can end, or frame, the coming-out process as finite and consider post-closet life possible and ideal (for example, Gagné, Tewksbury, & McGaughey, 1997; Hutson, 2010; Kus, 1985; McDonald, 1982; Seidman, 2002). From this perspective, a person who finds the closet inescapable—a person who finds no end to the coming-out process—may be perceived, by self and others, as deficient, immature, and unhealthy.

□

Premise #12: Coming out is considered an inescapable, ever-present process.

"Every time you get into a new situation, there's the issue of negotiating disclosure" Michael says in an interview. "Coming out is a proactive act that always puts you at risk. Everyday interactions become moments of such risk, again and again, for the rest of a gay person's life" (2008). Tyler, another interviewee, agrees: "I don't think I could say that I'm ever completely out. Coming out is a process you do over and over again. Most people don't walk into rooms wearing 'Hi, I'm gay' T-shirts" (2007).

"Where heterosexuality is presumed," Henry Urbach writes, "coming out can never be accomplished once and for all;" the "sustenance of gay identity (where straight identity is presumed) depends on continuous acts of declaration" (1996, p. 69). A. C. Liang states that persons with same-sex attraction are "faced with the burden of having to decide with every interaction whether or not to self-disclose" (1997, p. 293). Janet Halley makes a similar observation:

because the assumption of heterosexuality applies in virtually every social interaction—from the encounter of teacher with student, salesperson with shopper, mother with daughter, Supreme Court Justice with clerk—even the most forthright and fearless gay man or lesbian cannot "come out" once and for all in a single public disclosure. (1989, p. 647)

Eve Sedgwick agrees, noting that

the deadly elasticity of heterosexist presumption means that . . . people find new walls springing up around them . . . every encounter with a new classful of students, to say nothing of a new boss, social worker, loan officer, landlord, doctor, erects new closets whose fraught and characteristic laws of optics and physics exact from at least gay people new surveys, new calculations, new . . . requisitions of secrecy or disclosure. (1990, p. 68)

"Being 'out' always depends to some extent on being 'in,'" Judith Butler says. Being out "gains its meaning only within that polarity," thus making it necessary for a person to "produce the closet again and again in order to maintain [her- or himself] as 'out'" (1991, p. 16). Out-ness is a matter of degree changing with context (Berzon, 2002; Chirrey, 2003; Crimp, 1993; Plummer, 1995).

Consider, for instance, a story in *Rolling Stone* about Adam Lambert, a musician who gained notoriety from being a contestant on *American Idol*. Lambert is said to have come out—at least for *Rolling Stone* and *Idol* audiences—in this story. Even though "backstage at [American] Idol" everyone knew of Lambert's same-sex attraction, and even though Lambert lived "for eight years as a gay man," Vanessa Grigoriadis writes, Lambert had previously "thought about coming out in the press" but "didn't want audiences to focus on the issue" (2009, p. 54). He also wanted to "'be in control of [the coming-out] situation'" (p. 52). Lambert's experience with and philosophy of disclosure illustrates not only how a person may try to control the timing of disclosure but also how leaving the closet does not happen with or in a single utterance—coming out never ends as new audiences make for new times to disclose.

Unless a person would, in the words of Tyler, "walk into rooms wearing 'Hi, I'm gay' T-shirts," or unless a person is situated in a homo-normative context (for example, a pride parade, a bar catering to predominantly same-sex LGBQ clientele), the person must find a way to come out as every new (hetero-normative) encounter makes for a new time to claim same-sex attraction and/or a LGBQ identity, a new time to worry about others, a new time to balance safety and protection with openness and honesty.

Furthermore, if coming out never ends, or if a person can't ever complete the coming-out process, then the person will always be in the closet in relation to some audiences—and, consequently, always has the possibility of being held accountable for hiding, lying, omitting information, being selfish or reckless—and, consequently, always has the possibility of being held accountable for being unhealthy and unhappy, immature and immoral, dishonest and politically irresponsible, shameful and self-hating.

☐

Leaving the closet is the time often thought to end a person's struggle with sexuality, the culmination and release of personal tension stemming from the possession of same-sex attraction and/or a LGBQ identity (Hegna, 2007). But although some struggles and tensions cease with coming out, new struggles and tensions form—all of which are made possible by the aforementioned premises. In the next chapter I illustrate these struggles and tensions and, in so doing, show how the closet can constitute a LGBQ person's existence.

CHAPTER FIVE

Paradoxes of the Closet[1]

I am an instructor of a Public Speaking course. The first assignment is a "Success Speech" designed for students to speak about a personal achievement. As I do with many assignments, I participate; I want to further introduce myself to the students as well as provide an example of how an outlined speech might sound. I decide to tell of my success with coming out to my father, my success with telling him that I am gay. Initially, I receive a positive response, but a few days later I receive a call from the chairperson of my department.

"Tony, the president of the university called me today," he reports in a serious tone. "She told me that a student's parents complained about you 'being out' in the classroom."

"Who would complain about that?" I ask.

"The parents don't think that 'being gay' is a part of the 'university curriculum,'" he says. "The president agrees."

Frustrated, sad, and frightened, I respond: "I don't want to hide from students especially in a speech asking me to discuss an achievement. What should I do?"

"You should be out in the classroom," he says, "but rethink how you do it."

The conversation ends and I reflect on the complaint against my claim to be a particular kind of person (gay) and for coming out too soon. An identity I claimed and the timing of my disclosure threatened a student, a student who will probably dislike me and my gay body for the remaining 13 weeks of the course. I decide that I came out too early in the semester and now worry about losing my job.

□

In the classroom I do not avoid discussions of same-sex attraction. I often use examples of lesbians and gay men, and talk about issues facing nonheterosexual communities. However, instead of coming out in the first few weeks, I now come out either mid-semester or not at all. I have not received another formal complaint about my sexuality in the classroom, but I continue to receive a variety of informal criticisms about when and whether I come out.

In courses where I come out mid-semester, I often received charges, from students and colleagues, of being manipulative for waiting too long, dishonest for keeping my sexuality secret, and politically motivated for trying to advance a "gay agenda" (that is, by forcing others to contend with same-sex attraction).

In courses when I say nothing, I often receive, minimally, a comment of passive support (for example, "Maybe you can come out next semester"), to aggressive chastising for being dishonest and self-hating and for not being a good gay role model. I cannot recall an instance when someone has supported me for *not* disclosing my sexuality, for deciding to stay in the closet in relation to students. Furthermore, many of these criticisms have been about not only a (contextually) marginal and devalued attraction but also the amount of time I kept the attraction hidden (Brown-Smith, 1998).

And so I struggle, every semester and in each new class, with the timing of my disclosure, recognizing that I may receive criticism with whatever coming-out action I take—whether I come out or do not, and, if I do, whether I come out at the beginning, middle, or end of a semester. I also struggle with how whatever decision I make reflects on me and my credibility as a teacher; I worry that I may be marked as someone too politically aggressive or someone uncomfortable with who he claims and feels to be.

□

Just because a person feels comfortable coming out doesn't mean that same-sex attraction will no longer be an issue; coming out isn't the "end of the struggle" (Burgess, 2005, p. 126). As long as the closet exists as a construct for making sense of same-sex attraction, the presence of the closet in a person's life can function as a metaphor she or he comes to live by (Lakoff & Johnson, 1980).

Furthermore, when coming out is conceived of as a never-ending, lifelong process—a process a person can never complete once and for all—new dilemmas emerge for the person, particularly with when, where, and how to (not) reveal information about her or his attraction. Consider, for instance, Tyler's thoughts about coming out to unfamiliar others:

> If someone asks me if I am gay, am I going to deny it? No. But am I going to come forward with the information? Not necessarily. I wouldn't walk into a bank and say I'd like to make a deposit and that I'm gay. It's not that I'm not out, but rather that my sexuality is not necessary information for the situation. (2007)

Tyler says that his sexuality is not "necessary information" for making a deposit, but I disagree: the closet, as a relational construct, is a construct for which Tyler himself or others—a bank teller, LGBQ activists, mental health professionals—might hold him accountable. Tyler may be ridiculed *for* coming out—for example, the bank teller saying that Tyler's sexuality is not necessary information for making a deposit—or for *not* coming out—for instance, Tyler feeling frustrated for not disclosing, an activist calling Tyler politically irresponsible for being unable to disclose his gayness, or a mental health professional saying that because he didn't disclose he might suffer from shame.[2]

In this chapter I illustrate two contemporary dilemmas made possible by the closet, coming out, and same-sex attraction: the formation and working of interactional paradox, particularly among strangers and acquaintances; and the search and need for acknowledgment of same-sex attraction, particularly from close, personal others such as friends and family. I consider these dilemmas contemporary, because even though a person may feel comfortable with coming out, expectations of the closet can still make for complications and contradictions in everyday interaction (for example, coming out) and in meaningful relationships (for instance, seeking recognition and validity of same-sex attraction).[3]

Paradox

A paradox is a situation in which "contradiction" deduced from "consistent premises" exists (Watzlawick, Beavin, & Jackson, 1967,

p. 188); a situation in which a person has the possibility of being held accountable—by her- or himself and others—for taking the wrong course of action, making the wrong move; an "untenable" situation in which a person's "feelings are denuded of validity" and "acts are stripped of their motives, intentions, and consequences" (Laing, 1969, p. 124); a situation in which "compliance itself is not good enough" and "noncompliance is completely out of the question" (Watzlawick, Weakland, & Fisch, 1974, p. 71). Paradox does not develop in a person but from her or his interactions with others; people produce paradox together.

For a person with same-sex attraction, interactional paradox exists when nine premises of the closet, coming out, and same-sex attraction exist:

1. Same-sex attraction is tied to the closet.

2. Same-sex attraction is not easily accessible; it must be constituted through discourse and action. If this attraction was easily accessible, no one would have to come out; others would know of a person's attraction based on how the person looks or sounds.

3. The closet makes sense only in relation to hetero-normative contexts—contexts that frame people as heterosexual until proven otherwise.

4. The closet construct requires a person to leave the metaphorical space by saying or doing something indicative of (not easily accessed) same-sex attraction.

5. Coming out is potentially dangerous not only because others might find same-sex attraction inappropriate or immoral but also because a person may expose a history of secrecy, lies, and reckless acts. In other words, if life in the closet—the time pre-coming out—motivates a person to find ways of keeping same-sex attraction private, then coming out may disclose (questionable) ways a person achieved such privacy.

6. Coming out is sometimes perceived as necessary and important, mature and healthy, honest and politically responsible; conversely, not coming out is unhealthy and shameful, immature, dishonest, and politically irresponsible.

7. Coming out is sometimes conceived of as unimportant, inappropriate, and selfish; conversely, not coming out demonstrates care and respect.

8. Coming out is sometimes conceived of as discrete; there is an end to the process.

9. Coming out is sometimes conceived of as inescapable; there is no end.

Paradox occurs when a person stays safely in the closet—recognizing that coming out can be dangerous—but is held accountable for being unhealthy or shameful, immature, dishonest, or politically irresponsible when (not easily accessed) same-sex attraction leaks.

Paradox occurs when a person not only tries to stay out—that is, arrive to the (perceived) end of the coming-out process—but also recognizes that coming out never ends, because new interactions require new disclosures of same-sex attraction.

Paradox occurs when a person realizes that she or he is most fully out by coming out immediately upon meeting unfamiliar others but also learns that coming out puts her- or himself at risk in such encounters.

Paradox occurs when a person with same-sex attraction is held accountable—by self and others—for taking a wrong course of action, making the wrong move: there are consequences for a person who comes out or does not, who comes out too soon or not soon enough, who completes the coming-out process or finds completion impossible, or who comes out most of the time, some of the time, or never at all.

In the next four sections I describe and analyze four paradoxical interactions in which I, as a person with same-sex attraction, felt held accountable, by myself and others, according to the aforementioned premises. Similar to Marvasti's description of interactions that made his "skin tone relevant" (2006, p. 527), I write of interactions that made my sexuality—particularly my same-sex attraction and gay identity—relevant. I then analyze these interactions to show how paradox is manifest in and created by interaction.

Hiking (Out) with Strangers

I put on my backpack and approach the start of a 14-mile overnight hike. I am with my friends and mentors, Carolyn and Art, and two acquaintances of theirs, Cindy and Susan—two strangers to me, with me, for two days and one night.

Typically, I am fine interacting with strangers for a short time. But with the length of time we will spend together, I feel sure the unfamiliar others will ask about my life, particularly my relationships, research and writing interests, and teaching. And I feel anxious: I put pressure on myself for deciding when and how to inform others of my gay identity as well as tell them about my research, writing, and teaching interests, many of which deal with same-sex attraction.

I fear negative responses to my identity and my work, particularly from people who find same-sex attraction inappropriate or immoral. Consequently I consider coming out potentially dangerous. Negative experiences with identifying as gay flood my memory: a cousin who, after I said, "I am gay," no longer allows me to visit; Brett, the ex-boyfriend who may have killed himself after coming out to his father; the person interviewing me for a job who told me, on the interview, that he was gay but no one else at his workplace knew—he was scared it would tarnish his case for promotion; the high school acquaintance who emailed me for advice on getting out of reparative therapy; the student who told me that after coming out to his mother and father they told him that he was "no longer their son"; and the student who reported me to the president of the university for being out in the classroom.

These experiences provide some of the context for the anxiety I feel as I approach a long, overnight hike with two strangers. I want to enjoy the experience but cannot *not* concern myself with whether, when, and how to disclose whom I like to love and what I like to study. I can keep my same-sex attraction and research secret, but I know it may be difficult should mundane questions about my relationships or research enter the conversation—questions such as: "Are you married?" "Do you have a girlfriend?" and "What do you teach about and study?"

But secrecy has problems, too. If I come out later into the hike, the strangers may consider me manipulative (Phellas, 2005) or ashamed of my sexuality (Yoshino, 2006). The (potentially dangerous) reactions I experience on coming out may thus happen not because another person finds same-sex attraction inappropriate and/or immoral but because I kept my (not easily accessed) attraction hidden too long or because the others were upset that I wrongly assumed that they would be less than okay with this attraction. With self-disclosure being "embedded in the history of past disclosures" (Bochner, 1984, p. 610;

Rawlins, 1983), an omission of personal information might mark me as having told a lie (Brown-Smith, 1998).[4]

I could come out immediately upon meeting unfamiliar others, but this might make for discomfort as well. I perceive "Hi, I'm Tony and I'm gay" a tactless greeting. Though it may make me feel better to reveal my sexuality to others, the fear that my statement might make others uncomfortable makes me uncomfortable. What if these others view gayness as inappropriate and/or immoral or feel as though I came out too early? I decide against coming out immediately, and, instead, wait and hope for a more comfortable time to disclose.

"What do you do for a living?" Susan asks, a common one-liner that is about as safe as talking about the weather—usually.

"I teach college," I respond. I do not say "I am also a researcher and writer," because these statements may invite her to ask what I research and write *about*. Given that my topic is often same-sex attraction, discussing my research and writing can mark me as gay. Even though I can identify numerous heterosexual-identified scholars who write about same-sex attraction, I recognize that one who researches and writes about same-sex attraction may be initially marked and consequently evaluated as *not* heterosexual, at least until heterosexuality is validated through discourse or action (for example, saying "I'm straight.").

I recall advice I received from an interviewer for an academic job I did not get (2008). "Say you research and write about 'sexuality,' not 'gay identity,'" the interviewer said. "I know you write about gay identity, and I am okay with it. But I also know that you made others participating in the job search uncomfortable—they found the topic of gay identity inappropriate and immoral."

I remember dissonance overcoming my body: I felt sad for making other people uncomfortable, disingenuous for thinking about masking my work as more general ("sexuality") than specific ("gay identity"), angry that others still consider gay identity inappropriate and immoral, and regret for hearing that had I changed a few words I may have been offered the job. I continue to feel unsure about the threshold of coming out—the threshold of needing and wanting to be open and honest with others while still being able to be open and honest with myself (Bochner, 1984; Rawlins, 1983).

Now I am in a similar situation, worried about how strangers may be offended by or uncomfortable with my gay identity and/or hearing about work that may, consequently, mark me as gay. But I feel disingenuous to say I study sexuality—such intentional masking feels like a lie. I also think of friends, family, and pro-gay commentators who refer to being out as healthy, a sign of maturity, and politically beneficial (for example, Signorile, 2007; Yoshino, 2006); choosing to *not* tell is rarely considered a virtuous, viable option.

I make a compromise with myself: not wanting to start off on the "wrong foot," I feel fine saying "I teach college" at the start of the trip, but only as long as I force myself to come out during the upcoming hours.

"What do you do for a living?" I ask Susan.

"I'm a dental assistant," she responds. "I primarily help dental surgeons with surgery."

"Sounds interesting," I remark.

"Oh, it is. I have some great stories."

"Do tell!" Carolyn says. "Entertain us—we have at least six more miles to hike today, and six more tomorrow."

"There was this time a male patient underwent anesthesia," Susan begins. "His girlfriend was in the room, and apparently the patient had done some time in prison."

I start to feel uncomfortable . . . again.

"The anesthesia started making the patient disoriented just as the male surgeon entered the room," she continues. "And in front of his girlfriend the patient begins talking about his attraction for men and starts flirting with the surgeon."

I have a few ideas about where this story might go: Susan may describe the surgeon's response to the patient's flirting, the girlfriend's response to her boyfriend's flirting, and/or Susan's own reaction. But regardless of the story's direction, I sense Susan may evaluate same-sex attraction, either implicitly with the tone of her voice or explicitly with direct commentary.

I know I must act, but do I step in and say, "I am attracted to men" to protect her from saying something offensive? Do I let her say something offensive, and *then* tell her that I am gay? Do I let her say something offensive and hope that I can keep my attraction hidden for the remainder of the hike?

"Apparently, the patient had a few boyfriends in prison," Susan continues.

Nervously, I decide to protect Susan and me by steering the conversation in another direction. "Did the girlfriend know of his attraction to men?"

"I don't think so," she responds. "But in prison he . . ."

"I bet his flirting with the surgeon made the girlfriend uncomfortable," I interrupt.

"I guess it may have," she says, sounding somewhat confused.

The tone of her voice indicates that the story has ended, the subject changed. I sense that I do not have to worry about being offended by an antigay remark or having to come out . . . yet.

(Mis)Reading Sexuality

I arrive to an all-male-clientele salon. Dan introduces himself and says he will cut my hair. I find Dan quite masculine: he has a firm gait, deep voice, and a somewhat-disheveled, relaxed appearance. He guides me to the hair-cutting station. Throughout the cut, we talk about sports, politics, and where we're from.

"Illinois," I say.

"Concord, North Carolina," he responds. "I miss it."

Although I didn't initially think about his sexuality, Dan's masculine appearance and his missing of small-town North Carolina motivates me to think that he is heterosexual. Stereotypes emerge: gay men often do not miss rural hometowns and are rarely hypermasculine. Though I study and teach about sex, gender, and sexuality, I still cannot disband deeply held assumptions. It doesn't help that the next part of our conversation is about attractive women.

"You know what it's like working around hot women all day?" he asks as a female employee walks by.

I hesitate. Is he making an observation about the difficulties, or the benefits, of men and women working together in one space? Does he want me to comment on his "hot" statement and say that I would love to work around hot women? Because I just met Dan, I find it awkward to say "I am gay" and am not sexually attracted to (hot) women.

"Um, sure," I respond uncomfortably and ambiguously, assuming that he's asking if I know about men and women working together.

The conversation stops, and I sense that he is nearly finished with my hair.

"Want something to drink?" he asks.

"No thanks."

"Okay," he says. "I'll be right back. I have to get some water."

When he returns, I notice he has something in his lip. I look into the mirror, see him spit into a cup, and realize that he has been chewing tobacco for most of the haircut. I cringe. He's hypermasculine, misses the rural place of his youth, asks about hot women, and is chewing tobacco, another stereotypical, masculine, heterosexual act; I have never met a woman or a gay man who chews. These additional characteristics add to my anxiety: as a gay person, hypermasculine men scare me. They were the bullies in high school. They are the people I see bash gays. They are the people that I find most uncomfortable with same-sex attraction.

He coats my neck with shaving cream and pulls out a straight-edged razor.

"So do you have a girlfriend?" he asks while caressing my neck with the sharp blade.

"Damn question!" I say to myself. He's not asking if I am bisexual or gay or queer, but is assuming that I like people of a different sex. How do I respond?

"Nope," I reply.

I feel guilty for typifying Dan and clinging to unquestioned heterosexual assumptions. I also feel guilty for not speaking of my attraction. Should I have come out? Should I have arrived to the salon and said "Hi, I'm Tony, and I'm gay?" Should I have come out when he asked if I knew what working around "hot women" was like? Do I tell him that I am not attracted to women? Even though I am single, should I have pretended to have a boyfriend when he asked if I had a girlfriend? I could have lied, but would that have eliminated self-condemnation?

A few weeks later a (male) friend says he's been dating Dan for a few months. I am amazed. Assuming that Dan identifies as gay, I approach him the next time I am at the salon.

"Why didn't you tell me that you were gay?" I ask.

"Why didn't you tell me that *you* were gay?" he responds.

"I didn't think it was appropriate," I say. "You scared me. I thought you were straight."

"Sorry," he says, "but I didn't think telling you was appropriate, either. I assumed you were straight, too."

I believe Dan initially marked me as heterosexual, evidenced by him asking if I knew what it was like "working around hot women" and if I had "a girlfriend." Even though attractive men worked at the salon, Dan did not ask if I knew what it was like working around hot men or if I had a boyfriend. For Dan, my heterosexuality was assumed, thus suggesting that my gay identity, for him, was not easily accessible.

Consequently I had to say something to indicate my attraction or get him to ask about my identity (for example, by asking "Why didn't you tell me that you were gay?" and hoping that he would infer or ask about my identity or attraction).

Likewise, I marked Dan as heterosexual as evidenced by my fear of coming out to him, surprise with finding out he was dating a man, and asking him about not coming out to me. Had I believed Dan to be gay, I would not have worried about my safety. My assumptions illustrate not only heteronormativity and the inaccessibility of gay identity (and, consequently, the need to come out of the closet, to say or do something indicative of same-sex attraction), but also how Dan and I stigmatized gay identity in our encounters by assuming and per-petuating heterosexuality; if either of us didn't consider gay identity contentious, then why didn't either of us ask about the other's attrac-tion and/or be direct about ours?

Even after I came out to Dan, I still left our encounters feeling guilty, shameful, and dishonest—guilty for (intentionally) omit-ting information, "not correcting a falsehood" (Brown-Smith, 1998, pp. 28–29), and for reinforcing the "interpersonal strain" of hetero-normativity, a strain that suggests "it's fine" to be gay as long as it is not discussed (Feigenbaum, 2007, p. 7; Glave, 2005); shameful for not seeming proud and comfortable with an identity I claim; and dishon-est for reifying an inaccurate assumption. But I also felt torn between what I could have done differently: I could have entered the salon and said, "I am gay," but know that, in so doing, would have feared for my safety. However, by not coming out immediately, I knew I could be held accountable—by Dan, others, and myself—for feelings of guilt and shame for having told a "lie of omission" (Brown-Smith, 1998, p. 29) should my gay identity leak to Dan at a later time.

Dining Out, Staying In (the Closet)

I arrive at Damen's, one of my favorite fast food restaurants. I place my order and take a seat. Since she's not busy, the cashier comes and sits at my table. I tell her that I'm moving to Chicago. She asks if I'm moving with my girlfriend.

"No," I say.

Should I tell this cashier, an acquaintance, that I'm gay? Do I say, "No, I'm not moving with my girlfriend or boyfriend, because I am single?" I assumed that she assumed I identified as heterosexual by (a) perceiving me as a man and (b) asking about the possibility of being in a relationship with a woman. Why couldn't, or didn't, I say that I date men? Even though I believe that I am comfortable with same-sex attraction, mundane encounters like these make me question myself; they make coming out difficult.

The cashier asked if I was moving with my girlfriend. I was not moving to Chicago with a girlfriend and so decided to say "no." However, I believe her question also implies that I would be in a relationship with a woman, evidenced by her not asking if I would move with a boyfriend, partner, or significant other. Her statement illustrates how heteronormativity manifests itself in discourse: since my same-sex attraction was not easily accessible to her—an inaccessibility thereby marking me as heterosexual—I would have to make my same-sex attraction known by either saying or doing something indicative of this attraction.

But again she did not ask if I identified as gay, bisexual, queer, or straight, only if I was moving with my girlfriend. Thus, by saying "No, I am not moving with a girlfriend" and adding "I wouldn't have a girlfriend, because I am gay," I worried that she might respond not only with disdain for gayness but also with "I didn't ask about your sexuality." I therefore decided to say only "No." However, as in the previous encounters, I left the interaction feeling trapped in guilt, shame, and dishonesty.

Moving (and Staying) In

A male tenant moves into my apartment building. When we first meet, he asks what I do as a career.

"I'm in graduate school," I say. "I read and write and teach."

"What do you write about?" he asks.

Hesitantly, I respond with "I write about ways people talk about nature."

Guilt devours me: I am scared to say I write about sexuality, same-sex attraction, and the closet. I am not ready to come out to a person during our first meeting, and I assume that speaking of what I write about might mark me as gay.

But now, having said, "I write about ways people talk about nature," I also worry about when to disclose. I know I'll talk with him again. Do

I tell him what I write about at a later time? "Why didn't you tell me initially?" he might ask. Even if he only thinks such a sentiment, he may perceive me as being shameful about my work and myself. The possibility exists. And what I think he thinks is just as important as what he thinks (Blumer, 1969; Laing, 1969; Mead, 1962 [1943]).

I worried about coming out to a stranger by discussing my work, to a person whose stance on same-sex attraction I did not know. I did not want him to harm me or my apartment, take my mail, or damage my car. I did not want to hear gay slurs regularly or receive "unwanted attention" from him and his friends (Gerber, 1996, p. 46).

Furthermore, having said "I write about ways people talk about nature" (or "I write about sexuality"), I felt as though I told a "lie of omission" (Brown-Smith, 1998, p. 29), should my other writing topics emerge at a later time. The neighbor may eventually hold me accountable not only for potentially writing about topics that are contextually marginal and devalued but also for telling a lie in our initial encounter. Regardless of whether or not my specific writing topics emerge, I hold myself accountable for our past interactional practices as well as those I might use in forthcoming encounters.

Analyzing Interactional Paradox

I leave these interactions torn between what I should have said and done and what I actually said and did. I could have come out to these people but, as a result, may have experienced negative evaluation and rejection, hostility, and possibly violence. I did not know these people—particularly their views about same-sex attraction—and by being open and honest I risked safety and protection (Bochner, 1984; Rawlins, 1983).

Coming out in such everyday interactions make other relational dilemmas possible as well. I find it socially awkward to walk into a classroom or hair salon or fast food restaurant and say "I am gay" or tell strangers of my attraction immediately upon meeting. Being that some of these people assumed my heterosexuality, speaking about gay identity may "breach" the hetero-normative assumptions that govern their everyday interactions (Garfinkel, 1967). Consequently I may make others uncomfortable not only for making same-sex attraction a topic of discussion but also for speaking about the (marginal and devalued) attraction. I may then be marked as awkward, selfish, and politically motivated, as wanting to advance the mythic "gay agenda."

I could make sure to come out to these people in our next encounters—the next time I hike with the same people, get a haircut, visit the restaurant, or see my neighbor—but recognize that I may then be considered manipulative for postponing disclosure or a liar for omitting information (Brown-Smith, 1998). Even if I postpone disclosure or omit information in order to maintain safety, I may still be held accountable for my (intentional) hiding acts should information about my attraction emerge at a later time. Furthermore, the longer I wait to disclose, the longer I construct a history of postponement and omission, a history that for one-time encounters may not matter but may matter to people to whom I will be exposed time and again.

I am also not aware of research that advocates for *not* coming out; not disclosing is often framed as bad, unhealthy, and politically irresponsible, an act of silence that is an "assault" on my "civil rights" (Yoshino, 2006). And so I hurt myself by not coming out and open myself not only to my own ridicule but also to ridicule from others for not being myself, with myself and with others.

In analyzing these encounters, I illustrate how I trap myself by Mead's (1962 [1934]) "generalized other," particularly how I try to incorporate the "attitudes" of "other persons" into my conduct and how I try to "justify" my and others' actions (Scott & Lyman, 1968). I trap myself by trying to discern the threshold of coming out—the threshold of needing and wanting to be open and honest with another while still being open and honest with myself. I trap myself knowing that I risk safety and protection in coming out if the other fears, hates, or is disgusted by gay people; knowing that I risk being awkward, selfish, and politically motivated for coming out too soon; knowing that I risk feeling shameful and dishonest for coming out too late or not at all; and knowing that I risk being regarded (or regarding myself) as manipulative, unhealthy, and politically irresponsible for postponing disclosure and omitting information should my (not easily accessed) identity emerges at a later time. I feel trapped in what Laing (1969) calls an "untenable position" (p. 124), a position where my acts may be "stripped of their motives, intentions, and consequences," a position in which "compliance itself is not good enough" and "noncompliance is completely out of the question" (Watzlawick, Weakland, & Fisch, 1974, p. 71). I feel trapped in paradox.

Complicating Paradox: The Search for Acknowledgment

The film *A Single Man* (Ford, 2009) documents the struggle of George Falconer, a man whose (male) partner of 16 years, Jim, dies in a car accident. What fascinates me about George's struggle is the lack of acknowledgment he receives from others. Two scenes resonate in particular. First, Jim's cousin calls George to tell him that Jim's parents do not want George to know about Jim's death. The cousin also says that Jim's funeral is reserved for "close family," a comment said to George to imply that Jim's family doesn't consider George "family" and consequently is not welcome to attend the funeral.

The second instance of a lack of acknowledgment happens with George's best (female) friend, Charlie. Before Jim, George and Charlie engaged in a brief but intimate sexual affair. George then met Jim but continued to maintain a close friendship with Charlie. After Jim's death George and Charlie spend an evening together talking, dining, and dancing. During this time Charlie tells George not only that his relationship with Jim was not a "real" relationship but also that she thinks his attraction to Jim was a substitute for something he couldn't or had not yet found—a real, legitimate heterosexual relationship.

Throughout this book, I have illustrated how coming out is dangerous, uncertain, and often emotional. I have also illustrated how a person always has the potential, in interaction, to be held accountable—by self and others—for taking a wrong course of action, making the wrong move when coming out. However, even if this person makes the right move—that is, feels comfortable with the timing of disclosure and doesn't receive criticism from others about what was disclosed and how and when disclosure happened—another dilemma can emerge: the person's same-sex attraction, post-coming out, may never be considered legitimate or ever acknowledged again by others. The purpose of this section is to interrogate meanings of out-ness post-coming out. In particular I highlight relational dilemmas that can emerge *after* a person informs another about her or his same-sex attraction, dilemmas made possibly by a lack of acknowledgment of this attraction.

For instance, what happens when a son decides to tell his mother about his meaningful and intimate relationships with men but is never again asked, by his mother, about these relationships? Is this son "out" to his mother? Does her *lack* of talk about his same-sex relationships suggest a lack of acceptance?

Or what if a woman comes out to her brother, but after the initial coming-out event, he refuses to ask about or discuss her intimate and meaningful same-sex affairs? Should the woman come out to him, time after time, in search of more frequent acknowledgment and thus risk being perceived as aggressive or as trying to advance the "gay [and lesbian] agenda"? Can, or should, this woman be marked as unhealthy or politically irresponsible for not reintroducing or regularly discussing her attraction? Unique post-coming-out paradoxes can surface again.

I mentioned in Chapter 4 that the U.S. military policy of Don't Ask, Don't Tell (DADT) stipulates that a person can be discharged if she or he engages in "homosexual conduct"—that is, "a homosexual act, a statement that the member is homosexual or bisexual, or a marriage or attempted marriage to someone of the same gender" (Anonymous, 1993, p. A16). A person with same-sex attraction can serve in the military but only as long as the attraction is not observed or known and reported by and to others—that is, as long as the person stays closeted.

DADT unfortunately encourages—requires—a LGBQ person to lie, hide, and omit information in order to serve in the military, but this policy is troubling for another reason as well: it prohibits a person from discussing her or his intimate and meaningful same-sex relationships. Some military personnel have told me that heterosexual relations should not be acknowledged either. However, they are not only acknowledged but are also not regulated, especially in that the military offers spousal benefits and accommodations to heterosexual couples—benefits and accommodations not extended to those in committed, intimate, and meaningful same-sex affairs.

DADT is specific to the U.S. military—but what happens in "civilian" life if a person and/or a relationship adheres to a similar policy? What happens if people prohibit a discussion of same-sex attraction, saying that they believe it is okay for a person to possess such attraction only as long as the person does not talk about or engage in conduct that might indicate such attraction?

In 2003 I told my father that I found men attractive. He proceeded to tell other relatives, who, immediately on hearing the news, called me or wrote me letters saying they still loved me. But such efforts at acknowledging my same-sex attraction evolved into exceptions. As I write this in 2010, none of these relatives has ever acknowledged my same-sex attraction again or has asked about my committed, intimate, and meaningful relationships with men. Even when I try to approach my attraction by casually speaking of my partner, such conversations end quickly, often with the person I am talking to assuming a tense posture, eliminating eye contact, mentioning she or he is happy for me and then changing the topic, and/or saying my relationship is no one's business.

This phenomenon speaks to a DADT existence among my family (Harris, 2003). The situation complicates the meanings of coming out as well. For instance, I would say I am out to these relatives—they have received information about my same-sex attraction. I also believe they are actively aware of my attraction—before learning of it, they perpetually asked about my relationships with women. However, now no talk happens about my committed, intimate, and meaningful relationships; I came out into silence.

And I wonder: Do I tell my relatives that I would like acknowledgment of my attraction? Do I continue to try to talk about my attraction with them? Am I out to others if the others do not validate my attraction? Additional questions about coming out emerge: What if a person comes out to others—others who (supposedly) "accept" the person's attraction but who never again recognize, explicitly, the person's attraction? Must a person come out again and again to the same person?

Ragan Fox presents a more complicated coming-out dilemma. Fox's father, suffering from Alzheimer's disease, constantly asked Fox if he had met "any nice, Jewish girls." Fox said he would respond with "Dad, we've been through this; I'm gay" and added that he felt like the only gay man "who had to come out to his father 556 times!" (2010, p. 8). Thomas Waugh (2009) describes a similar situation with his mother, a person to whom he once came out but who now, with the onset of Alzheimer's, continues to ask about his wife. Can we say Fox is out to his father and Waugh is out to his mother, a father and a mother who, motivated by Alzheimer's, not only perpetually forget about their child's same-sex attraction but also inquire about their heterosexuality? What does coming out mean for Fox and for Waugh, for Fox's father and Waugh's mother, and for each of the parent-child relationships?

A similar coming-out situation happened to Dave, a friend who was hospitalized for pneumonia. During the hospitalization his mother came to visit, a visit that required her to drive almost four hours, an unplanned visit to see him for one of the six nights he'd spend in the hospital. During her stay a female nurse walked into the room, "an attractive woman," his mother observed. When the nurse walked out, Dave's mother asked if he "saw a wedding ring."

"No, Mom. Why would I notice?" Dave said.

"Because it's natural to notice," she replied. "It's natural for a man to notice if a woman is married, because if she's not wearing a ring that means she's available."

"Mom, gay men don't notice these things."

"I didn't know you were gay," she said.

A pause filled the room.

"I've got a headache," she said after a few seconds. "I need to eat. I don't want to discuss this anymore." She left abruptly and angrily, and Dave remained confused: he told her that he was gay twelve years ago, eight years ago, five years ago, and again last year.

Dave's situation, particularly his mother's claim to not know about Dave's sexuality, complicates coming out. What should Dave do? Should he constantly remind his mother of his same-sex attraction? Even though he believes he was out to her for many years, was he ever out if she says she didn't know about his sexuality? Even if his mother continues to deny or forget about his attraction, what should Dave do, for this *relationship*, to encourage his mother to acknowledge his attraction? As Liang believes, coming out is "unsuccessful" and has not happened if a "heterosexual presumption" about a person continues to exist (1997, p. 292).

Hyde argues that "positive acknowledgment"—making time and space for others in our lives—is a "moral thing to do" (2004, p. 96). By contrast, silent or negative acts of acknowledgment—acts of racism, sexism, ageism, homophobia, and acts that disregard important parts of a person's life—can "expose" the person to a "fate of social death" (p. 64), a fate absent integrity (Garrick, 1997), and a fate constituted, however slight, by feelings of anxiety, despair, and unworthiness (Hyde, 2006). As Garrick observes, "we cannot live a healthy life without recognition" (2001, p. 96).

I sometimes hear the sentiment that a person's same-sex attraction is "no one's business" (Cooper, 1996, p. 176; Gupta, 2009), is a "purely a personal matter" (Panikkar, 2009, p. 241), and is a "strictly private affair" (Ankleshwaria, 2009, p. 200). Although I agree to some extent—there are private characteristics of our intimate relations with others we may choose not to disclose—a double standard exists if others talk about female-male, heterosexual relations but simultaneously find same-sex relations unworthy or inappropriate for discussion—a double standard that resembles Pierce's description of a bigot:

> [When a] bigot sees gay people holding hands in public, they
> [*sic*] say the gays are pushing their lifestyle on any observers,
> whereas when heterosexuals hold hands in public, it is sweet. For
> the bigot there are two ways of being affectionate in public, one
> for normal people and one for those who are contaminated by
> gayness. (2007, p. 18)

When talk of relationships happens in everyday conversation—best noted when a woman is asked if she has a boyfriend, when a man is asked if he has a girlfriend, and when a person is asked about (heterosexual) marriage—then the silence around intimate, same-sex boyfriends, girlfriends, and relationships does become everyone's business.

For instance, Michael described a time when a woman asked if he was married. He responded with "'Well, I live with my partner,'" and she responded with "'Oh! I'm sorry that I presumed.'" Michael disrupted a common assumption the woman had about his intimate relationship with another person: he presumed that since she asked about marriage, and given that same-sex marriages aren't socially and legally recognized in a majority of states and nations, she asked about his relationship with a woman. What I emphasize, however, is that her question about marriage is a question that makes a person's intimate relationships a part of everyday conversation (Foster, 2008). If we think that a person's intimate relationships should be "no one's business," then we should not ask about boyfriends, girlfriends, marriage, and other intimate and meaningful forms of coupling. But if we believe these topics are appropriate to discuss, then same-sex boyfriends, girlfriends, marriages and other intimate and meaningful forms of coupling must be appropriate, too.[5]

And thus I ask: Whose business is same-sex attraction after the initial coming-out event? Intimate friends and family? Strangers? Does same-sex attraction become social business—become meaningful—only when it is asked about, by others, in everyday conversation? Should a person with same-sex attraction proactively and perpetually put forth information about this attraction to someone to whom she or he has previously disclosed?

□

Even though I consider myself comfortable with same-sex attraction, I leave some of my everyday interactions with strangers and acquaintances feeling trapped by paradox—trapped in contradiction made possible by conditions, characteristics, and premises of the closet, coming out, and same-sex attraction; trapped knowing that in most every new interaction, I may be held accountable, by self and others, for being manipulative, dishonest, self-hating, and politically irresponsible with whatever closet-related action I take—for coming out too soon or not soon enough, for coming out most of the time, some of the time, or never at all.

I also emerge from my everyday interactions wanting—desiring—acknowledgment, wanting recognition of my intimate and meaningful same-sex affairs, especially from friends and family. I want to be asked "Are you seeing anyone?" by the same people who asked this of me pre-coming out. I want to be asked "How is Jerry [my partner]?" I want to hold Jerry's hand, safely, in public and be invited to family gatherings. I want to call him "honey" and "sweetie" around heterosexual others without worrying about these others cringing or becoming uncomfortable (Glave, 2005, p. 121). I want others—especially close, personal others—to consider our relationship legitimate, important, and appropriate to discuss most everywhere, most anytime (Foster, 2008; Van Gelder, 1998). I want my—our—relationship recognized and validated.

CHAPTER SIX

Making Change, Writing Hope

Hate is like taking poison.
The only person you hurt is yourself.

BETTY KILBY (in Drash, 2010)

Although my grief over Brett's death served as a significant reason to write about same-sex attraction, I started thinking about and theorizing this attraction years ago when I felt immersed in confusion, despair, and fear—confusion from learning about this attraction and, consequently, the closet; despair from living in the closet, that is, knowing about my attraction but feeling as though I could speak of it only to select people; and fear of disclosing my attraction, of coming out. I then stumbled on the complexity of paradox, particularly how my attraction—once I became comfortable with it—continued to complicate many of my everyday interactions.

Another reason to write stemmed from a desire to make change and write hope, to show people, all people, that conflict made possible by the closet, coming out, and the possession of same-sex attraction "need not be as it is" (Hacking, 1999, p. 6). There are techniques to maneuver everyday paradox. There are lessons—joys—that come with same-sex attraction. There are ways to appreciate and acknowledge one another more.

And hence, my purpose for this chapter: I use the tools of metacommunication and queer theory to develop ways to change the characteristics and, consequently, experiences of the closet and coming out. In particular I illustrate techniques a LGBQ person can use to navigate paradox in interaction. I also work to make the closet, coming out, and same-sex attraction relational phenomena—phenomena that affect not only the LGBQ person but also her or his close, personal others. I highlight lessons I have learned and values that come from identifying as gay. And I put theory and experience into practice by grounding possibilities of remaking the closet, coming out, and same-sex attraction in everyday life.

Metacommunication and Queer Theory: Possibilities for Change

In order to make change and write hope in terms of the closet, coming out, and same-sex attraction, I turn to the purposes and strategies of metacommunication and queer theory. Metacommunication is "communication about communication" (Bateson, 2000, p. 215) and happens when people talk about conditions, premises, and paradoxes of relating (Bateson, 1951; Watzlawick, Weakland, & Fisch, 1974). Metacommunication is important because it can alter, clarify, and lessen the interactional workings of these conditions, premises, and paradoxes. However, metacommunication is difficult if a person does not have the language or conceptual and experiential distance to reflect on such often-hidden, constitutive phenomena.

Queer theory is a "philosophy" that works to create equitable and meaningful social change. Queer theory does so by (1) diffusing, polluting, and creating dissonance around what passes as "normal"; (2) (re) appropriating language, stereotypes and texts, practices and beliefs, in unique, innovative ways; (3) revelling in possibility, always working against what passes as stable, certain, and rigid; and (4) taking a vigilant and political approach to social interaction, an approach that recognizes that symbols and bodies matter (Holman Jones & Adams, 2010).

Metacommunicating about the closet, coming out, and same-sex attraction means discussing the conditions, characteristics, premises, and paradoxes tied to and made possible by these phenomena—many of which I discerned throughout this book (Chapters 2, 3, and 4). "Queering" the closet, coming out, and same-sex attraction means creating dissonance around these conditions, characteristics, premises, and paradoxes with the purpose of creating equitable and meaningful social change.

For instance, in Chapter 2, I outlined seven conditions of the closet—conditions that, based on my analysis of my experience, others' commentary, and representations of same-sex attraction, must be met before coming out ever seems possible. Changing the conditions—the conceptual framework of the closet—seems to be one way to change, or to queer, experiences tied to the metaphorical space, specifically the experiences of living and leaving the closet, everyday paradoxes of coming out, and other patterns of interaction tied to same-sex attraction.[1]

Or if, as a gay man, I recognize that I am more comfortable with hiding information about my past, isolating myself from others, or engaging in reckless acts (Chapter 3), I may reconsider the necessities of hiding, isolating, and being reckless. Or by recognizing that I reside in paradox for (not) disclosing same-sex attraction in everyday interaction (Chapter 5), I may focus less on the need to come out and more on how to negotiate the possibility of always being considered deceptive, manipulative, immature, dishonest, and/or self-hating. Or if I realize that the disclosure of same-sex attraction and reactions to this disclosure may constitute a significant memory of and turning point in my relationships (Chapter 4), I might now ask: Why *this* moment and *these* reactions, especially when more positive moments and reactions exist? Why is it that when I talk about my father and me, I often talk about coming out to him and his reaction? Why don't I talk about how he sought advice from another father of a gay son on how to respond to my coming out? And why don't I talk about the times we feel good together? By discerning conditions, premises, and paradoxes of the closet, coming out, and same-sex attraction, I feel better equipped to metacommunicate about and queer these phenomena.

In this chapter I discern seven interrelated strategies—"tools"—in which metacommunication and queer theory might change conditions of the closet and premises of being closeted and coming out, and paradoxes of same-sex attraction. In particular I focus on (1) embracing paradox, (2) evading paradox, (3) manipulating sexuality through discourse and action, (4) innocently manipulating the metaphorical "frontstage," (5) coming out as heterosexual, (6) reframing personal accountability in terms of the closet and same-sex attraction, and (7) conceive of coming out as relational. Like all tools, these strategies sometimes work and sometimes break, are sometimes inappropriate and sometimes apt, are sometimes politically savvy and sometimes not.

Becoming Interactionally Competent: Embracing Paradox

One way a person can navigate paradoxes of the closet, coming out, and same-sex attraction is by developing an "interactional competence" of these phenomena. Such competence happens when (not) coming out is not (personally) considered a problem, when the reason for (not) doing so involves "choice and not terror, not intimidation, not victimization, nor any of the range of attitudes that can fall under the umbrella effect of oppression" (Delany, 1996, p. 25).

George Herbert Mead argues that an intelligent social actor incorporates the "attitudes" of "other persons" into her or his own conduct (1962, p. 69). For a person with same-sex attraction, such incorporation means including ways others might respond to (not) coming out. For instance, when a person knows the exhaustive need both to not come out *and* to always come out and embraces the idea that she or he may be assessed as inappropriate regardless of the length of time that information is omitted and disclosure is postponed, then the person can better prepare for ascriptions of being awkward, politically motivated, and selfish, guilty, shameful, and dishonest, manipulative, unhealthy, and politically irresponsible; she or he adjusts to possible conduct of the other *before* encountering others, adopts a "different act" before others act (p. 43). By recognizing and embracing the possibility of always residing in paradox, a person can work to make interactional peace regarding same-sex attraction, a peace knowing that a definitive state of relational certainty can never be achieved, regardless of what is said or done.

Bypassing Reaction, Evading Paradox

In Chapter 4 I illustrated how the act of coming out and others' immediate reactions to this act—those seconds, minutes, hours, and days—often serve as significant, scarring moments in a LGBQ person's life. In Chapter 5 I noted that one paradox of coming out is the difficulty with being held accountable for disclosing too soon and/or not soon enough. Based on these characteristics, two possibilities exist for bypassing immediate reactions and evading paradoxes tied to time.

First, it seems important to give a person's close, meaningful others license to tell their close, meaningful others about the person's same-sex attraction. For example, it might help a daughter if her father tells relatives about her same-sex attraction, or if a gay man's best friend relays his attraction to other important and meaningful friends who are not in immediate contact. In so doing, the daughter and the man bypass witnessing others' immediate, possibly painful and scarring reactions; those first few seconds, minutes, hours, and days would happen without direct, embodied observation by the person with same-sex attraction. The daughter or man would also not have to worry as much about the timing of coming out—that is, coming out too soon or not soon enough. Giving people license to tell others about a one's sexuality indicates a broader observation about self-disclosure: sometimes there are benefits to asking or allowing another person to tell others about you.

Second, it is important for coming out to happen in public forums, especially with online social networking sites such as Myspace, Facebook, and Twitter. For instance, on Facebook, in the section that asks about who I am "Interested In" I can mark "Men." For people who perceive or know me as male, I can thus explicitly mark my same-sex attraction—that is, come out—without having to say it in live, embodied interaction. Thus far, I have acquaintances, friends, and relatives who (I assume) have seen my "Interested-In-Men" designation. I did not have to worry about the timing of my coming out or witness their immediate reactions.

Furthermore, Facebook allows me to mark my "Relationship Status" as "In a Relationship," "Married," or "Engaged" and, if desired, name the person with whom I am coupled. I can document the existence of my relationship and, consequently, make the acknowledgment of my relationship possible for people viewing my Facebook page. And even if a person does not comment on the relationship, she or he can still "see" its existence; it cannot be relegated to silence as easily as it can in live, embodied interaction.[2]

Manipulating Sexuality through Discourse and Action

Two premises of coming out make this strategy possible: (1) coming out makes sense only when same-sex attraction is not easily accessible; and (2) a person is considered to have come out when she or he validates the existence of same-sex attraction.

In Chapter 4 I mentioned how same-sex attraction—attraction manifest by, or tied to, LGBQ identities—lacks definitive, permanent, easily accessible visible and aural traits. Consequently it is an attraction that must be confirmed, repeatedly, in discourse and action. I can say a woman is a lesbian, but that does not mean she has same-sex attraction, lives in the closet, or will eventually come out as a lesbian. For her to come out, she needs to validate her same-sex attraction through discourse or action—for example, by saying "I am a lesbian." If same-sex attraction was easily accessible, coming out— the revealing of this attraction—would be unnecessary, since others would know of a person's attraction based on how she or he looks or sounds; the person would never have to say anything, never have to come out.

When same-sex attraction is characterized in these ways, then a person can attempt to move between sexualities for particular purposes. For instance, I say "I am gay" in most every course I teach. Once my coming-out act happens, I sometimes have students who identify as "Evangelical Christians" set up a time, outside class, to meet. (As of this writing, I have had five of these "meetings.") In the meetings the student will ask if she or he can "save" me from my inappropriate and/or immoral lifestyle. I do not want to critique Evangelical Christian dogma or these persons' "caring" attempts to save me but rather emphasize one way that I try to "queer"—that is, create dissonance—in these encounters.

The conversations often go something like this: "Why did you want to meet?" I'll ask. "I want to talk with you about your gay lifestyle," the student says. "I'm not gay," I'll respond. "You said you were," the student will reply. "I'm not right now," I'll answer.

What does it say about sexuality if a person identifies as gay one day, bisexual the next, and heterosexual the following week? While refusing to identify as gay may seem self-hating and not politically savvy, alternating sexuality through discourse can make some persons question what sexuality is. Consequently I believe that claiming and then refusing a gay identity is a queer act of "deliberate transgression" (Foucault, 1978, p. 6)—a "confusion technique" (Watzlawick, Weakland, & Fisch, 1974, p. 101)—that may motivate a person to reframe her or his understanding of same-sex attraction. Thus far, none of the students know what to say about or have challenged my perceived fluidity.

I also find it difficult to confront religious dogma directly. I have witnessed conversations that go something like "gays are sinful" with a retort of "I don't think so." A debate begins without any definitive conclusion, and an interactional stalemate forms. This is another reason why manipulating same-sex attraction's not easily accessed and self-claimed characteristic—why naming ourselves differently in interaction—can break and remake dominant, conceptual frames tied to the closet.

Sexuality can also be manipulated through action. I often try to use my (perceived) sexed (male), gendered (masculine), and sexualized (gay) body—and stereotypes about this body—to generate confusion, blur categories, and motivate questioning. For instance, two men once called me a "homo-phoney"—a man who identified as homosexual (gay) but did not have any "homosexual qualities." There was the colleague who said I was not "gay enough" to talk about same-sex attraction, and the professor who, because I "acted straight" believed that I desired intimate relationships with women, not men. There was the student who didn't think I was gay because I acted masculine, and another student who told me that other students thought either that I lied about my same-sex attraction or that I was transgendered—a (masculine) man whose sex was female and who liked men. Even though I simultaneously work against and perpetuate the script of the effeminate gay male, such comments suggest that I sometimes queer this script and create dissonance toward normative conceptualizations of sex, gender, and sexuality (Adams & Holman Jones, 2008).[3]

(Innocently) Manipulating the Frontstage

The closet comes to exist when a person realizes that she or he harbors a secret, that same-sex attraction is not easily accessible. However, as I illustrated in Chapter 5, when a person makes (secret, not easily accessed) same-sex attraction perpetually known, she or he risks being perceived as awkward, politically motivated, and selfish. Thus, it seems important to find ways of using bodies to create intentional-but-unobtrusive, unapologetic dissonance (Faber, 2002; Muñoz, 1999; Phelan, 1993), to purposefully "leak" the backstage (Schrock & Boyd, 2006, p. 58) while trying to come across as "innocently involved" in interaction (Goffman, 1969, p. 88), to take a heightened awareness, a vigilant approach, to coming out in everyday encounters *without seeming to do so.*

For a person with same-sex attraction, one way to intentionally, unobtrusively, and unapologetically come out is by making this attraction known through the manipulation of "frontstage" and "backstage" characteristics of interaction (Goffman, 1959). The frontstage comprises context, audiences, and anything a person sensually emits: sight (such as physical appearance), smell, sound (such as talk), touch, and, in intimate encounters, taste. Contrarily, the backstage comprises information often unknown to or inaccessible by audiences: a person's thoughts, intentions, and strategies for accomplishing particular tasks.

Consider, for instance, my experience in the checkout of a grocery store: a male customer ahead of me pays, grabs his bags, and walks away from the grocery bagger and the cashier. Upon his departure but out of his hearing range, I hear the cashier tell the bagger that the customer "was a flaming faggot." Both laugh as I move forward in the line.

The cashier begins to scan my groceries while the bagger bags. Both still laugh about the cashier's flaming faggot remark and neither pays much attention to me.

The casher soon says what I owe. Although I usually pay for my groceries with a credit card, I decide, this time, to use a check, a check that has "Working for Lesbian, Gay, Bisexual, and Transgender Equal Rights" printed above the signature line. My move to pay by check will, I hope, force the cashier to ask for my ID in order to verify the check's signature and therefore possibly see the printed text.

"May I see your ID?" he asks.

"Sure," I respond as I innocently retrieve my wallet. I give him the ID. He looks at the signature and then compares it to the check. It is here where he pauses. I know that he's reading the print above the signature line, and I know that he begins to know that I know he laughed at the flaming faggot who passed through the checkout line before me.

"Uh . . . thank you," he says, followed by "I'm sorry for what I said about that man."

"No problem," I respond. "Thanks for your help."

Because of his remark, I assumed the cashier was not a "flaming faggot." I also assumed that the cashier didn't think I was one—I don't think he would have made the remark if he did, particularly because he didn't say flaming faggot in the presence of the man he called flaming. Unsure of how to approach the remark, I tried to conceive of a way to make my (not easily accessed) gay identity unobtrusively and unapologetically known or, had I not identified as gay, to find a way to mark myself unobtrusively and unapologetically as a LGBQ ally (Adams & Holman Jones, 2008). In this interaction I used my assumptions of the cashier's identity and my assumptions of his assumptions about my identity to negotiate paradox as well as (I hope) make a politically charged, seemingly neutral point.

A person can intentionally but unobtrusively manipulate conditions, premises, and paradoxes of the closet, coming out, and same-sex attraction in other ways as well. A person can embrace contradictory assumptions about sex, gender, and sexuality; for example, a man can engage in acts of hyper-masculinity while innocently making his gay identity known; in so doing, he rubs against the assumption that a masculine man cannot be gay (Adams & Holman Jones, 2008; Butler, 1999; Escoffier, 2003; Frank, 1993; Halberstam, 2005; Meyer, 1995; Sedgwick, 1993; Walker, 1993). A person can wear articles of clothing that do not necessarily say "I am queer" but rather possess an ambiguous symbol that may motivate someone to ask about the symbol—for instance, a logo affiliated with a lesbian, gay, bisexual, or queer organization. A person can make a comment about an attractive person of the same sex—for example, a woman saying to a friend "I find Jodie Foster attractive" while making sure the comment is loud enough for others to hear. And, as I mentioned earlier, a person can come out on social networking pages such as Myspace, Facebook, and Twitter—a kind of outing that seems matter-of-fact, innocent, and unapologetic.

Coming Out as Heterosexual

In hetero-normative contexts, heterosexuality is often disregarded and assumed, not *explicitly* discussed (Butler, 1999; Foster, 2008; Yep, 2003); I hear "Do you think he's gay?" far more than "Do you think he's straight?" Hetero-normative contexts frame a person as heterosexual until proven otherwise and, consequently, make the act of identifying as heterosexual unnecessary and require a person to come out—that is, explicitly validate same-sex attraction through discourse or action.

Speaking about heterosexuality in hetero-normative contexts can thus function as an unnecessary form of discursive visibility (Gator Gay-Straight Alliance, 2004; Jacobs, 2007; Skelton, 1997; Wilkinson & Kitzinger, 1994). Coming out as heterosexual makes heterosexuality something talked about rather than disregarded and assumed; it becomes a *queer* act of speaking, an act of "deliberate transgression" (Foucault, 1978, p. 6) that, by disrupting taken-for-granted, heteronormative conventions, may create dissonance about heterosexuality's privileged status.

Coming out as heterosexual can also expose awkwardness in, and preparation for, a disclosure of sexuality. If coming out is a never-ending process—new situations make for new times to disclose—the feeling of never being able to fully disclose one's heterosexuality can become tedious and tiresome. Furthermore, since heterosexuality is often disregarded and assumed, identifying as heterosexual can come to feel awkward in that a person speaks unnecessarily of a disregarded and assumed trait.

I am not suggesting that coming out as heterosexual parallels a LGBQ person's coming out. However, it makes sense that if persons of all sexualities were encouraged or expected to come out, then coming out might become less of a marked and meaningful event. In some contexts identifying as straight may make little sense, but in others it is a strategy that could create new concerns about sexuality and same-sex attraction.

Reframing Accountability

Although I do not think everyone who has same-sex attraction experiences the closet and encounters paradox in the ways I describe, and although a LGBQ person may not feel as though the conditions of coming out apply to her or his experience, I believe that the closet, coming out, and paradoxes of same-sex attraction are relational phenomena: *others* may hold a person accountable for these phenomena in a variety of ways, at a variety of times, and in a variety of places. As long as the closet is talked about, believed in, and researched, a person always has the potential, in interaction, to be held accountable for the construct and, consequently, always has the potential to experience paradox. Thus, even though I foreground my experiences of paradox, I believe my discussion has relevance for anyone who believes in and/or interacts with a person who knows of and believes in the closet.

Consequently everyone should acknowledge—and be held accountable for—the relational paradoxes a person can experience in terms of the closet. It is ignorant to say that a person does not risk safety in coming out to others, unfortunate for a person to feel guilty, shameful, and dishonest for not coming out, and naïve to consider a person awkward, selfish, and politically motivated for coming out too early and/or manipulative, unhealthy, and politically irresponsible for coming out too late or not at all. If we make any of these assessments about LGBQ persons, then we must reflexively assess ourselves and recognize that we may be holding the person to contradictory standards.

If any action a person takes with coming out has the potential to be deemed "illegitimate" and "unreasonable" (Scott & Lyman, 1968), then a different kind of accounting must exist for a person whose attraction—and conditions and premises of this attraction—make conflict; for a LGBQ person, there must be room, in interaction, for positive evaluations of (not) coming out, for coming out too soon and/or not soon enough. I believe we should exempt persons with same-sex attraction not from accountability but rather from negative evaluations made *solely* on whether and how coming out happens.

Making Coming Out Relational

I remember uttering the phrase "I am gay" to my father. He responded by not speaking to me for six months. When I told my mom I found men attractive, she supported my attraction as long as I promised to never tell relatives—she feared they would abandon her for having a gay son. Thus, at some family gatherings I entertain being asked if "I have a girlfriend" and justify why I am not married. In December 2005 my cousin did not want my boyfriend and me in her house—she refused to have gays contaminating her space. Saying "I am gay" influenced my relationship with her, too.

It is easy to criticize my father, mother, and cousin for these disheartening responses. It is easy to say that they are selfish and hurtful. It is easy to say that I am silenced in some familial contexts and should thus work to eliminate this silence by way of dialogue, debate, avoidance, or argument. However, persons-in-relationships are not isolated phenomena, and, although I may not like hearing another's response, I must make an attempt to work with and respect it. A person can have rational reasons (Shweder, 1986), from her or his perspective, to fear or dislike same-sex attraction (Tillmann-Healy, 2001). Thus a person with same-sex attraction cannot necessarily expect or demand another to respond favorably to coming out.

Throughout much this book I described a person's burdens and dilemmas with the closet. In this section I reframe the coming-out event from an individualistic narrative that places a significant amount of burden on the LGBQ person to a narrative that makes all persons accountable for its affiliated burdens. Reframing is a move to alter the "conceptual framework" of an event (Watzlawick, Weakland, & Fisch, 1974, p. 104) in order to offer new understandings of the "same circumstance" (p. 109). Reframing coming out as relational means recognizing the myriad of ways that others are involved in and implicated by the closet and, in so doing, offering new understandings of these phenomena. The closet, coming out, and same-sex attraction are *shared* responsibilities, ones we must all negotiate *together*; they're phenomena made possible by joint interaction, of people being, working, relating together; everyone is accountable.

For instance, Chapter 1 includes a story about Ugandan officials wanting not only to exterminate persons with same-sex attraction but also to incarcerate people who do not turn these others in to authorities (Sharlet, 2010). This situation illustrates how a same-sex attraction is a shared responsibility, one implicating everyone: people with same-sex attraction have the possibility of being executed solely for this attraction, and heterosexual people have the possibility of being incarcerated for knowing others who possess same-sex attraction.

Or consider the situation of Gareth Thomas, a well-known rugby player once married to a woman. While married, he struggled with his sexuality: he knew he desired men, but he didn't speak of this attraction to close, meaningful others, particularly with Jemma, his wife. Looking back, he realized that this hurt not only him but also her: "He could keep lying to everyone else, keep lying to himself, but to Jemma, to that innocent woman?" (Smith, 2010, p. 61) Consequently, staying in the closet—suppressing same-sex attraction—can hurt everyone. Even if a person disagrees with the validity or importance of same-sex attraction, there must be concern for others tangled in/ loving someone with same-sex attraction but who feels as though she or he cannot make this attraction known.

Furthermore, when a person comes out, she or he implicates people in her or his close and meaningful sphere; a closet is constructed around addressees (Aoki, 2005; Hom, 1995; Seidman, Meeks, & Traschen, 1999). "When gay people in a homophobic society come out, perhaps especially to parents or spouses," Eve Sedgwick says,

> it is with the consciousness of a potential for serious injury that is likely to go in *both* directions. The pathogenic secret itself . . . can circulate contagiously *as* a secret: a mother says that her adult child's coming out of the closet with her has plunged her, in turn, into the closet in her conservative community. (1990, p. 80)

A relational understanding of coming out means considering how closets work for the LGBQ person *and* others affiliated with this person. For instance, when Sharon Lim-Hing came out to her family—*said* something to them about her same-sex attraction—family members quit sending invitations for family events; they seemed supportive of her attraction but only as long as it was not discussed. "This tolerance," she writes, "tells me that I'm still part of the family but that being gay or having a gay person in the family is shameful" (1990/91, p. 21).

Or consider a mother-son interaction in the film *Were the World Mine* (Gustafson, 2008):

"Why are you gay? What did I do?" the mother asks.
     "You didn't make me queer," the son [Timothy] replies. . . .
     "Nobody did. I'm just queer. Okay? So deal with it."
     "Go to hell," she responds. "I do deal with it, Timothy. Every day I deal with it. You aren't the only one who has it rough around here. Every single day I come out of the closet, just like you. You know this is not just your problem. It's both of ours, and I'm trying."

Later in the film, the mother speaks of her son's queer-ness to two acquaintances, both of whom ridicule her for having a queer son. The film illustrates a parent's personal struggle with a child's queer identity as well as complications the parent may experience from telling others about the child.

"I don't necessarily think about how I'm going to take a person's response to my coming out," Tyler says in an interview.

But I always think about how the other person is going to feel, how the person is going to handle it, if the person is going to be upset. I believe it is unfair to come out to someone who does not have time to deal with the disclosure. It is also unfair if you don't think the other will react. This is something I told my boyfriend. He wanted me to be there when he came out to his mom. I told him that would be unfair to her. With me there she could not express herself how she wanted. With just him, she could. If she wanted to scream, she could scream. If she wanted to cuss, she could cuss. I think that when a person comes out, the person needs to worry about how the other is going to feel. (2007)

A heterosexual person (or closeted LGBQ person) may react negatively to coming out for many reasons. The person may feel as though she or he motivated, or contributed to, the onset of the marginal and devalued attraction. For instance, Armesto and Weisman note that parents can "experience shame and guilt as a result of a child's disclosure that he or she is gay"; they are often more concerned with "mentally undoing some aspect of themselves ('If I had done this differently, then . . .')" (2001, p. 148).

A person's negative reaction may also stem from the perception that a person with same-sex attraction has been too secretive or living a "lie" pre-disclosure—especially if the LGBQ person explicitly and aggressively confirmed perceptions of heterosexuality. Thus, others may need support if they have a minimal amount of knowledge of the reasons why a LGBQ person may feel as though she or he could not have come out sooner (Elizur & Ziv, 2001).

"Identity by association"—the idea that a person is a particular kind of person because of her or his relationships with other kinds of people—is another reason a person's same-sex attraction can pose difficulties for others (Boyd, 2006, p. 179; see also Aoki, 2005; Garfinkel, 1967; Taylor, 2000; Walker, 1993). A person affiliated with someone whom others consider inappropriate and/or immoral may worry about whether these others consider her or him inappropriate and/ or immoral, too. For instance, a person who says "I have a gay friend" risks being perceived as gay and/or being condemned for associating with someone who is gay; a parent who says, "I have a daughter who is a lesbian" may be thought of as a bad parent; and a child who has a LGBQ parent may be punished because of the parent's sexuality (T. C. Fox, 2010; Tam & Heinz, 2010).

The identity-by-association idea also provides further insight into the coming-out process. A person does not necessarily come out when she or he discloses information about someone else. A person comes out when she or he is invested in a disclosure and is concerned about how others will respond. I may have a friend who identifies as queer, but I do not come out by saying "I know a person who is queer." I do, however, come out if I am invested in this utterance—that is, if I worry that others may think of me as queer or might condemn me for associating with a queer person, or may conceive of me as a bad parent if the queer person is my child. When a person comes out, she or he reveals potentially harmful or controversial information.

For instance, I lived the first 20 years of my life in Danville, Illinois, a rural, factory and farming town of about 30,000 people. Generations of my family lived in this town, and, with the exception of three cousins, all still remain. I visit this town a few days each year, although I haven't lived in Danville for more than a decade.

My father owns a restaurant in Danville, a business that has been in his family for more than 40 years. If my father believes that my coming out to others in the town will hurt his business—his livelihood and way of financial survival—then how can I ethically invade his space—the town—and make my same-sex attraction visible, an attraction that many in Danville may still perceive as inappropriate and/or immoral?[4] What gives me the right to jeopardize *his* business when I do not live in the area? Here, I consider my concealment an act of "social obligation" (Henry, 1965, p. 100).

But when should a person take a stand? What happens if a lesbian is empathetic toward close, meaningful loved ones, but these others find her attraction disgusting time after time? Should she continue to accommodate their disgust and simultaneously try to make her feelings known? What happens when a father forces a son to undergo reparative therapy, because the son's attraction is a problem for his father? What happens if the father chooses to no longer speak to his son, because the son refuses to change? Should the son still make an effort to understand, accommodate, and even respect his father?

I believe there is a limit to understanding others' reactions to same-sex attraction, particularly when others assess the attraction a "problem." To suggest that same-sex attraction is a problem and must somehow be "fixed" is unethical, or, at the very least, a position for which a middle ground of agreement or acceptance may be difficult to find. Although a relational understanding of coming out may allow for initial, negative reactions to same-sex attraction, the attraction cannot be a problem forever; negative reactions must cease eventually. Negative evaluations happen far too often and can motivate a variety of undesirable acts (for example, suicide). Such evaluations would also seem only to encourage a person to stay closeted.

LGBQ persons should not refrain from discussing intimate and meaningful same-sex relations forever. As previously mentioned, Hyde argues that "acknowledgment" is a "communicative behavior that grants attention to others and thereby makes room for them in our lives" (2004, p. 63). Negative forms of acknowledgment such as silence or disregard "expose people to [a] fate of social death" (p. 64; see also Glave, 2005) thus making "positive acknowledgment" a "moral thing to do" (p. 63). Embracing Hyde's call suggests that acknowledgment of a person's same-sex attraction, particularly her or his intimate and meaningful relations with same-sex others, is necessary. Otherwise, positive acknowledgment does not exist, because silence serves as a negative, dismissing act.

And here is a larger dilemma that complicates the possibility of negative response: a person's perception that others might respond negatively to coming out might motivate this person to *not tell*—the person may find safety and protection more important than openness and honesty (Bochner, 1984; Rawlins, 1983). Consequently, the person continues to live (in) the closet around these others and may thereby continue to build on a history of secrecy, omissions of information, self-condemning acts, and, perhaps, lying.

Making coming out relational means treating all persons involved as responsible for the closet. Making coming out relational means recognizing how the disclosure of same-sex attraction implicates others and recognizing the variety of ways people may choose to disclose and the variety of ways people may respond. Making coming out relational means conceiving of the process as an interpersonal (rather than individual) affair, a process in which a LGBQ person tries to disrupt harmful, hetero-normative assumptions while also trying to express concern for hurtful others.

I realize that understanding these reactions against same-sex attraction may run counter to progressive politics as well as an increased social acceptance of LGBQ persons, and may also seem a bit dangerous for a person who is newly out, but in making coming out relational I call us all to try to understand—not necessarily accept—negative-responding others, even if such understanding might make us uncomfortable. I want acceptance of and respect for same-sex attraction, and I want an acknowledgment of intimate, meaningful same-sex affairs by families and schools, churches and workplaces, nations and states. But I also do not want to carelessly dismiss others' understandings of same-sex attraction. I do not have to accept such understandings, only recognize that negative responses to coming out may be simultaneously justified *and* inexcusable.

Same-Sex Attraction: Lessons Learned

Throughout this work, I have highlighted many negative characteristics of the closet and coming out in order to change and improve experiences tied to same-sex attraction. However, before I conclude, I want to highlight four positive characteristics of these phenomena—characteristics that same-sex attraction and my identification with a gay identity have taught me.

First, identifying as gay has taught me that love doesn't see categories. I feel as though I have fought, and continue to fight, to be able to love a man, a person classified the "same" as me—male. And what I have learned from such fighting is that love and relationships cannot be dismissed solely because of such categories as sex, gender, race, age, class, religion, and/or ability; love transcends labels. People form intimate and meaningful relationships for different reasons, and relationships can never be adequately described or dismissed based on the convergence or divergence of such identities. The only criteria I have for love or a legitimate, meaningful relationship is mutual consent and equality.[5]

A second, related observation is that I have come to realize and respect the multiple forms attraction, sexuality, and relationships might take. There are open and three-way relationships, and relationships that combine a variety of sexes and genders. There are people with fetishes, people who have never had vaginal, anal, and/or oral sex, and people who desire a variety of sex acts and as much as possible. There are people who prefer being single, coupled for life, want 15 children, or never want kids.

Third, I recognize the existential need for acknowledgment. One thing I realized from my experiences of same-sex attraction is that positive forms of acknowledgment, of confirmation, for this attraction (and my intimate, same-sex relationships) make me feel good and worthy. As Hyde (2006) observes, the lack of positive acknowledgment, of making legitimate time and space for others in our lives, can contribute to feelings of anxiety, despair, and unworthiness—it can expose a person to "social death." This may be one reason why suicide rates for LGBQ persons are high—they may have experienced too much disconfirmation about whom they like. Their existence is not confirmed, explicitly, and, if it is, it is not confirmed in affirming ways.

Fourth, as a gay man, I spend much time trying to make my same-sex attraction and my intimate and meaningful relationships a part of everyday conversation, not shrouded in silence; I yearn for caring acknowledgment. In so doing, I have come to question the validity of other topics relegated to the silences of everyday conversation, topics such as racism, religion, illness, ability, ageism, immigration, and death. Had I not questioned, and rebelled against, the normality of heterosexuality, I might still be engaging in what I consider risky, unhealthy behaviors—for me, these included a reckless disregard of others, excess and careless alcohol use, and self-hating, unprotected sexual acts. I seek to engage in a similar questioning and rebelling against normalizing acts that promote human disregard, such as the abrasive, dehumanizing requirements of gaining citizenship in particular places, the valuing and privileging of able bodies in everyday life, and hidden social barriers that prohibit some people from gaining employment, health care, or happiness.

□

I leave this project knowing that I will continue to struggle with the closet, coming out, and same-sex attraction, because I have a history of heterosexuality, ex-girlfriends, visits to (female) strip clubs, and lies about liking women—a history for which others can and do still hold me accountable, for example, by asking about why I "lied" to myself for so long, why I teased women, and why I ever said I found women attractive. I leave knowing that I also have a hidden history of same-sex attraction, reckless acts, and intimate and invasive same-sex experiences—a history for which others can and do still hold me accountable, for instance, by asking about why I felt a need to hide, why I was dishonest and didn't come out earlier, and why I ever engaged in reckless acts.

I leave knowing that the organization Heterosexuals Organized for a Moral Environment frequently come onto my college campus, position themselves at the doors of the student union, and distribute fliers that say homosexuals live "20–30 years shorter than normal," lesbians have a "higher breast cancer rate" than heterosexual women, and "male homosexuals" have "significantly higher rates" of AIDS, anal cancer, and syphilis. "The rational way to deal with homosexual behavior," the fliers continue,

> is to treat it like we treat smoking, a comparatively less dangerous and less costly behavior. We should discourage it in a way consonant with our democratic principles. Haven't Americans demonstrated that they can reject smoking while not rejecting and hating those who smoke?

I leave knowing that the respect—and, at minimum, tolerance—of same-sex attraction does not yet exist, even on what I consider to be a progressive, urban college campus.

But I also leave thinking—hoping—that the closet, coming out, and same-sex attraction are becoming less controversial. I leave knowing that acceptance of same-sex attraction in the United States continues to increase significantly (Blow, 2010), and U.S. media are infiltrated with "out celebrities" and "role models" (Puente, 2010).[6] I leave knowing that children are identifying as LGBQ as early as middle school, the validity and rights of same-sex relationships continue to be recognized globally (for example, Spain, Mexico, Netherlands), and the illegality of homosexuality in particular regions (for instance, India, Uganda, Poland) continues to get challenged or overturned.

I also leave hoping that this book will help propel change, hope, and unconditional love—love without conditions, qualifiers, or regrets—and hoping that we all attend to and value others more. I leave knowing that I am not invincible—I could die tomorrow in a car crash or on a walk on my way home from school, or that I may come down with an abrupt, incurable illness. And I leave knowing that I must continue to use my abilities and resources—my privileges—to continue to speak with others about the closet, coming out, and same-sex attraction—to work to tell not only my stories but also the stories of others unable and/or afraid to speak.

EPILOGUE

August, 2003. A Cher concert in Indianapolis, Indiana. An early birthday gift for Brett. A last trip together before death entered our story.

At the concert I sit on the end of a row, seat 1. Brett sits next to me in seat 2. A couple, a man and a woman, occupies seats 3 and 4, and seats 5 and 6 contain two women, an assumed couple, too. At intermission, the man in seat 3 leans to Brett. "Hey, there are two pretty ladies sitting next to my wife and me," he says. "You two men should introduce yourselves."

"They're not our type," Brett responds bluntly, then looks at me and laughs.

After the concert we begin the five-hour drive home. Talk of Cher occurs for the first 30 minutes but ceases when Brett says he feels tired. I put my hand on his bare leg not covered by inked-stained shorts and tell him to rest. He places his head on my shoulder and goes to sleep, a familiar and comfortable position we maintain for most of the trip.

□

December, 2003. We break up but decide to live together until he moves to Oklahoma, and until I move to Florida.

□

June, 2004. The last time Brett and I will see each other for months. He enters my room wearing his usual plaid green pajama pants and worn grey T-shirt, and climbs on my twin mattress. I turn on k.d.

lang's *Drag* CD, one of our favorites, and then join him on the bed. Despite months of turmoil we peer into each others' eyes and begin to cry. We connect again and bond by holding, crying, talking, realizing we each could love and still love each other, something we both doubted.

"I'm going to miss you," I say.

"I already miss you," he replies.

We know we'll miss each other, know we love each other, know that we'll no longer be able to wheel Seymour, our potted tree, around to meet house guests, no longer be able to take comfort in pot-smoke-filled rooms, no longer be able to share care for a fish.

□

October, 2004. Tampa, Florida. Brett, a two-hour layover at the airport. Tony, a two-hour break between teaching. A lunch at Pizza Hut.

□

January, 2005. Springboro, Ohio. A night together at a Knights Inn. Though we telephoned often, this is the last time we see each other.

□

March, 2006. A call from a friend.

"Brett's dead," she says through tears. "His sister just called me. You should call her."

Our conversation ends, and I call the sister, a person I have never met. "Hi, Sarah? This is Tony Adams. I lived with Brett in Carbondale," I say, a strategic phrasing of words. Even though at this time I assumed Brett was out to his family, I refrain from calling him my ex-boyfriend. I retreat into the closet about our history, wanting to feel out the interaction before saying "we dated," wanting to keep the sister on the phone and not encourage her to hang up. "You sick fuck," I could hear her say. "My brother wasn't gay." It was a comment I feared, and so "I lived with Brett in Carbondale" sufficed.

"I know," she says. "I've heard about you." I wonder what "heard about you" means, but I'm scared to ask. She continues by describing how he died and what the doctors said, did, and tried to do. The details—a blur.

"I bought him a yellow pony, a plush pony no bigger than a hand," I say nervously.

"I've seen it," she replies. "I know the pony you're talking about."

"He used to call me 'My Little Tony,' a play off 'My Little Pony.' 'My Little Tony,' that's what he'd say. Could I have it?"

"Of course," she says. "I'll send it to you next week."

☐

The pony, the item that Brett took wherever he traveled, the only item I asked for when he died. "I know the pony you're talking about," the sister says. "I'll send it to you next week."

☐

I'm still waiting.

☐

I want to attend Brett's funeral and see his body one last time, but before I book a flight, two of our mutual friends tell me the story of Brett coming out to his father. And I think: What happens if family and friends refuse to speak of Brett's same-sex attraction and his past of intimately and meaningfully loving men? What happens if the family doesn't know of this past? What happens if I arrive at the funeral and someone asks who I am?

I decide against attending. Although funerals are typically for the survivors of death, I am concerned about becoming angry about the choices that might be made to celebrate Brett's life, choices about his likes and dislikes, choices about his friends and lovers.

I also decide against attending out of concern for my safety. If Brett's father reacted negatively to Brett's coming out as the alternate story suggests, then I am scared of being a gay man, an ex-boyfriend, in his father's presence. Furthermore, the funeral is in rural Oklahoma. Folk wisdom in some LGBQ social circles advise against visiting such settings. These places often cultivate harm; LGBQ people move or live in them at heightened risk. I recall images of Matthew Shepard. I think about the story of *Brokeback Mountain* (Proulx, 1999). I get nauseous remembering my experiences of living most of my life in a conservative rural area.

□

I write for you Brett, someone who, according to entries on his online obituary, "loved without letting on that [he] loved" (Cole); could "take a stressful day, turn it 90 degrees, and help you to see the humor in it" (Alley-Young); would sing Cher songs when it "got too quiet" (Prell).

□

Death of an ex-lover: an event after which life never seems quite the same. Brett's death, a year and a half after our year and a half together, makes new thoughts, feelings, and behaviors possible: obsessively, I watch squirrels play in the tree outside my window. I walk by myself for hours, enjoying the ability to walk. I thank something— a god, a force, higher being(s)—that I can feel, experience, be. New behaviors made possible by a person I once loved and still love. Brett's death: a motivation to have fun being, a motivation to recognize that what you say may be the last thing you say, recognize that what you say matters.

□

Just know you make me smile.

Notes on Method, Criticism, and Representation

Chapter 1 introduced five questions that guided my writing of this book: (1) How is same-sex attraction discussed and lived? (2) What does it mean to come out of—and, consequently, stay in—the closet? (3) When and how does—and should—coming out happen? (4) How does a person's same-sex attraction affect not only the self but also others? (5) How can I work to make experiences of same-sex attraction and the closet more humane?

These questions, in turn, made three methodological questions possible: (1) How might I study the closet—a metaphorical space and abstract construct? (2) How do I study coming out—an act of self-disclosure difficult to witness as it is lived? (3) How can I study same-sex attraction—a private attraction only accessible and primarily constituted in discourse and action?

In this appendix I illustrate the ways in which I addressed these methodological questions. I first define autoethnography and discern the benefits and consequences of using the method to study same-sex attraction. I then describe the techniques I used to study the closet and coming out. I conclude with a discussion about how I assembled this book. In so doing, I provide a methodological guide for studying ephemeral and invisible phenomena such as the closet, coming out, and same-sex attraction.

Autoethnography

I am an autoethnographer. I study culture in all its material and ephemeral manifestations as well as investigate the unique, interactional dynamics of cultural members. I value my experience of cultural phenomena, strive for "thick descriptions" (Geertz, 1973) of cultural happenings, and find storytelling an important practice and mode of representation. To thoroughly outline the premises and practices of autoethnography, I begin by outlining the premises and practices of *ethnography* and *auto*biography.

Ethnography

An ethnographer is a person who studies, represents, and is defined by her or his relationship to a culture. A person becomes an ethnographer—does ethnography—by writing "thick descriptions" of cultural happenings (Geertz, 1973, p. 10). The purpose of these descriptions is to make "strange" aspects of a group familiar for "insiders" (cultural members) and "outsiders" (cultural strangers; see Maso, 2001). These descriptions are created by interviewing cultural members, participating in and observing cultural events and rituals (Geertz, 1973; Makagon, 2004), examining members' ways of speaking and relating (Ellis, 1986, 1995a, 2009; Lindquist, 2002; Philipsen, 1975, 1976), and analyzing such artifacts as clothing and architecture as well as texts such as books, movies, and photographs (Borchard, 1996; Goodall, 2006; Neumann, 1999). An ethnographer does not apply predetermined, sense-making structures to members' experiences but allows findings to emerge, inductively, from fieldwork (Jorgenson, 2002).

However, as an ethnographer interested in studying LGBQ cultures, I trip myself up on a methodological dilemma: I want to study LGBQ cultures—cultures constituted by and defined in relation to the closet, coming out, and same-sex attraction—but these cultures are often framed as one facet of, and secondary to, cultural experience, *not* as legitimate cultures themselves. Consequently, the claim "I study LGBQ cultures" makes little sense: if LGBQ cultures are not cultures, then how can I use ethnography—a method for studying cultural experience—to understand LGBQ cultural members, happenings, and experiences? By claiming to study LGBQ cultures, I claim to study cultures that some writers say do not exist.[2]

With a few exceptions (for example, Bronski, 2003; Herdt, 1992; Majors, 1994; Nicholas, 2004), most research on and about culture does not consider LGBQ communities as cultures. Many (inter)cultural communication books exclude discussions of LGBQ cultures (for instance, Asante, Miike, & Yin, 2007; Gudykunst & Moody, 2001; Monaghan & Goodman, 2007), and "culture" is still often synonymous with "region," "race," and "ethnicity" (Kim, 2002; Yep, 1998). When LGBQ communities are discussed, they are often framed as tangential to culture, as expressed by such phrases as "cultural views of homosexuality" (Yep, Lovaas, & Ho, 2001, p. 166), being "out in the [cultural] field" (Lewin & Leap, 1996; Rooke, 2010), and references to these communities as "subcultures" (Stein, 2010), "co-cultures" (Orbe, 1998), or "life-styles" (Herdt & Boxer, 1992).[3]

However, if culture is defined in terms of and made possible by a community's interactional practices, common values and beliefs, and shared experiences (for example, Braithwaite, 1994; Carbaugh, 1999; Ellis, 1986, 1995a; Geertz, 1973; Jorgenson, 2002; Lindquist, 2002; Philipsen, 1975, 1976), then LGBQ communities *are* cultures. Although not definitive or homogenous, LGBQ cultures can consist of such phenomena as camp (Meyer, 1995; Newton, 1979; Sontag, 1964; Whitney, 2006), gender inversion and nonconformity (Butler, 1999; Escoffier, 2003; Feinberg, 1993; Frank, 1993; Hutson, 2010; Sedgwick, 1993; Walker, 1993), same-sex attraction (Bolton, 1995; Ginsberg, 1974; Lee, 1979), and trauma and shame (Cornell, 2007; Cvetkovich, 2003; Downs, 2005; Halberstam, 2005; Halperin & Traub, 2010; Sedgwick, 2003). LGBQ cultures manifest themselves in, and are created by, such spaces as bars (Corey, 1996; Slavin, 2004), neighborhoods (Gorman, 1992; Kennedy & Davis, 1996), pride parades (Herrell, 1992; Johnston, 2005; Kates & Belk, 2001), and bathhouses (Berry, 2007; Hammers, 2009). In particular, lesbians and gay men have unique ways of interacting (Chesebro, 1981; Halperin, 2007; Hammers, 2009; Hayes, 1976; Jones, 2007; Leap, 1996; Nicholas, 2004; Stein, 2010; Tillmann, 2009c) and are populations that must often contend with and negotiate such canonical discourses as coming out of the closet (Brown, 2000; Sedgwick, 1990; Urbach, 1996), physical appearance and aging (Boxer, 1997; Goltz, 2009), and heteronormativity (Butler, 1993, 1999; Foster, 2008; Yep, 2003).[4]

But even if LGBQ cultures are cultures and, consequently, open to ethnographic research—which I believe they are—I encounter another problem: the impossibility of doing fieldwork *in* these cultures, a canonical, constitutive requirement for doing ethnography.

An ethnographer goes to, participates in, and observes a culture in order to describe, and, consequently, facilitate an understanding of the cultural members' interactional practices, common values and beliefs, and shared experiences (Brodkey, 1987; Buzard, 2003; Geertz, 1973; Goodall, 2001; Leeds-Hurwitz, 2005; Van Maanen, 1988). The ethnographer often leaves a "here"—a comfortable home—to do field-work in a "there"—an existentially exotic away, and, in so doing, works to become an "insider" in and/or remain an "outsider" to a culture's happenings.[5]

However, the spatial metaphors used to do ethnography—terms such as *fieldwork, here and there, insider and outsider*—are irrelevant to, and problematic for, the study of LGBQ cultures (Jackman, 2010). These cultures have no dominant place or space, no field, no here and no there, no definitive idea about what constitutes an insider and outsider. I do say that I do fieldwork in LGBQ cultures, but the spatial bias of ethnography trips me up on how LGBQ fieldwork is, and should be, done. For instance, where do I go to study the closet, the coming-out event, and same-sex attraction—constitutive characteristics of LGBQ cultures, but characteristics that are ephemeral, invisible, and not tied to space?

Granted, fields of LGBQ cultures do exist, fields where an ethnographer can go and leave, fields such as tearooms (Humphreys, 1975) and bathhouses (Berry, 2007; Hammers, 2009; Styles, 1979), neighborhoods (Kennedy & Davis, 1996; Levine, 1979) and pride parades (Herrell, 1992; Johnston, 2005; Kates & Belk, 2001), HIV-related facilities (Cherry, 1996) and bars (Corey, 1996; Slavin, 2004; Stein, 2010), suburbs (Lynch, 1992), community centers (Rooke, 2010), and softball fields (Tillmann-Healy, 2001). But emphasizing space as a condition of culture significantly prohibits any possibility of studying and understanding LGBQ cultures: only large or mid-sized cities have tearooms and bathhouses, neighborhoods and pride parades, HIV-related facilities and bars, suburbs and softball fields (Bronski, 2003; Majors, 1994). Tying LGBQ cultures to physical fields is not only limiting and impractical but also suggests that, with the exception of virtual fields, these cultures cannot exist outside of densely populated areas.[6]

Furthermore, many of the aforementioned characteristics of LGBQ cultures lack fields, characteristics such as camp, gender inversion and nonconformity, same-sex attraction and trauma. Lesbians and gay men, in particular, possess particular ways of speaking not grounded in physical space, and, as illustrated throughout this book, persons joined by the possession of same-sex attraction must often negotiate ephemeral and invisible phenomena, such as the closet, coming out, and hetero-normativity.

And so I ask: How does an ethnographer study cultures that lack visible characteristics and physical fields, characteristics such as the closet, coming out, and same-sex attraction? How might an ethnographer study whether a person is and is not out of the closet? Am I an insider to LGBQ cultures when I come out, an outsider when I do not? When is a person in and out of LGBQ cultures, there and not there?

To study LGBQ cultures ethnographically, a researcher needs not only to justify LGBQ populations as legitimate cultures but must also reframe ethnography's methodological reliance on, and use of, space. In particular, an ethnographer of LGBQ cultures must trouble, reframe, or dismiss space-bound metaphors of, and requirements for, being here or there, in the field or not. For me, this means documenting profound, painful, and unexpected conversations I have about the closet and coming out on cocktail napkins, in computer files, and by journaling, all the while acknowledging that these notes may be used, at a later time, as data; it means always being immersed in possible LGBQ discursive fields, never knowing when same-sex attraction will inform or become an explicit part of my experience.

The ethnographer of LGBQ cultures must also find a way to study invisible and ephemeral phenomena, such as the closet, coming out, and same-sex attraction. For me, this means reflecting on and using my experience with the closet, talking with others about their experience with coming out, and examining mass-mediated representations of same-sex attraction.

Autobiography

Autobiography is also part of *auto*ethnography. When a person writes an autobiography, she or he retrospectively writes episodes from her or his life. However, an autobiographer usually does not live through these experiences in order to make them a part of the autobiography; as Freeman notes, "one often does not know 'what is happening' until the moment is past, until it can be located within some broader constellation of events, read for its significance in some larger whole" (2004, p. 64; see also Freeman, 2010). An autobiographer—in doing autobiography—relies on memory, interviews with others, and texts such as photographs, journals, and recordings (Delany, 2004; Denzin, 2006; Didion, 2005; Goodall, 2006).

Autobiographers must also attend to conventions of writing and understand how the autobiographical genre works (Bruner, 1993; Mandel, 1968; Tullis et al., 2009); there is a need to know how to tell a good story—how to create a literary thrust, develop characters, and make a good read (Couser, 1997)—and a need to know and attend to the expectations and politics of grammar and print (Adams, 2008; Lorde, 1984).

(Auto)Ethnography

When a person does autoethnography, she or he interviews cultural members, participates in and observes cultural events and rituals, examines members' ways of speaking and relating, analyzes cultural artifacts, and values the use of personal experience (Ellis, 1995b, 2004; Ellis & Bochner, 2000). But using personal experience does not mean an autoethnographer can tell only her or his story. Rather, the autoethnographer must be able to distance her- or himself from and reflect on personal experience. As Mitch Allen, a publisher of autoethnographies, says,

> you have to look at experience analytically. Otherwise [you're] telling [your] story—and that's nice—but people do that on *Oprah* [a U.S.-based television program] every day. Why is your story more valid than anyone else's? What makes your story more valid is that you are a researcher. You have a set of theoretical and methodological tools and a research literature to use. That's your advantage. If you can't frame it around these tools and literature and just frame it as "my story," then why or how should I privilege your story over anyone else's I see 25 times a day on TV? (2006)

Autoethnography requires a researcher to make personal experience meaningful for others, and, consequently, say something about cultural experience and/or motivate cultural change (for example, Bochner, 2002a; Ellis, 2002a, 2002b, 2007, 2009; Marvasti, 2006; Tillmann, 2009b).

An autoethnographer must also have a heightened sensitivity to the "literary values" and "narrative thrust" of a text (Richardson, 2009,

p. 346). Autoethnographers value creativity and performative ways of representing research (for instance, Denzin, 2003; Diversi & Moreira, 2010; Pelias, 2005; Pineau, 2000) and, consequently, treat sterile, storytelling practices as inadequate or problematic. Furthermore, autoethnographers strive for narrative truth (Bochner, 2002b); they understand the fallibility of memory (Freeman, 2010) and consider truth contextual, contested, and complicated (Denzin, 2004, 2007; Tullis et al., 2009).

Using Autoethnography to Study LGBQ Cultures

To study LGBQ cultures autoethnographically—cultures absent physical fields—I relied on four kinds of data: (1) my experience of the closet and coming out; (2) informal and unsolicited conversations I had with others about same-sex attraction; (3) interviews with persons who identify as LGBQ; and (4) mass-mediated representations of the closet, coming out, and same-sex attraction.

Personal Experience

As an autoethnographer, I treat my experiences of a culture as meaningful and valuable. In particular, I retrospectively write about personal experiences that stem from, or are made possible by, being a part of a culture and/or from embracing a particular cultural or personal identity. I distance myself from these experiences in an attempt to discern and analyze patterns of these experiences as evidenced by repeated characteristics, responses, feelings, and topics of discussion. In so doing, I make patterns of a culture familiar for insiders and outsiders, make personal experience meaningful cultural experience.

I find the use of personal experience valuable for two primary reasons. First, personal experience allows insight into everyday, lived moments of the closet, coming out, and same-sex attraction—constitutive phenomena of LGBQ cultures. I am able to tap into and analyze my "firsthand familiarity" (Blumer, 1968, p. 38) with these characteristics and, as such, observe what happens in social life under my nose (p. 50).

The second reason I find personal experience useful is because as a self-identified gay man I have participated in LGBQ cultures for nearly a decade. I make my gay identity known most everywhere.

Most of my family knows I find men attractive, and I openly discuss my same-sex relationships with friends and acquaintances, colleagues, students, and strangers. Thus I am regularly held accountable, by self and others, for many of the assumptions of the closet, coming out, and same-sex attraction outlined in this book; they inform, emerge in, and are reinforced by many of my interactions.

But I do not just get to tell my story of the closet, coming out, and same-sex attraction. Couser (1997) suggests that for legitimate and valuable life writing to occur— for others to find personal experience important—an author must say something new about cultural experience by way of countering dominant narratives, adding to hegemonic storylines, disrupting storytelling convention(s), and/or developing a new genre of writing.[7] If stories seem repetitive, they may be perceived to lack value (Adams, 2008).

Writing about my experience as a gay man would not seem too innovative or exciting—this has been done many times in many ways. What I need to do is to find the "gaps" (Goodall, 2001) in existing research about and writing on the closet, coming out, and same-sex attraction. And these gaps are one way I approached assembling this book.

For instance, in my research I documented unique experiences of the closet, coming out, and same-sex attraction that are not often included in discussions about these phenomena. The formation of the closet—how "coming in" happens—is not a topic writers have discussed in explicit, nuanced, and concise ways (Chapter 2). The time of "being closeted" is not discussed in these ways, either (Chapter 3). Leaving the closet—the time of "coming out"—is a dominant story; however, I attempted to engage in a meticulous understanding of the event (Chapter 4). I consider paradoxes of the closet—coming out to strangers and acquaintances—and the search for acknowledgment from friends and family as contemporary, understudied dilemmas tied to same-sex attraction (Chapter 5). Using information from these chapters, I then developed strategies a person could use to disrupt harmful closet-experiences and everyday paradoxes, and concluded with lessons I have learned from identifying as gay (Chapter 6).

Informal, Unsolicited Conversations; or, Researching Life as Lived

I mention characteristics of my coming-out disclosures because there have been many situations in which persons who identify as LGBQ, or who struggle to identify as LGBQ, have asked me about my experiences with and advice about the closet and coming out. Consequently, I have participated in many informal and unsolicited conversations about same-sex attraction.

There was the person interviewing me for a job who told me, on the interview, that he was gay but no one else at his university knew; he feared it would tarnish his case for tenure.

There was the student who, the week after I came out to the class, wrote in a class paper that she likes women but refuses to talk about it with anyone—as of this writing, three years later, she says she still has come out only to one other person.

There was the high school acquaintance, who, after seeing on my Facebook.com page that I like men, called for advice on getting out of reparative therapy, therapy that tried to change—that is, "correct"— his same-sex attraction.

There was the student who told me, in my office, that his mother and father said he was "no longer their son," kicked him out of the house, and refused contact.

There was the friend whose father was "outed" to her after having an affair with a man, who emailed to ask for advice on humane and respectful ways to tell him that she loves him and that his attraction to men is okay.

In classrooms and my office, in restaurants and bars, in online environments and at festivals and churches, I never know when someone will ask or tell me about struggles with the closet, coming out, and same-sex attraction. Furthermore, such conversations continue as my gay identity—particularly my public embrace of this identity—encourages others to share their dilemmas and secrets with me, trusting that I would not ridicule them or out them to others. They not only consider me an insider—someone who may have experiences similar to theirs—but also someone they trust and consider safe. I am not just "one of them;" I am one of them who will not say a word about who they claim or feel to be; these persons believe they have much to lose, if their same-sex attraction is revealed.

Such informal and unsolicited conversations are important ethnographic material: Even though they happened unsystematically and serendipitously, they illustrate how fieldwork can happen in relation to LGBQ cultures, particularly because such "natural" discourse offers glimpses of the closet and coming out that more organized and intentional efforts to gather information about these phenomena do not. They offer an "accidental," "surprising," and "unplanned" glimpse into LGBQ experience (Poulos, 2008, p. 47), one that allows me to attend to "life itself"—the world of "everyday encounters" (Freeman, 2004, p. 73). By treating these conversations as data, I move beyond the "rarefied atmosphere of the interview" and explore "people's lives *outside* the research context" (p. 73).

Informal and unsolicited conversations also require me to use great care: ethically, I must protect the privacy of these persons by masking or altering identifying details such as context, topics discussed, and a person's race, gender, or name. Even though these conversations are part of my experience, LGBQ persons still encounter many personal and social pressures. Consequently, they need to be protected, aggressively, especially if they are being used in ways they may never want or know. While fabrication can influence the understanding of these conversations, protection and concern for the persons involved trump the need for actual, historical truth; the essence and meaning of the conversations are important, not necessarily the precise recounting of identifying details (Bochner, 2002b; Freeman, 2010; Tullis et al., 2009).

Furthermore, I consider these conversations a part of my experience as teacher, mentor, and friend to others with same-sex attraction. Consequently, I find them relevant for autoethnography. The situations distinguish cultural experiences of LGBQ persons from the experiences of other kinds of people, and are situations I frequently experience—ones that speak to the secrecy, fear, and isolation persons with same-sex attraction may encounter.

I also do not believe these conversations would have happened had I identified as heterosexual or had I not said anything about being gay. I recognize that this belief may suggest that a heterosexual or non-out LGBQ person cannot study LGBQ cultural experience, but to some extent I agree: the closet, coming out, and same-sex attraction—constitutive characteristics of LGBQ cultures—are important phenomena to study. Informal and unsolicited conversations provide necessary insights into these phenomena. As long as a heterosexual or non-out LGBQ person can come across as trustworthy and safe, then the person may be able to access unique relational facets of LGBQ cultures, particularly if she or he has been asked about effective ways to come out, ways of improving harmful relational situations tied to same-sex attraction, and/or if she or he is familiar with LGBQ barriers and resources (for example, Tillmann-Healy, 2001).

Interviews

In addition to using my experience with and informal, unsolicited conversations about the closet, coming out, and same-sex attraction, I interviewed persons about their experiences with these phenomena. However, out of concern for safety and an ethic of care, I interviewed only persons (a) out to me who were (b) willing to speak about their experiences of same-sex attraction. Although safety and care are important for interviews, they are even more crucial when a person speaks about same-sex attraction; given that consequences for coming out still exist, and knowing that what a person says may appear in a public document (this book), only some people may participate (Rao & Sarma, 2009). Given these assumptions, I chose to interview friends and acquaintances about their experiences with same-sex attraction.

I conducted two kinds of interviews: interactive interviews (Ellis, Kiesinger, & Tillmann-Healy, 1997) and life story interviews (Bruner, 1986). Interactive interviews are best used for acquiring an "in-depth and intimate understanding of people's experiences with emotionally charged and sensitive topics" (Ellis, Kiesinger, & Tillmann-Healy, 1997, p. 121). Interactive interviews usually occur with friends or acquaintances who have experience with the topics discussed. Interactive interviews are collaborative endeavors between researchers and participants, endeavors in which all persons probe one another, together, about issues that transpire in conversation. Interactive interviews usually consist of multiple interview sessions and are situated within the context of emerging, interpersonal relationships.

I conducted interactive interviews with five lesbians and four gay men about their experiences with homophobia. I did not use a predetermined set of questions for these interviews but often started our conversation with "How do you define coming out?" "What does it mean to be LGBQ?" and/or "Have you ever experienced homophobia?" I allowed conversations to proceed organically with everyone sharing experiences. I then wrote up our conversations, met with each person to discuss my report of the conversation, and incorporated their feedback into my writing.

Life story interviews provide insight into how people make sense of their lives (Atkinson, 2002, 2007). Believing that experience is best described through story, Bruner (1986) conducted life story inter-views with a family of four: a father, a mother, a son, and a daughter. He first asked each person to tell her or his life story in one half hour. He then spent another half hour asking each person about how she or he constructed the life story. Bruner concludes by suggesting that patterns of a story influence the structure of lived experience; an in-extricable connection exists between the stories a person tells and the life she or he lives.

I conducted life story interviews with four, self-identified gay men all of whom were friends of mine. Using Bruner (1986) as a model, each interview consisted of three meetings. In the first meeting I asked each man to record his life story in 30 minutes. In the second and third meetings I formulated comments and questions based on information shared in the recording from the first meeting. These comments and questions included my responses to each man's re-cording, topics that needed greater specification, and topics the men did not discuss but that, because of my knowledge of them, I felt had affected their lives. For instance, if I knew that a man's same-sex at-traction influenced his experiences, but the man did not discuss this attraction or influence, I asked about his experiences with same-sex attraction as well as why he left these experiences out of his story. These interviews provided more information than interactive inter-views but required a greater time commitment.

Mass-Mediated Representations of Same-Sex Attraction

I also found mass-mediated representations of same-sex attraction important, particularly because these representations provide public, easily accessible insights into relational experiences of the closet and coming out as well as help to constitute ideas about and experiences of LGBQ cultures; they show what being LGBQ means and how the closet and coming out might look and feel. For this project I examined (a) life writings by persons who possess same-sex attraction and (b) televised, film, and audio representations of the closet and coming out.

Life writings (for example, memoirs, autobiographies, and journals) address significant temporal experiences of same-sex attraction—experiences across childhood, adolescence, and adult-hood. These texts also provide insight into acts and interactions dif-ficult for a researcher to witness. For instance, the act of coming out to another person is difficult to observe. Researchers of same-sex attraction must thus rely on self-reports of the event. "My boyfriend wanted me to be there when he came out to his mom," Tyler says in an interview.

> I told him that would be unfair for her. With me there, she would be unable to express herself like she would want to. Without me, she could do whatever she wanted. If she wanted to scream she could scream. If she wanted to cuss she could cuss. (2007)

As an act of self-disclosure, coming out is rarely witnessed by outsiders as lived, and it is not an event for which a researcher can choose to be present. Sometimes a person may ask another to witness the event—as Tyler's boyfriend asked of Tyler—but being able to observe the event in action is rare. And as Tyler observes, being present for this kind of disclosure may show disrespect for the person to whom a person comes out.

For this project I examined eight life writings—*Surviving Madness* (Berzon, 2002), *Gary in Your Pocket* (Fisher, 1996), *Body, Remember* (Fries, 2003), *What Becomes of the Brokenhearted* (Harris, 2003), *Covering* (Yoshino, 2006), *Mean Little Deaf Queer* (Galloway, 2009), *Times Square Red, Times Square Blue* (Delany, 1999), and *Truth Serum* (Cooper, 1996)—and six anthologies—*Word Is Out* (Adair & Adair, 1978), *Boys Like Us* (Merla, 1996), *A Member of the Family* (Preston, 1992), *When I Knew* (Trachtenberg, 2005), *From Boys to Men* (Gideonse & Williams, 2006), and *Whistling in the Dark* (Rao & Sarma, 2009).

Life writings have unique limitations. Not every person has narrative privilege—the safety to write and publish a life story or the ability or desire to navigate conventional and political requirements for publishing (Adams, 2008; Couser, 1997; Freeman, 2010; Lorde, 1984). Furthermore, self-reports of interaction—not only life writings but also reports gleaned from interviews and personal experience—do not allow a researcher to observe the unobstructed, lived characteristics of coming out—characteristics that would have occurred regardless of and unhindered by a researcher's presence (Bochner, 1989; Soukup, 1992).

However, other kinds of mass-mediated representations (for example, television, film, audio programs) of the closet, coming out, and same-sex attraction can accommodate the self-reporting limitation of life writings, interviews, and personal experience. Although scripted, edited, limited by time, and sometimes stereotypical, these representations portray same-sex attraction in relational contexts and can thus represent and constitute, for audiences, how the closet and coming out looks and feels. In other words, these representations can inform (live) social interaction—providing strategies for persons—all persons—to better navigate same-sex attraction as lived; art can imitate life, but life can also imitate art.

For this project I examined representations of the closet, coming out, and same-sex attraction featured in sitcoms such as *Will & Grace*, films such as *Sordid Lives, Were the World Mine, For the Bible Tells Me So*, and *A Single Man*, and episodes of the *Savage Love Podcast*.

Assembling the Book: Working with and Representing the Data

In Chapter 1 I mentioned that my goal was to provide a "thick description" (Geertz, 1973, p. 10) and, consequently, facilitate understanding of the closet, coming out, and same-sex attraction—constitutive characteristics of LGBQ cultures. To accomplish this goal, I treated my personal experience, informal and unsolicited conversations, interviews, and mass-mediated representations of same-sex attraction as valuable sources of "data"—as long as the sources illuminated experiences of the closet, coming out, and same-sex attraction.

My work with these sources was recursive: I first engaged in "initial coding" (Charmaz, 1983) of the sources, a process in which I discerned themes, inductively, across the sources—themes evidenced by repeated words, phrases, and storylines. Once I discerned themes, I then noticed these themes, deductively, when I reviewed existing and forthcoming data sources (Denton & Zelley, 2010).

For instance, when I first coded my experience, conversations, interviews, and mass-mediated representations, I noticed four major themes: a time before ever being able to come out (Chapter 2); a time of being out to oneself but not others (Chapter 3); a time of coming out to others (Chapter 4); and a time post-coming out (Chapter 5). I also noticed minor themes—the conditions, characteristics, and premises—of these major themes. Thus, I organized not only this book thematically but also the contents of each chapter.

However, once I developed these themes, I then noticed them in existing and forthcoming data sources. For instance, I might read a book or article, have an experience, or watch a film that spoke to one or more of the themes. I would then include the material in this book, especially if the material skillfully illustrated an argument or observation. Even though I trapped myself by preformed themes, leaving out sources that further illuminated these themes felt neglectful.

Furthermore, my training in communication carries particular assumptions that guided my development of themes. I was interested in *interaction*, particularly how people relate, what happens when different assumptions and perspectives align and collide, and how conflicts develop. I attended to ways people used and interpreted language, constructed and understood discourse, and engaged in harmful relational practices. My focus on interaction thus made particular features of the closet, coming out, and same-sex attraction more salient than others. For instance, I was not interested in psychological characteristics of a person who identifies as LGBQ or if the person suffered from "internalized homophobia." Rather, I was interested in how this person's relationships were influenced by her or his embrace of same-sex attraction and how, in turn, the person's relationships affected her or his experience of the closet.

□

I used a variety of writing techniques to represent my themes. I used a collage of texts—my experiences, others' experiences, mass-mediated representations, and extant research—to create a "layered account" (Ronai, 1995, 1996) of the closet, coming out, and same-sex attraction. I used square bullets to denote shifts between my themes—shifts between times and space, experiences and persona (Ronai, 1992). I rearranged sequences of some events and changed names and places to "take pressure off" real people and organizations (Fine, 1993, p. 287; see also Richardson, 1992). I compressed a significant amount of time into the text, and I made decisions about the "emphasis, tone, syntax," and "diction" of my writing (Mandel, 1968, p. 218).

I also used different "voices"—points of view—in writing. Sometimes I used first-person voice to tell a story, typically stories I personally experienced. I did so to present an intimate, immediate, and involving "eyewitness account" of a situation (Caulley, 2008, p. 442). Sometimes I used second-person voice to bring readers into a scene, to actively witness, with me, the experience, to be a part of rather than distanced from an event (for example, Glave, 2005; McCauley,

1996; Pelias, 2000). I also used second-person voice for moments I felt shameful to claim (see Chapter 3). Sometimes I used third-person voice to establish the context of an interaction, report my findings, and present what others do, say, or write.

I used characteristics of "showing" and "telling" as well (Adams, 2006; Hampl, 1999; Lamott, 1994). Showing "brings readers into the scene" (Ellis, 2004, p. 142) in order to evocatively "experience an experience" (Ellis, 1993, p. 711). Through the use of conversation I showed events that felt emotionally rich. Conversely, telling positions readers at a distance, provides an overview of a situation rather than an evocative experience of it and uses description that lacks the immediacy of dialogue and sensuous engagement. I told about events that felt fragmented and emotionally empty, events in which intellect took priority over emotion.

Criticisms

I must address four criticisms of this work. First, I have been told that, for some, *the closet no longer exists or matters*. In response to nearly every presentation or publication I have completed about the closet, an audience member or reviewer has said that the closet has lessened in significance and, consequently, is no longer a worthy topic of research. Persons with same-sex attraction have supposedly progressed beyond the metaphorical space; we live in a "post-closet" world (Hutson, 2010).

Second, coming out and the closet signify a *Eurocentric understanding of sexuality and same-sex attraction* (Jolly, 2001; Kong, Mahoney, & Plummer, 2002; La Pastina, 2006; Labi, 2007; Lee, 2003; Phellas, 2005; Rao & Sarma, 2009). A Eurocentric understanding often assumes that persons who engage in any kind of intimate same-sex act must be lesbian, gay, bisexual, and/or queer.

Third, *gay identity—an identity tied to, and made possible by, the closet—is a White identity* (Anzaldúa, 1991; Fung, 1996; Halberstam, 2005; Johnson, 2001; King, 2005; Lee, 2003; McCune, 2008; Perez, 2005; Ross, 2005; Yep, 2007). In the United States "gay marriage" is often positioned as one of the most pressing issues for persons with same-sex attraction. However, this is often a pressing issue only for privileged, often White, people. Other issues are overshadowed and disregarded because of the focus on marriage—issues such as racism, religion, economic disparity, access to healthcare, immigration, and homelessness.

Fourth, *gay identity is male-biased and misogynistic* (Halberstam, 2005; Jones, 2007; Tillmann, 2009a). "Gay" can be used as a general, neutral descriptor of both men and women (for example, "gay marriage") and used to distinguish men and male experience (for instance, "gays and lesbians"; Hubert, 1999). Lesbians—women who possess same-sex attraction—are also excluded from definitions of sex (acts), particularly when/if sex is conceived of as something that happens only when an (original, present-at-birth) penis penetrates a vagina and/or when a penis ejaculates; these criteria exclude any possibility of female-female sexual relations (Butler, 1991; Frye, 1983; Hans, Gillen, & Akande, 2009; Johnston, 1975). "I was never in danger of being thrown in jail for practicing sodomy," Julia Creet writes. "Not surprisingly, what constitutes homosexual sex in the public eye has always hung on the penis" (1991, p. 29).[8]

Furthermore, some people believe that men can be gay—and, consequently, able to come out of the closet—only if they assume a passive, penetrated role in sex. In this usage, a gay label does not apply to active, masculine penetrators. A man who "has sex with another man has little to do with 'gayness,'" Nadya Labi writes. "The act may fulfill a desire or a need, but it doesn't constitute an identity" (2007, p. 74). It is "being a bottom" that is "shameful" as bottoming "means playing a woman's role" (p. 78). This criterion not only illustrates a Eurocentric understanding of sexuality but also speaks to the masculine and misogynistic biases of gay identity, specifically how "playing a woman's role" is framed as shameful (Frank, 1993; Halberstam, 2005; Rao & Sarma, 2009).

I engaged these criticisms in three ways. First, I wrote for people who believe in and are held accountable for the closet. The metaphor continues to manifest itself in a variety of painful and puzzling ways, and coming out continues to create relational rifts and makes news headlines. To say the closet no longer exists is ignorant and impractical. If you believe the closet no longer matters, you may not have seen much value in this project.

Second, I made my discussion relevant for people who possess same-sex attraction, not only those who adhere to (Eurocentric) gay (male) identity. I did this by focusing on the embrace and revelation of same-sex attraction, not only the embrace and revelation of gay identity. Same-sex attraction can exist absent gay identity, but gay identity does not often exist absent same-sex attraction. I also tried to incorporate intersex, queer, transsexual, and transgender research into my discussion, and so qualified such terms as "sex," "gender," and "sexuality."

Third, I made the closet, coming out, and same-sex attraction *relational* phenomena by illustrating how *others* could hold a person accountable for these phenomena in a variety of ways, at a variety of times, and in a variety of places. Even though I identify as (and, consequently, write from the perspective of) a White, middle-class, able-bodied, college-educated, gay man living in the United States, and even though I interviewed and analyzed more writings by gay men, and even though a person with same-sex attraction may not feel as though the closet describes her or his experience, *others* may make meaning of, and, consequently, evaluate a person by way of the closet, coming out, and same-sex attraction. I wrote assuming that persons with same-sex attraction would negotiate the closet at some time whether they wanted to or not, and I tried to make my observations resonate with anyone who has been held accountable, unwittingly, for the closet.

In making the closet, coming out, and same-sex attraction relational phenomena, I rendered them phenomena everyone—straight, lesbian, gay, bisexual, queer, and so on—must negotiate. As I described earlier in the book, one reads stories about Ugandan officials wanting to exterminate persons with same-sex attraction and put persons who know of others with this attraction in prison if they do not turn these others in to authorities (Sharlet, 2010). This situation illustrates how same-sex attraction makes everyone accountable. *Everyone* with same-sex attraction has the possibility of being executed, and *anyone* who knows of others with same-sex attraction has the possibility of being incarcerated. The closet, coming out, and same-sex attraction are not just White issues or male battles; a person will be killed or incarcerated if she or he is Black (and gay), female (and a lesbian), or heterosexual (and knows someone with same-sex attraction).

☐

When writing this book, I did not strive to test predictions, control outcomes, or make generalizations about LGBQ cultures (Poulos, 2008, p. 47). I also did not believe my observations would or should resonate with everyone. Rather, I embarked on an autoethnographic journey to understand the closet, coming out, and same-sex attraction—a journey designed to help make the experience of these phenomena more humane or tolerable for others, and a journey to atone for mistakes of my past, to apologize to people I've taken for granted and to those I once wished harm, and to allow me to better recognize and accept my "inner demons" (Freeman, 2010, p. 35). I embarked on a journey with the hope of encouraging us all to learn ways of acknowledging and appreciating one another more.

Prologue

1. I received Joshua's permission to use his words in this book.

Chapter One

1. For a more comprehensive treatment of method, see the appendix.
2. This is a fairly new perspective on sexual identity. Historically, a person could possess same-sex attraction and even engage in same-sex sexual acts without ever having to identify as homosexual; socially, a homosexual identity was not constituted by object choice or sexual act but rather by a person's enactment of gender. As Rüling writes: "Homosexual women have many characteristics, inclinations, and abilities which we usually consider as valid for men" (2006 [1904], p. 29), adding that homosexual women who engage in feminine acts do so in order to "hide their homosexuality" (p. 37). Meyer (1995) argues that cross-dressing functioned as a dominant, "public marker" of homosexuality in the United States before 1950; Johnson (2004) agrees, noting that homosexual men marked sexuality by way of "distinctive clothing styles and mannerisms" (p. 45). If coming out rests on the disclosure of a homosexual/LGBQ identity, then a person cannot come out if she or he doesn't identify with or feel as though this identity applies to her or him. I return to this idea in Chapters 2 and 4; however, my purpose of mentioning this

history here is to show why a discussion of sexuality simultaneously requires a discussion of sex and gender.

3. Intersexed persons call this assumption into question. There
are people with clitorises that look like small penises and small
penises that look like clitorises. There are people with ovaries,
two X chromosomes, and visible vaginas, labias, and clitorises
but high amounts of testosterone. And there are people who produce sperm, possess X and Y chromosomes, and have visible
penises and testicles but who possess high amounts of estro-
gen (Coventry, 2000; Dreger, 2006; Fausto-Sterling, 1993, 2000;
Greenberg, 2002).

4. I thank Steve Schoen for introducing me to Buck Angel. To learn
more about Buck Angel, visit www.BuckAngel.com.

5. Each of these assumptions makes the others possible. The goal
of the gay chemical is to make enemy soldiers attracted to one
another. If the soldiers consisted of both men and women and if
they were heterosexual, then they would already be attracted to
one another (thus causing a unit to fail). Furthermore, turning
a coed unit of soldiers gay would be futile: instead of men coupling with women and women coupling with men, men would
couple with men and women with women. For the chemical to
work, enemy soldiers must be (a) of one sex and (b) heterosexual, that is, not already attracted to one another.

6. Although the use of a gay bomb may seem absurd, the gay bomb
metaphor was used at another time as well. In 1955 Arthur Guy
Mathews wanted newspapers across the United States to run the
headline "EXTRA, EXTRA! COMMUNISTS ARE NOW CONVERTING AMERICAN
YOUTH TO HOMOSEXUALITY TO DEFEAT US FROM WITHIN!" This conversion,
similar to the purpose of the gay bomb, would make the new
homosexuals "shriek, scream, cry, and break down into hyster-
ical states of psychoses when they are called upon to carry arms
to defend our shores from the enemy." The goal of homosexual
conversion was to make youth "physically weak" and, as such,
was considered by Mathews as "Stalin's Atom Bomb" (cited in
Johnson, 2004, p. 37). Unlike the more recent gay bomb, this
bomb assumes that men who become gay become feminized
and are thus made weak and helpless, a homophobic *and* misogynistic assumption.

7. Consider the case *Littleton v. Prange* (1999). Christie Littleton
was born male (sex) and underwent sex reassignment surgery,
an act that allowed her not only to change her birth certificate
from "male" to "female" but also to marry a man in Texas, a

heterosexual consummation further classifying her as female, since same-*sex* marriages were illegal in the state. Seven years after marriage, Jonathon, her husband, died as a result of medical error. Christie filed a malpractice suit against the doctors, but the defense argued that Christie was and will always be male because of her sex-at-birth and thus could not marry a man (because same-*sex* marriage was illegal). The defense won the argument, invalidating Christie's marriage to Jonathan (Greenberg, 2000).

8. Throughout this book I focus on the experiences of the closet and coming out as narrated by self-identified, sex-at-birth women and men—"cis-women" and "cis-men" (Stryker, 2008). My treatment of the closet should resonate with people who identify as transgender/sexual as well, but I do not claim to speak for or justly represent experiences of trans-people, particularly because I assume that a trans-person's experiences of the closet and coming out—experiences often intertwined with sex/gender ambiguities—may be different from the experience of a cis-woman or a cis-man. In other words, a trans-person may negotiate coming out processes similar to cis-women and -men, but, unlike cis-women and -men, the trans-person must also attend to disclosures of and responses to changes in sex and gender (Kailey, 2005; Schrock & Boyd, 2006).

Chapter Two

1. Although Delany (1999) uses this passage to critique interpellation, I believe he adequately describes how a closet begins to form and what must happen before a person could ever identify as LGBQ.

Chapter Four

1. Trans and LGBQ identities often share similar struggles with sex and gender. However, unlike LGBQ identities, transidentities are not constituted by same-sex attraction; a person can be trans-*and* heterosexual.

2. Even though Kagan's unmarried and childless status also contributed to people questioning her heterosexuality, I believe

gender inversion—as illustrated by the image—served as a significant impetus for such questioning.

3. Chapter 1 provides a more comprehensive overview of sex, gender, and sexuality.

4. In hetero-normative contexts, heterosexual attraction is often assumed and thus not discussed. One reason pride parades exist is to disrupt hetero-normative assumptions, illustrated best by the phrase "We're here! We're queer! Get used to it!" Another reason pride parades exist is to encourage persons with same-sex attraction to feel okay and normal about themselves and their relationships; by way of celebration and encouragement, they allow for temporary acceptance and appreciation—at least for a day, a weekend, or a month.

Chapter Five

1. Parts of this chapter and the next originally appeared in T. E. Adams (2010), Paradoxes of sexuality, gay identity, and the closet, *Symbolic Interaction 33*, 234–256. I thank the Society for the Study of Symbolic Interaction and the University of California for permission to reprint.

2. I recognize that coming out may not seem necessary for such a transactional interaction. However, my concern is that I have never read research that distinguishes between contexts, types of interaction, and coming out. Research tends to frame coming out as good and not coming out as bad, always and everywhere; nuances of context and interaction unfortunately proceed unacknowledged.

3. A note on form: I write this chapter in a less fragmented way than previous chapters. This is intentional. For me, the times of learning, living, and leaving the closet felt (and still feel) fragmented. Once I felt increasingly comfortable with my sexuality, I felt as though I knew how the closet could work as well as the ways in which I might manage coming out to strangers, acquaintances, friends, and family. However, new closet-related dilemmas soon emerged, particularly with everyday disclosures and the lack of acknowledgment by others of my intimate and meaningful same-sex relationships. But these troubles do not feel as fragmented and confusing as learning about, finding my way through, and coming out of the metaphorical closet space.

Consequently, I write these troubles not as fragmented and chaotic but as more secure, calm, and particular.

4. Willman distinguishes between "deliberate ambiguity"—not revealing "intricacies" of her personal life to acquaintances and strangers—and "deceptive ambiguity"—intentionally hiding her sexuality (2009, p. 207). In so doing, she makes a fine distinction about intentionality with regard to omitting information about same-sex attraction. However, even if her intentions about being silent about same-sex attraction are made known, *others* may still consider the act of omission a problem and consequently hold her accountable for being unhealthy or shameful, immature, dishonest, or politically irresponsible when her (not easily accessed) attraction later becomes known.

5. I am also not sure why saying "I am LGBQ" has, in some contexts, become synonymous with saying what the person does in private, behind closed doors. A person saying "I am heterosexual" says nothing about her or his sexual activities—only the sex of others to whom the person is attracted. I know many people who identify as heterosexual, but I have no idea about their sexual activities or desires. I may be able to infer some acts, but I do not know, with any certainty, what they do in private.

Chapter Six

1. Some of the conditions are difficult to manipulate. For example, it is impractical to quit using any language tied to same-sex attraction. Efforts could be made to discuss same-sex attraction earlier in a variety of contexts (for example, schools, families), but the need to have language in order to discuss same-sex attraction is not a condition easily conducive to change. It is also difficult to change the *marginal* characteristic of same-sex attraction, since heterosexuals seem to outnumber LGBQ persons. And I do not believe that same-sex attraction can or should go away on demand.

2. I recognize that a person might lie about her or his sexuality on Myspace, Facebook, and/or Twitter. But a person can lie about sexuality in everyday interaction, too. I can say I am gay today, bisexual tomorrow, queer the next, and heterosexual the following week. If I am stuck in the closet, I may feel a need to lie about my heterosexuality, too.

3. I recognize that such manipulation is quite simple, maybe too simple. However, if my goal is to create dissonance, then such comments suggest, to me, that dissonance happens, at least for some people. But this is one way to create dissonance, not the only way or the most ideal.

4. As I write this, Danville's local newspaper, *The Commercial News*, published "Too Much Sin in the World Today" (Lamar & Lamar, 2010), "Public Opinion Should Rule" (Jones, 2010), and "Pitts Misses the Whole Message" (Cunningham, 2010), three letters to the editor describing the immorality of same-sex attraction. I feel as though this is a common sentiment in the conservative community.

5. I recognize that mutual consent is complicated by variables such as age and ability. For instance, I do not think it is right for person who is 40 years old to couple with someone who is 10, even if both agree to the relationship. I also do not think a person should take advantage of someone whose understanding may be impaired or complicated by cognitive ability. But such examples are why I qualify my definition: if either person, in a possible relationship, tries to take advantage of another, then I do not believe a legitimate, mutually meaningful relationship exists.

6. As of this writing, out celebrities include Adam Lambert, Jane Lynch, George Takei, Meredith Baxter, Wanda Sykes, Lance Bass, Clay Aiken, Ricky Martin, Ellen DeGeneres, Rosie O'Donnell, Perez Hilton, Rachel Maddow, Wilson Cruz, Anna Paquin, Chely Wright, Darryl Stephens, Mary Cheney, Sean Hayes, Cynthia Nixon, Oscar Nuñez, Neil Patrick Harris, T. R. Knight, Lily Tomlin, Melissa Etheridge, Kelly McGillis, and Rufus Wainwright.

Appendix

1. In Chapter 1, I only briefly discussed the method for this project; I did not want methodological jargon to take away from the flow of the story. Thus I created this appendix to explain how I assembled this book. Although some of the information is redundant, this more thorough overview of method should serve as a template for studying controversial and not easily accessed phenomena such as the closet, coming out, and same-sex attraction.

2. Some reviewers have said that contemporary ethnographers take a broad orientation to defining culture. I respond ambivalently, knowing this is said with good intentions, but I do not see much evidence. Many books and journals about culture do not consider LGBQ communities as cultures. If LGBQ communities are mentioned, they are often referred to as co-cultures, subcultures, or lifestyles. And so I say to these reviewers: when I see LGBQ communities being treated as cultures more often and in a variety of research contexts, I will then believe that contemporary ethnographers take a broad orientation to defining culture.

3. An inverted take on this observation: I am not aware of research that investigates LGBQ cultural views of a particular region, race, or ethnicity—for example, "How do gay men view South Africans" or "How do lesbians view Asian-Americans?" I see only regional, racial, or ethnic (cultural) perspectives of same-sex attraction and homosexuality, not lesbian, gay, bisexual, or queer (cultural) perspectives of region, race, or ethnicity (for instance, Bennett & Battle, 2001; Desai, 2001; González, 2007; Kee Tan, 2001; La Pastina, 2006; Labi, 2007; Phellas, 2005; Rao & Sarma, 2009; Yep, Lovaas, & Ho, 2001).

4. "Homosexual" as a term descriptive of same-sex attraction did not exist until 1869; "gay," "lesbian," "bisexual," and "queer" did not serve as descriptors of same-sex attraction until the early to mid-20th century. Consequently, LGBQ cultures could not exist until persons started using these words to describe a group of (similar) people (Hacking, 1990; Meyer, 1995). Furthermore, since sexuality is not often discussed during a person's youth, LGBQ cultures are often learned about and develop for persons during the teenage years (Gideonse & Williams, 2006; Hayes, 1976).

5. Some reviewers have said that contemporary ethnography has moved beyond strict ties to space and the field. Again, I respond ambivalently, knowing this is said with good intentions, but I am not seeing much evidence. With some exception (for example, Markowitz, 2001), I do not know of ethnographies that explicitly disregard or aggressively critique the spatial bias of and requirement for fieldwork.

6. Virtual fields of LGBQ cultures exist (for instance, Campbell, 2004; Whitesel, 2010), but again the field-metaphor limits: LGBQ cultures are not tied to or constituted by these fields. I also do not believe that LGBQ cultural phenomena such as the closet, coming out, and same-sex attraction can be studied in a specific, physical or virtual field.

7. Couser says this best about writings on breast cancer: "it is symptomatic of the maturing of the breast cancer narrative that new narratives evince the need for a new angle; once the genre has been established, the experience of cancer is not necessarily sufficient to justify a narrative" (1997, p. 70).

8. The use of a penis and/or penile ejaculation are key criteria for sex, the latter criterion being best observed in the discourse of the Monica Lewinsky-Bill Clinton affair: It was Clinton's ejaculation on Monica's dress that signified "sexual relations" happened; if the/his semen did not exist, sex may not have occurred. I am not saying that physical contact between Lewinsky and Clinton did not happen but that if Clinton's penis did not ejaculate, their relations may not have been called "sexual." I define "sex" as acts involving intimate emotional and physical arousal, not necessarily acts motivating orgasm or acts contingent on penises and vaginas.

REFERENCES

Adair, N., & Adair, C. 1978. *Word is out: Stories of some of our lives.* New York: Dell.

Adam, B. D. 2000. Love and sex in constructing identity among men who have sex with men, *International Journal of Sexuality and Gender Studies* 5(4), 325–339.

Adams, T. E. 2002, November. Two's company: Living the gay life "straightly." Paper presented at the annual meeting of the National Communication Association, New Orleans, LA.

———. 2003a. Packaged wilderness: Problematizing simulated- and tele-vised-nature experience. Unpublished master's thesis, Southern Illinois University, Carbondale.

———. 2003b, November. Apparently I'm a "homo-phoney": Being accused of being "straight." Paper presented at the annual meeting of the National Communication Association, Miami, FL.

———. 2005. Speaking for others: Finding the "whos" of discourse, *Soundings* 88, 331–345.

———. 2006. Seeking father: Relationally reframing a troubled love story, *Qualitative Inquiry 12*, 704–723.

———. 2008. A review of narrative ethics, *Qualitative Inquiry 14*(2), 175–194.

———. 2009. Mothers, faggots, and witnessing (un)contestable experience, *Cultural Studies↔Critical Methodologies,* 9(5), 619–626.

———. 2010. Paradoxes of sexuality, gay identity, and the closet, *Symbolic Interaction 33*(2), 234–256.

Adams, T. E., & Holman Jones, S. 2008. Autoethnography is queer. In N. K. Denzin, Y. S. Lincoln, & L. T. Smith (Eds.), *Handbook of critical and indigen-ous methodologies* (pp. 373–390). Thousand Oaks, CA: Sage.

Advocate.com. 2010, August 17. Russian billionaire: Kill all gays. Accessed August 17, 2010, www.advocate.com/News/Daily_News/2010/08/17/Russian_Billionaire_Kill_Gays_and_Lesbians/.

Aldridge, B. 2004. Best face forward: The constitution of selves in autoperformance. Unpublished master's thesis, Southern Illinois University, Carbondale.

Alexander, J., & Losh, E. 2010. "A YouTube of one's own?" "Coming out" videos as rhetorical action. In C. Pullen & M. Cooper (Eds.), *LGBT identity and online new media* (pp. 37–50). New York: Routledge.

Alley-Young, G. 2006, March 10. Untitled [obituary guestbook entry]. Accessed September 1, 2007, www.legacy.com/TulsaWorld/GB/GuestbookView.asp x?PersonId = 16918149&PageNo = 3.

Ankleshwaria, D. 2009. [Untitled interview]. In R. R. Rao & D. Sarma (Eds.), *Whistling in the dark: Twenty-one queer interviews* (pp. 199–213). Thousand Oaks, CA: Sage.

Anonymous. 1993, July 20. The Pentagon's new policy guidelines on homosexuals in the military, *The New York Times*, p. A16.

Anonymous. 2007, June 14. What's next, gay lasers? *Tampa Bay Times*, p. 14.

Anzaldúa, G. 1991. To(o) queer the writer—Loca, escritora y chicana. In B. Warland (Ed.), *InVersions: Writings by dykes, queers, and lesbians* (pp. 249–263). Vancouver: Press Gang.

Aoki, E. 2005. Coming out as "We 3": Using personal ethnography and the case study to assess relational identity and parental support of gay male, three-partner relationships, *Journal of GLBT Family Studies 1*(2), 29–48.

Armesto, J. C., & Weisman, A. G. 2001. Attributions and emotional reactions to the identity disclosure ("coming out") of a homosexual child, *Family Process 40*(2), 145–161.

Asante, M. K., Miike, Y., & Yin, J. 2007. *The global intercultural communication reader*. New York: Routledge.

Associated Press. 2007, February 18. "I don't hate gay people," Hardaway now says. *MSNBC.com*. Accessed March 9, 2007, www.msnbc.msn.com/id/17160685/.

Atkinson, R. 2002. The life story interview. In J. F. Gubrium & J. A. Holstein (Eds.), *Handbook of interview research* (pp. 121–140). Thousand Oaks, CA: Sage.

———. 2007. The life story interview as a bridge in narrative inquiry. In D. J. Clandinin (Ed.), *Handbook of narrative inquiry* (pp. 224–245). Thousand Oaks, CA: Sage.

Barefoot, Ron. n.d. Gentle wisdom. Accessed March 2, 2007, www.pflag.com/pages/0021.html#intuition.

Bateson, G. 1951. Information and codification: A philosophical approach. In J. Ruesch & G. Bateson (Eds.), *Communication: The social matrix of psychiatry* (pp. 168–211). New York: W.W. Norton.

———. 2000. *Steps to an ecology of mind*. Chicago: University of Chicago Press.

Bell, D., & Valentine, G. 1995. Queer country: Rural lesbian and gay lives, *Journal of Rural Studies 11*(2), 113–122.

Bennett, J. A. 2003. Love me gender: Normative homosexuality and "ex-gay" performativity in reparative therapy narratives, *Text and Performance Quarterly 23*(4), 331–352.

Bennett, J. A. 2006. In defense of gaydar: Reality television and the politics of the glance, *Critical Studies in Media Communication* 23(5), 408–425.

Bennett, M., & Battle, J. 2001. "We can see them, but we can't hear them": LGBQ members of African American families. In M. Bernstein & R. Reimann (Eds.), *Queer families, queer politics: Challenging culture and the state* (pp. 53–67). New York: Colombia University Press.

Berlant, L. 1997. *The queen of America goes to Washington City.* Durham, NC: Duke University Press.

Berry, K. 2007. Embracing the catastrophe: Gay body seeks acceptance, *Qualitative Inquiry* 13(2), 259–281.

Berzon, B. 2002. *Surviving madness: A therapist's own story.* Madison: University of Wisconsin Press.

Betsky, A. 1997. *Queer space: Architecture and same-sex desire.* New York: William Morrow and Company.

Bloom, A. 2002. *Normal.* New York: Vintage.

Blow, C. M. 2010, June 4. Gay? Whatever, dude. *The New York Times.* Accessed June 30, 2010, www.nytimes.com/2010/06/05/opinion/05blow. html?_r = 1&hp.

Blumer, H. 1969. *Symbolic interactionism.* Englewood Cliffs, NJ: Prentice Hall.

Bochner, A. P. 1984. The functions of human communication in interpersonal bonding. In C. C. Arnold & J. W. Bowers (Eds.), *Handbook of rhetorical and communication theory* (pp. 544–621). Boston: Allyn and Bacon.

————. 1989. Interpersonal communication. In E. Barnouw (Ed.), *International encyclopedia of communications* (Vol. 2, pp. 336–340). New York: Oxford University Press.

————. 2002a. Love survives, *Qualitative Inquiry* 8(2), 161–169.

————. 2002b. Perspectives on inquiry III: The moral of stories. In M. L. Knapp & J. A. Daly (Eds.), *Handbook of interpersonal communication* (3rd ed., pp. 73–101). Thousand Oaks, CA: Sage.

Bockman, P. 1996. Fishing practice. In P. Merla (Ed.), *Boys like us* (pp. 73–81). New York: Avon.

Bolton, R. 1995. Tricks, friends, and lovers: Erotic encounters in the field. In D. Kulick & M. Willson (Eds.), *Taboo: Sex, identity, and erotic subjectivity in anthropological fieldwork* (pp. 140–167). New York: Routledge.

Borchard, K. 1998. Between a hard rock and postmodernism: Opening the Hard Rock Hotel and Casino, *Journal of Contemporary Ethnography* 27(2), 242–269.

Bornstein, K. 1994. *Gender outlaw.* New York: Routledge.

————. 2006. *Hello, cruel world.* New York: Seven Stories.

Boxer, A. M. 1997. Gay, lesbian, and bisexual aging into the twenty-first century: An overview and introduction, *Journal of Gay, Lesbian, and Bisexual Identity* 2(3/4), 187–197.

Boyd, H. 2006. The wife. In J. A. Kane-DeMaios & V. L. Bullough (Eds.), *Crossing sexual boundaries: Transgender journeys, uncharted paths* (pp. 179–192). Amherst, NY: Prometheus.

Braithwaite, D. O. 1994. Viewing persons with disabilities as a culture. In L. A. Samovar & R. E. Porter (Eds.), *Intercultural communication: A reader* (7th ed., pp. 148–154). Belmont, CA: Wadsworth.

Brodkey, L. 1987. Writing ethnographic narratives, *Written Communication* 4(1), 25–50.

Brodwater, T. 2006, October 20. Anti-gay sign goes up in Post Falls. *Spokesman Review*. Accessed October 20, 2006, www.spokesmanreview.com/breaking/story.asp?ID = 7701.

Bronski, M. 2003. Gay culture. In L. A. Samovar & R. E. Porter (Eds.), *Intercultural communication: A reader* (10th ed., pp. 138–144). Belmont, CA: Wadsworth.

Brouwer, D. 1998. The precarious visibility politics of self-stigmatization: The case of HIV/AIDS tattoos, *Text and Performance Quarterly* 18(2), 114–136.

———. 2004. Corps/Corpse: The U.S. military and homosexuality, *Western Journal of Communication* 68(4), 411–430.

Brouwer, D. C., & Hess, A. 2007. Making sense of "God Hates Fags" and "Thank God for 9/11": A thematic analysis of Milbloggers' responses to Reverend Fred Phelps and the Westboro Baptist Church, *Western Journal of Communication* 71(1), 69–90.

Brown, M. P. 2000. *Closet space: Geographies of metaphor from the body to the globe*. New York: Routledge.

Brown-Smith, N. 1998. Family secrets, *Journal of Family Issues* 19(1), 20–42.

Bruner, J. 1986. Life as narrative, *Social Research* 54, 11–32.

———. 1993. The autobiographical process. In R. Folkenflik (Ed.), *The culture of autobiography: Constructions of self-representation* (pp. 38–56). Stanford, CA: Stanford University Press.

Bryant, S. P. 2005. *Hung*. New York: Doubleday.

Burgess, S. 2005. Did the Supreme Court out in *Bush v. Gore*? Queer theory on the performance of the politics of shame, *Differences* 16(1), 126–146.

Burnie, J. 2008, March 25. Why can't my family accept that I'm gay? *Daily Record*. Accessed March 25, 2008, www.dailyrecord.co.uk/comment/columnists/lifestyle-columnists/joan-burnie/2008/03/25/why-can-t-my-family-accept-that-i-m-gay-86908-20362137/.

Butler, J. 1990. Performative acts and gender constitution: An essay in phenomenology and feminist theory. In S.-E. Case (Ed.), *Performing feminisms: Feminist critical theory and theatre* (pp. 270–282). Baltimore: The John Hopkins University Press.

———. 1991. Imitation and gender insubordination. In D. Fuss (Ed.), *Inside/out: Lesbian theories, gay theories* (pp. 13–31). New York: Routledge.

———. 1993. *Bodies that matter: On the discursive limits of "sex."* New York: Routledge.

———. 1997. *Excitable speech: A politics of the performative*. New York: Routledge.

———. 1999. *Gender trouble: Feminism and the subversion of identity* (2nd ed.). New York: Routledge.

Butler, J. 2004. *Undoing gender*. New York: Routledge.

Buzard, J. 2003. On auto-ethnographic authority, *The Yale Journal of Criticism* *16*(1), 61–91.

Campbell, J. E. 2004. *Getting it online: Cyberspace, gay male sexuality, and embodied identity*. New York: Harrington Park.

Carbaugh, D. 1999. "Just listen": "Listening" and landscape among the Blackfeet, *Western Journal of Communication 63*(3), 250–270.

Caulley, D. N. 2008. Making qualitative research reports less boring: The techniques of writing creative nonfiction, *Qualitative Inquiry 14*(3), 424–449.

CBC News. 2007, May 30. Montreal woman refused service at gay bar says rights violated. Accessed May 31, 2007, www.cbc.ca/canada/montreal/story/2007/05/30/qclestud.html?ref = rss.

Charmaz, K. 1983. The grounded theory method: An explication and interpretation. In R. M. Emerson (Ed.), *Contemporary field research: A collection of readings* (pp. 109–125). Prospect Heights, IL: Waveland.

Chávez, K. R. 2004. Beyond complicity: Coherence, queer theory, and the rhetoric of the "Gay Christian Movement," *Text and Performance Quarterly 24*(3/4), 255–275.

Chee, A. 2006. Dick. In T. Gideonse & R. Williams (Eds.), *From boys to men: Gay men write about growing up* (pp. 103–118). New York: Carroll & Graf.

Cherry, K. 1996. Ain't no grave deep enough, *Journal of Contemporary Ethnography 25*(1), 22–57.

Chesebro, J. W. 1981. *Gayspeak: Gay male and lesbian communication*. New York: The Pilgrim Press.

Chirrey, D. A. 2003. "I hereby come out": What sort of speech act is coming out? *Journal of Sociolinguistics 7*(1), 24–37.

Clatterbaugh, K. C. 1997. *Contemporary perspectives on masculinity: Men, women, and politics in modern society* (2nd ed.). Boulder, CO: Westview Press.

Cobb, M. 2006. *God hates fags: The rhetorics of religious violence*. New York: New York University Press.

Cole, R. 2006, May 20. Untitled [obituary guestbook entry]. Accessed September 1, 2007, www.legacy.com/TulsaWorld/GB/GuestbookView.aspx?Person.Id = 16918149&PageNo = 1.

Cole, S. W., Kemeny, M. E., Taylor, S. E., & Visscher, B. R. 1996. Elevated physical health risk among gay men who conceal their homosexual identity, *Health Psychology 15*(4), 243–251.

Colman, D. 2005, June 19. Gay or straight? Hard to tell, *The New York Times*, p. 9.1.

Cooper, B. 1996. *Truth serum*. Boston: Houghton Mifflin.

Cooper, M. 2010. Lesbians who are married to men. In C. Pullen & M. Cooper (Eds.), *LGBT identity and online new media* (pp. 75–86). New York: Routledge.

Corey, F. C. 1996. Performing sexualities in an Irish pub, *Text and Performance Quarterly 16*(2), 146–160.

Cornell, D. 2007. The shadow of heterosexuality, *Hypatia 22*(1), 229–242.

Corrigan, P. W., & Matthews, A. K. 2003. Stigma and disclosure: Implications for coming out of the closet, *Journal of Mental Health* 12(3), 235–248.

Cory, D. W. 1951. *The homosexual in America*. New York: Greenberg.

Couser, G. T. 1997. *Recovering bodies: Illness, disability, and life writing*. Madison: University of Wisconsin Press.

Coventry, M. 2000, October/November. Making the cut, *Ms. 10*, 52–60.

Creet, J. 1991. Lesbian sex/gay sex: What's the difference? *Out/look 11*, 29–34.

Crimp, D. 1993. Right on, girlfriend! In M. Warner (Ed.), *Fear of a queer planet: Queer politics and social theory* (pp. 300–320). Minneapolis: University of Minnesota Press.

Cunningham, B. 2010, October 17. Pitts misses the whole message [letter to the editor]. *The Commercial-News*. Accessed October 20, http://commercialnews.com/letters/x847469491/Pitts-misses-the-whole-message.

Cvetkovich, A. 2003. *An archive of feelings: Trauma, sexuality, and lesbian public culture*. Durham, NC: Duke University Press.

Dao, J. 2010, May 28. As "don't ask" fades, military faces thorny issues. *The New York Times*. Accessed June 30, 2010, from www.nytimes.com/2010/05/29/us/politics/29gays.html.

Davidson, A. I. 1985. Sex and the emergence of sexuality, *Critical Inquiry* 14(1), 16–48.

de Bruxelles, S. 2007, June 2. Boy, 15, lay down in front of train after gay taunts. Accessed June 10, 2007, www.timesonline.co.uk/tol/news/uk/article1873278.ece.

Delany, S. R. 1996. Coming/Out. In P. Merla (Ed.), *Boys like us: Gay writers tell their coming out stories* (pp. 1–26). New York: Avon.

———. 1999. *Times Square red, Times Square blue*. New York: New York University Press.

———. 2004. *The motion of light in water*. Minneapolis: University of Minnesota Press.

Denton, M., & Zelley, E. D. 2010. *Applying communication theory for professional life: A practical introduction*. Thousand Oaks, CA: Sage.

Denzin, N. K. 2003. *Performance ethnography: Critical pedagogy and the politics of culture*. Thousand Oaks, CA: Sage.

———. 2004. The war on culture, the war on truth. *Cultural Studies↔Critical Methodologies* 4(2), 137–142.

———. 2006. Mother and Mickey, *The South Atlantic Quarterly* 105(2), 391–395.

———. 2007. The secret downing street memo and the politics of truth: A performance text, *Cultural Studies↔Critical Methodologies* 7(2), 99–109.

Desai, G. 2001. Out in Africa. In J. C. Hawley (Ed.), *Postcolonial, queer: Theoretical intersections* (pp. 139–164). Albany: State University of New York Press.

Dictionary.com. n.d. Coming out. Accessed March 23, 2007, http://dictionary.reference.com/browse/coming%20out.

Didion, J. 2005. *The year of magical thinking*. New York: A. A. Knopf.

Diversi, M., & Moreira, C. 2010. *Betweener talk: Decolonizing knowledge production, pedagogy, and praxis.* Walnut Creek, CA: Left Coast Press.

Donnelly, E. 2009, June 29. Allowing gays in the military would be unfair and hurt troop morale. *U.S. News & World Report.* Accessed June 30, 2010, http://politics.usnews.com/opinion/articles/2009/06/29/allowing-gays-in-the-military-would-be-unfair-and-hurt-troop-morale.html.

Downs, A. 2005. *The velvet rage: Overcoming the pain of growing up gay in a straight man's world.* Cambridge, MA: Perseus.

Drash, W. 2010, May 20. When kin of slaves and owner meet. *CNN.* Accessed May 20, 2010, www.cnn.com/2010/LIVING/05/20/slavery.descendants.meet/?hpt=Sbin.

Dreger, A. D. 2006. Intersex and human rights. In S. E. Sytsma (Ed.), *Ethics and intersex* (pp. 73–86). Dordrecht: Springer.

Duffey, T. 2006. When a spouse comes out: As told from a straight spouse's point of view, *The Family Journal 14*(1), 88–91.

Edwards, T. 2005. Queering the pitch? Gay masculinities. In M. S. Kimmel, J. Hearn, & R. W. Connell (Eds.), *Handbook of studies on men and masculinities* (pp. 51–68). Thousand Oaks, CA: Sage.

Elizur, Y., & Ziv, M. 2001. Family support and acceptance, gay male identity formation, and psychological adjustment: A path model, *Family Process 40*(2), 125–144.

Ellis, C. 1986. *Fisher folk: Two communities on Chesapeake Bay.* Lexington: University Press of Kentucky.

———. 1993. "THERE ARE SURVIVORS": Telling a story of a sudden death, *The Sociological Quarterly 34*(4), 711–730.

———. 1995a. Emotional and ethical quagmires in returning to the field, *Journal of Contemporary Ethnography 24*(1), 68–98.

———. 1995b. *Final negotiations: A story of love, loss, and chronic illness.* Philadelphia: Temple University Press.

———. 1998. "I hate my voice": Coming to terms with minor bodily stigmas, *The Sociological Quarter, 39*(4), 517–537.

———. 2002a. Shattered lives: Making sense of September 11th and its aftermath. *Journal of Contemporary Ethnography 31*(4), 375–410.

———. 2002b. Being real: Moving inward toward social change, *Qualitative Studies in Education 15*(4), 399–406.

———. 2004. *The ethnographic I: A methodological novel about autoethnography.* Walnut Creek, CA: AltaMira Press.

———. 2007. Katrina and the cat: Responding to society's expendables, *Cultural Studies↔Critical Methodologies 7*(2), 188–201.

———. 2009. *Revision: Autoethnographic reflections on life and work.* Walnut Creek, CA: Left Coast Press.

Ellis, C., & Bochner, A. P. 2000. Autoethnography, personal narrative, reflexivity. In N. K. Denzin & Y. S. Lincoln (Eds.), *Handbook of qualitative research* (2nd ed., pp. 733–768). Thousand Oaks, CA: Sage.

Ellis, C., Kiesinger, C. E., & Tillmann-Healy, L. M. 1997. Interactive interviewing: Talking about emotional experience. In R. Hertz (Ed.), *Reflexivity and voice* (pp. 119–149). Thousand Oaks, CA: Sage.

Emeigh, J. G. 2006, April 13. Tech prof reports threat to police. *The Montana Standard*. Accessed April 15, 2006, from www.mtstandard.com/articles/2006/04/13/newsbutte/hjjdjfigjcfjjj.txt.

Escoffier, J. 2003. Gay-for-pay: Straight men and the making of gay pornography, *Qualitative Sociology 26*(4), 531–555.

Faber, A. 2002. Saint Orlan: Ritual as violent spectacle and cultural criticism, *The Drama Review 46*(1), 85–92.

Falconi, V. 2006, October 11. The importance of coming out. *Daily Mississippian*. Accessed April 21, 2007, http://media.www.thedmonline.com/media/storage/paper876/news/2006/10/11/Opinion/The-Importance.Of.Coming.Out-2342761.shtml.

Fausto-Sterling, A. 1993. The five sexes: Why male and female are not enough, *The Sciences (33)*2, 20–24.

———. 1995. How to build a man. In M. Berger, B. Wallis, & S. Watson (Eds.), *Constructing masculinity* (pp. 127–134). New York: Routledge.

———. 2000. The five sexes, revisited, *The Sciences 40*(4), 18–23.

Feigenbaum, E. F. 2007. Heterosexual privilege: The political and the personal, *Hypatia 22*(1), 1–9.

Feinberg, L. 1993. *Stone butch blues*. Los Angeles: Alyson Books.

Fine, G. A. 1993. Ten lies of ethnography, *Journal of Contemporary Ethnography 22*(3), 267–294.

Ford, T. (Director). 2009. *A single man* [motion picture]. United States: The Weinstein Company.

Foster, E. 2008. Commitment, communication, and contending with heteronormativity: An invitation to greater reflexivity in interpersonal research, *Southern Communication Journal 73*(1), 84–101.

Foucault, M. 1978. *The history of sexuality: Volume 1* (R. Hurley, Trans.). New York: Vintage.

Fox, R. 2010. Re-membering daddy: Autoethnographic reflections of my father and Alzheimer's disease, *Text and Performance Quarterly 30*(1), 3–20.

Fox, T. C. 2010, March 15. Children denied Catholic schooling, lesbian couple speaks out. *National Catholic Reporter*. Accessed August 20, 2010, http://ncronline.org/news/faith-parish/children-denied-catholic-schooling-lesbian-couple-speaks-out.

Frank, B. 1993. Straight/strait jackets for masculinity: Educating for "real" men, *Atlantis 18*(1-2), 47–59.

Freeman, M. 2004. Data are everywhere: Narrative criticism in the literature of experience. In C. Daiute & C. Lightfoot (Eds.), *Narrative analysis: Studying the development of individuals in society* (pp. 63–81). Thousand Oaks, CA: Sage.

Freeman, M. 2010. *Hindsight: The promise and peril of looking back*. New York: Oxford University Press.

Fries, K. 2003 [1997]. *Body, remember*. New York: Dutton.

Frye, M. 1983. *The politics of reality: Essays in feminist theory*. Trumansburg, NY: Crossing Press.

Fung, R. 1996. Looking for my penis: The eroticized Asian in gay video porn. In R. Leong (Ed.), *Asian American sexualities: Dimensions of gay and lesbian experience* (pp. 181–198). New York: Routledge.

Fuss, D. 1991. Inside/out. In D. Fuss (Ed.), *Inside/out: Lesbian theories, gay theories* (pp. 1–10). New York: Routledge.

Gagné, P., Tewksbury, R., & McGaughey, D. 1997. Coming out and crossing over: Identity formation and proclamation in a transgender community, *Gender & Society 11*(4), 478–508.

Galloway, T. 2009. *Mean little deaf queer*. Boston: Beacon Press.

Gambone, P. 1996. Beyond words. In P. Merla (Ed.), *Boys like us* (pp. 98–114). New York: Avon.

Garfinkel, H. 1956. Conditions of successful degradation ceremonies, *The American Journal of Sociology 61*(5), 420–424.

———. 1967. *Studies in ethnomethodology*. Englewood Cliffs, NJ: Prentice-Hall.

Garrick, D. A. 1997. Ritual self-disclosure in the coming-out process, *Journal of Rural Studies 11*(2), 1–19.

———. 2001. Performances of self-disclosure: A personal history, *The Drama Review 45*(4), 94–105.

Gator Gay-Straight Alliance. 2004. I think I might be straight. Accessed December 1, 2007, http://grove.ufl.edu/~ggsa/pdf_docs/straightbrochure.pdf.

Geertz, C. 1973. *The interpretation of cultures*. New York: Basic Books.

Gelber, S. M. 1997. Do-it yourself: Constructing, repairing and maintaining domestic masculinity, *American Quarterly 49*(1), 66–112.

Gerber, D. A. 1996. The "careers" of people exhibited in freak shows: The problem of volition and valorization. In R. G. Thomson (Ed.), *Freakery: Cultural spectacles of the extraordinary body* (pp. 38–54). New York: New York University Press.

Gideonse, T., & Williams, R. 2006. *From boys to men: Gay men write about growing up*. New York: Carroll & Graf.

Gingrich-Philbrook, C. 1998. Disciplinary vision as gender violation: The stigmatized masculine voice of performance studies, *Communication Theory 8*(2), 203–220.

Ginsberg, A. 1974. Gay Sunshine Interview, *College English 36*(3), 392–400.

Glaadblog.org. 2010, January 14. GLAAD demands apology and retraction of dangerous anti-gay cartoon. Accessed January 15, 2010, http://glaadblog.org/2010/01/14/glaad-demands-apology-and-retraction-of-dangerous-anti-gay-cartoon/.

Glave, T. 2005. *Words to our now: Imagination and dissent*. Minneapolis: University of Minneapolis Press.

Glenn, E. N. 2000. The social construction and institutionalization of gender and race. In M. M. Ferree, J. Lorber, & B. B. Hess (Eds.), *Revisioning gender* (pp. 3–43). Walnut Creek, CA: AltaMira Press.

Goffman, E. 1959. *The presentation of self in everyday life*. New York: Doubleday.

———. 1963. *Stigma: Notes on the management of spoiled identity*. New York: Simon & Schuster.

———. 1967. *Interaction ritual: Essays on face-to-face behavior*. Garden City, NY: Anchor.

———. 1969. Strategic Interaction. In *Strategic Interaction* (pp. 85–145). Philadelphia: University of Pennsylvania Press.

Goltz, D. B. 2009. *Queer temporalities in gay male representation: Tragedy, normativity, and futurity*. New York: Routledge.

González, M. A. 2007. Latinos *on da down low*: The limitations of sexual identity in public health, *Latino Studies* 5(1), 25–52.

Gooch, B. 1996. Coming out. Going back in. Coming out again. Etc. In P. Merla (Ed.), *Boys like us: Gay writers tell their coming out stories* (pp. 82–87). New York: Avon.

Goodall, H. L. 2001. *Writing the new ethnography*. Walnut Creek, CA: AltaMira Press.

———. 2006. *A need to know: The clandestine history of a CIA family*. Walnut Creek, CA: Left Coast Press.

Gorman, E. M. 1992. The pursuit of the wish: An anthropological perspective on gay male subculture in Los Angeles. In G. Herdt (Ed.), *Gay culture in America* (pp. 87–106). Boston: Beacon Press.

Gray, E. R. 2001. Looking for a city: The ritual and politics of ethnography. In C. L. Dews & C. L. Law (Eds.), *Out in the South* (pp. 173–184). Philadelphia: Temple University Press.

Green, R. C. 2006. Signs. In T. Gideonse & R. Williams (Eds.), *From boys to men: Gay men write about growing up* (pp. 57–68). New York: Carroll & Graf.

Greenberg, J. A. 2000. When is a man a man, and when is a woman a woman? *Florida Law Review* 52, 745–768.

———. 2002. Definitional dilemmas: Male or female? Black or white? The law's failure to recognize intersexuals and multiracials. In T. Lester (Ed.), *Gender nonconformity, race, and sexuality* (pp. 102–124). Madison: University of Wisconsin Press.

Grever, C. 2001. *My husband is gay*. Berkeley, CA: The Crossing Press.

Grigoriadis, V. 2009, June 25. Wild idol: The psychedelic transformation and sexual liberation of Adam Lambert, *Rolling Stone* 1081, 50–57.

Gross, L. 1991. The contested closet: The ethics and politics of outing, *Critical Studies in Mass Communication* 8(3), 352–388.

Gudykunst W., & Mody, B. 2001. *Handbook of international and intercultural communication*. Thousand Oaks, CA: Sage.

Gupta, A. 2009. [Untitled interview]. In R. R. Rao & D. Sarma (Eds.), *Whistling in the dark: Twenty-one queer interviews* (pp. 166–174). Thousand Oaks, CA: Sage.

Gust, S. W., & Warren, J. T. 2008. Naming our sexual and sexualized bodies in the classroom: And the important stuff that comes after the colon, *Qualitative Inquiry 14*(1), 114–134.

Gustafson, T. (Director). 2008. *Were the world mine* [Motion picture]. United States: Wolfe Video.

Hacking, I. 1990. Making up people. In E. Stein (Ed.), *Forms of desire: Sexual orientation and the social constructionist controversy* (pp. 69–88). New York: Garland.

———. 1999. *The social construction of what?* Cambridge, MA: Harvard University Press.

Hailsham, V. 1955. Homosexuality and society. In J. T. Rees & H. V. Usill (Eds.), *They stand apart: A critical survey of the problems of homosexuality* (pp. 21–35). London: William Heinemann.

Halberstam, J. 2005. Shame and white gay masculinity, *Social Text 23*(3-4), 219–233.

Halley, J. E. 1989. The politics of the closet: Towards equal protection for gay, lesbian, and bisexual identity, *UCLA Law Review 36*, 915–976.

Halperin, D. M. 2007. *What do gay men want? An essay on sex, risk, and subjectivity.* Ann Arbor: University of Michigan.

Halperin, D. M., & Traub, V. 2010. *Gay shame.* Chicago: University of Chicago Press.

Hammers, C. 2009. An examination of lesbian/queer bathhouse culture and the social organization of (im)personal sex, *Journal of Contemporary Ethnography 38*(3), 308–335.

Hampl, P. 1999. *I could tell you stories: Sojourns in the land of memory.* New York: W.W. Norton.

Hans, J. D., Gillen, M., & Akande, K. 2009. Sex redefined: The reclassification of oral-genital contact, *Perspectives on Sexual and Reproductive Health 42*(2), 74–78.

Harris, E. L. 2003. *What becomes of the brokenhearted.* New York: Doubleday.

Hayes, J. J. 1976. Gayspeak, *Quarterly Journal of Speech 62*(3), 256–266.

Hegna, K. 2007. Coming out, coming into what? Identification and risks in the "coming out" story of a Norwegian late adolescent gay man, *Sexualities 10*(5), 582–602.

Henry, J. 1965. *Pathways to madness.* New York: Random House.

Herdt, G. 1992. *Gay culture in America: Essays from the field.* Boston: Beacon Press.

Herdt, G., & Boxer, A. 1992. Introduction: Culture, history, and life course of gay men. In G. Herdt (Ed.), *Gay culture in America: Essays from the field* (pp. 1–28). Boston: Beacon Press.

Herrell, R. K. 1992. The symbolic strategies of Chicago's gay and lesbian pride day parade. In G. Herdt (Ed.), *Gay culture in America: Essays from the field* (pp. 225–252). Boston: Beacon Press.

Holman Jones, S., & Adams, T. E. 2010. Autoethnography and queer theory: Making possibilities. In N. K. Denzin & M. G. Giardina (Eds.), *Qualitative inquiry and human rights* (pp. 136–157). Walnut Creek, CA: Left Coast Press.

Hom, A. Y. 1995. Stories from the homefront: Perspectives of Asian American parents with lesbian daughters and gay sons. In R. Leong (Ed.), *Asian American sexualities: Dimension of the gay and lesbian experience* (pp. 37–49). New York: Routledge.

Hopcke, R. H. 1993. Homphobia and analytical psychology. In R. H. Hopcke & K. L. Carrington (Eds.), *Same-sex love and the path to wholeness* (pp. 68–87). Boston: Shambhala.

Hopkins, P. D. 1998. How feminism made a man out of me: The proper subject of feminism and the problem of men. In T. Digby (Ed.), *Men doing feminism* (pp. 33–56). New York: Routledge.

Hubert, S. J. 1999. What's wrong with this picture? The politics of Ellen's coming out party, *Journal of Popular Culture* 33(2), 31–36.

Human Rights Campaign. 2005. *Resource guide to coming out for gay, lesbian, bisexual and transgender Americans.* Washington, D.C.: Human Rights Campaign Foundation.

Humphreys, L. 1975. *Tearoom trade: Impersonal sex in public places.* Hawthorne, NY: Aldine de Gruyter.

Hunt, M. 2007, April 16. Untitled. Accessed April 16, 2007, www.myspace.com /smada79.

Hunter, A. 1992. Same door, different closet: A heterosexual sissy's coming-out party, *Feminism & Psychology* 2(3), 367–385.

Hunter, D. 1996. The cure. In P. Merla (Ed.), *Boys like us: Gay writers tell their coming out stories* (pp. 284–292). New York: Avon.

Hutson, D. J. 2010. Standing OUT/Fitting IN: Identity, appearance and authenticity in gay and lesbian communities, *Symbolic Interaction* 33(2), 213–233.

Hyde, M. J. 2004. The ontological workings of dialogue and acknowledgment. In R. Anderson, L. A. Baxter, & K. N. Cissna (Eds.), *Dialogue: Theorizing difference in communication studies* (pp. 57–73). Thousand Oaks, CA: Sage.

———. 2006. *The life-giving gift of acknowledgment.* West Lafayette, IN: Purdue University Press.

Jackman, M. C. 2010. The trouble with fieldwork: Queering methodologies. In K. Browne & C. J. Nash (Eds.), *Queer methods and methodologies: Intersecting queer theories and social science research* (pp. 113–128). Burlington, VT: Ashgate.

Jackson, S. 2006. Gender, sexuality and heterosexuality: The complexity (and limits) of heteronormativity, *Feminist Theory* 7(1), 105–121.

Jacobs, A. T. 2007. I'm here! Am I queer? Analyzing the discourse of being openly closeted. Paper presented at the annual meeting of the National Communication Association, Chicago.

Jacquard, P. 2007, April 22. A matter of life and death, *The Advocate* 22.

Jandt, F. E., & Darsey, J. 1981. Coming out as a communicative process. In J. W. Chesebro (Ed.), *Gayspeak: Gay male and lesbian communication* (pp. 12–27). New York: The Pilgrim Press.

Johnson, D. K. 2004. *The lavender scare: The Cold War persecution of gays and lesbians in the federal government.* Chicago: The University of Chicago Press.

Johnson, E. P. 2001. "Quare" studies, or (almost) everything I know about queer studies I learned from my grandmother, *Text and Performance Quarterly 21*(1), 1–25.

Johnston, J. 1975, June. Are lesbians "gay"? *Ms.*, 85–86.

Johnston, L. 2005. *Queering tourism: Paradoxical performances at gay pride parades.* New York: Routledge.

Jolly, M. 2001. Coming out of the coming out story: Writing queer lives, *Sexualities 4*(4), 474–496.

Jones, L. K. 2010, August 25. Public opinion should rule [letter to the editor]. *The Commercial-News.* Accessed August 26, 2010, from http://commercial-news.com/letters/x281470562/Public-opinion-should-rule.

Jones, Jr., R. G. 2007. Drag queens, drama queens, and friends: Drama and performance as a solidarity building function in a gay male friendship circle, *Kaleidoscope: A Graduate Journal of Qualitative Communication Research 6*, 61–84.

Jorgenson, J. 2002. Engineering selves: Negotiating gender and identity in technical work, *Management Communication Quarterly 15*(3), 350–380.

Joshua. 2006, June 21. Old friends. Accessed September 1, 2007, http://blog.myspace.com/index.cfm?fuseaction=blog.view&friendID=2272761&blogID=135401139.

Kailey, M. 2005. *Just add hormones: An insider's guide to the transsexual experience.* Boston: Beacon Press.

Karslake, D. G. (Producer/Director). 2007. *For the Bible tells me so* [Motion picture]. United States: Atticus Group.

Kates, S. M., & Belk, R. W. 2001. The meanings of lesbian and gay pride day: Resistance through consumption and resistance to consumption, *Journal of Contemporary Ethnography 30*(4), 392–429.

Kee Tan, C. 2001. Transcending sexual nationalism and colonialism: Cultural hybridization as process of sexual politics in '90s Taiwan. In J. C. Hawley (Ed.), *Postcolonial, queer: Theoretical intersections* (pp. 123–137). Albany: State University of New York Press.

Kennedy, E. L., & Davis, M. 1996. Constructing an ethnohistory of the Buffalo Lesbian Community: Reflexivity, dialogue, and politics. In E. Lewin & W. L. Leap (Eds.), *Out in the field: Reflections of gay and lesbian anthropologists* (pp. 171–199). Urbana, IL: University of Illinois.

Khire, B. 2009. [Untitled interview]. In R. R. Rao & D. Sarma (Eds.), *Whistling in the dark: Twenty-one queer interviews* (pp. 256–264). Thousand Oaks, CA: Sage.

Kielwasser, A. R., & Wolf, M. A. 1992. Mainstream television, adolescent homosexuality, and significant silence, *Critical Studies in Mass Communication, 9*(4), 350–373.

Kim, M.-S. 2002. *Non-western perspectives on human communication: Implications for theory and practice.* Thousand Oaks, CA: Sage.

Kimmel, M. S., & Mahler, M. 2003. Adolescent masculinity, homophobia, and violence, *American Behavioral Scientist 46*(10), 1439–1458.

King, J. L. 2005. *On the down low.* New York: Harlem Moon.

Kirk, A. 2008. Coming out or staying in? The unfortunate specificity of the pedagogical "closet." Paper presented at the annual meeting of the Central States Communication Association, Madison, WI.

Kong, T. S. K., Mahoney, D., & Plummer, K. 2002. Queering the interview. In J. F. Gubrium & J. A. Holstein (Eds.), *Handbook of interview research* (pp. 239–258). Thousand Oaks, CA: Sage.

Kuhn, T. S. 1962. *The structure of scientific revolutions*. Chicago: University of Chicago Press.

Kus, R. J. 1985. Stages of coming out: An ethnographic approach, *Western Journal of Nursing Research* 7(2), 177–198.

La Pastina, A. C. 2006. The implications of an ethnographer's sexuality, *Qualitative Inquiry* 12(4), 724–735.

Labi, N. 2007. The kingdom of the closet, *Atlantic Monthly* 299, 70–82.

Laing, R. D. 1969. *Self and others*. New York: Pantheon.

Lakoff, G., & Johnson, M. 1980. *Metaphors we live by*. Chicago: University of Chicago Press.

Lamar, A., & Lamar, G. 2010, April 16. Too much sin in world today [letter to the editor]. *The Commercial News*. Accessed April 30, 2010, http://commercialnews.com/letters/x563621301/Too-much-sin-in-world-today.

Lamott, A. 1994. *Bird by bird: Some instructions on writing and life*. New York: Anchor.

Lawrence, D. H. 1914. The Prussian officer. In *The Prussian officer and other stories* (pp. 1–33). Freeport, NY: Books for Libraries Press.

Leap, W. L. 1996. *Word's out: Gay men's English*. Minneapolis: University of Minnesota Press.

Leary, T. 1957. *Interpersonal diagnosis of personality*. New York: Ronald Press Company.

Lee, J. A. 1979. The gay connection, *Urban Life* 8(2), 175–198.

Lee, W. 2003. Kuaering queer theory: My autocritography and a race-conscious, womanist, transnational turn, *Journal of Homosexuality* 45(2/3/4), 147–170.

Leeds-Hurwitz, W. 2005. Ethnography. In K. L. Fitch & R. E. Sanders (Eds.), *Handbook of language and social interaction* (pp. 327–353). Mahwah, NJ: Lawrence Erlbaum.

Levine, M. P. 1979. Gay ghetto, *Journal of Homosexuality* 4(4), 363–377.

Lewin, E., & Leap, W. L. 1996. *Out in the field: Reflections of lesbian and gay anthropologists*. Urbana: University of Illinois.

Liang, A. C. 1997. The creation of coherence in coming-out stories. In A. Livia & K. Hall (Eds.), *Queerly phrased: Language, gender, and sexuality* (pp. 287–309). New York: Oxford University Press.

Lim-Hing, S. 1990/91. Dragon ladies, snow queens, and Asian-American dykes: Reflections on race and sexuality, *Empathy* 2(2), 20–22.

Lindenberger, M. 2007, March 16. An evangelical's concession on gays. *Time*. Accessed March 26, 2007, www.time.com/time/nation/article/.0,8599,1599987,00.html.

Lindquist, J. 2002. *A place to stand: Politics and persuasion in a working-class bar*. Oxford: Oxford University Press.

Lorde, A. 1984. *Sister outsider*. Berkeley, CA: The Crossing Press.

Lynch, F. R. 1992. Nonghetto gays: An ethnography of suburban homosexuals. In G. Herdt (Ed.), *Gay culture in America* (pp. 165–201). Boston: Beacon Press.

Macintosh, L. 2007. Does anyone have a band-aid? Anti-homophobia discourses and pedagogical impossibilities, *Educational Studies 41*(1), 33–43.

Majors, R. E. 1994. Discovering gay culture in America. In L. A. Samovar & R. E. Porter (Eds.), *Intercultural communication: A reader* (pp. 165–171). Belmont, CA: Wadsworth.

Makagon, D. 2004. *Where the ball drops: Days and nights in Times Square*. Minneapolis: University of Minnesota Press.

Mandel, B. J. 1968. The autobiographer's art, *The Journal of Aesthetics and Art Criticism 27*(2), 215–226.

Markowitz, L. 2001. Finding the field: Notes on the ethnography of NGOs. *Human Organization 60*(1), 40–46.

Marvasti, A. 2006. Being Middle Eastern American: Identity negotiation in the context of the war on terror, *Symbolic Interaction 28*(4), 525–547.

Maso, I. 2001. Phenomenology and ethnography. In P. Atkinson, A. Coffey, S. Delamont, J. Lofland, & L. Lofland (Eds.), *Handbook of ethnography* (pp. 136–144). Thousand Oaks, CA: Sage.

McCauley, S. 1996. Let's say. In P. Merla (Ed.), *Boys like us: Gay writers tell their coming out stories* (pp. 186–192). New York: Avon.

McCune, J., & Jeffrey, Q. 2008. "Out" in the club: The down low, Hip-Hop, and the Architexture of Black masculinity, *Text and Performance Quarterly 28*(3), 298–314.

McDonald, G. J. 1982. Individual differences in the coming out process for gay men: Implications for theoretical models, *Journal of Homosexuality 8*(1), 47–60.

McDonough, M. 2006, April 18. Gays in Iraq fear for their lives. *BBC News*. Accessed April 18, 2006, http://news.bbc.co.uk/1/hi/world/middle_east/4915172.stm.

McGinty, M. 2006. Peristalsis. In T. Gideonse & R. Williams (Eds.), *From boys to men: Gay men write about growing up* (pp. 273–285). New York: Carroll & Graf.

McIntosh, M. 1968. The homosexual role, *Social Problems 16*(2), 182–192.

McLean, K. 2007. Hiding in the closet? Bisexuals, coming out and the disclosure imperative, *Journal of Sociology 43*(2), 151–166.

Mead, G. H. 1962 [1934]. *Mind, self, and society from the standpoint of a social behaviorist*. Chicago: University of Chicago Press.

Merla, P. (Ed.). 1996. *Boys like us*. New York: Avon.

Meyer, I. H., & Dean, L. 1998. Internalized homophobia, intimacy, and sexual behavior among gay and bisexual men. In G. Herek (Ed.), *Stigma and sexual orientation: Understanding prejudice against lesbians, gay men, and bisexuals* (pp. 160–186). Thousand Oaks, CA: Sage.

Meyer, M. 1995. The signifying invert: Camp and the performance of nineteenth-century sexology, *Text and Performance Quarterly 15*(4), 265–281.

Meyer, M. D. E. 2005. Drawing the sexuality card: Teaching, researching, and living bisexuality, *Sexuality & Culture 9*(1), 3–13.

Meyerowitz, J. 2002. *How sex changed: A history of transsexuality in the United States*. Cambridge, MA: Harvard University Press.

Michels, S. 2008, March 14. Politician's "anti-gay" speech sparks outrage. *ABC News*. Accessed April 4, 2008, http://abcnews.go.com/TheLaw/story?id = 4444956.

Miletic, D. 2007, May 29. Straight-out ban at gay venues sparks uproar. Accessed May 31, 2007, www.theage.com.au/articles/2007/05/28/1180205160437.html.

Minson, J. 1981. The assertion of homosexuality, *m/f 5-6*, 19–39.

Mohr, R. D. 1992. *Gay ideas: Outing and other controversies*. Boston: Beacon Press.

Monaghan, L., & Goodman, J. E. 2007. *A cultural approach to Interpersonal Communication*. Malden, MA: Blackwell.

Mosher, C. M. 2001. The social implications of sexual identity formation and the coming-out process: A review the theoretical and empirical literature, *The Family Journal 9*(2), 164–173.

Muñoz, J. E. 1999. *Disidentifications: Queers of color and the performance of politics*. Minneapolis: University of Minnesota Press.

Murphy, T. 2007, December 18. Gay vs. Trans in America, *The Advocate* 18–28.

Neumann, M. 1999. *On the rim: Looking for the Grand Canyon*. Minneapolis: University of Minnesota Press.

Newton, E. 1979. *Mother camp: Female impersonators in America*. Chicago: University of Chicago Press.

Nicholas, C. L. 2004. Gaydar: Eye-gaze as identity recognition among gay men and lesbians, *Sexuality and Culture 8*(1), 60–86.

Norton, J. 2008, May 23. The evil that *tbt** brings to our world [letter to the editor], *Tampa Bay Times,* p. 17.

Orbe, M. P. 1998. *Constructing co-cultural theory: An explication of culture, power, and communication*. Thousand Oaks, CA: Sage.

Oxford American desk dictionary and thesaurus. 2001. (2nd ed.). New York: Berkley.

Padva, G. 2004. Edge of seventeen: Melodramatic coming-out in new queer adolescence films, *Communication and Critical/Cultural Studies 1*(4), 355–372.

Panikkar, S. 2009. [Untitled interview]. In R. R. Rao & D. Sarma (Eds.), *Whistling in the dark: Twenty-one queer interviews* (pp. 225–246). Thousand Oaks, CA: Sage.

Pascoe, C. J. 2007. *Dude, you're a fag: Masculinity and sexuality in high school.* Berkeley and Los Angeles: University of California Press.

Pearson, C. L. 1986. *Good-bye, I love you.* New York: Random House.

Pelias, R. J. 2000. The critical life, *Communication Education 49*(3), 220–228.

———. 2005. Performative writing as scholarship: An apology, an argument, an anecdote, *Cultural Studies↔Critical Methodologies 5*(4), 415–424.

Perez, H. 2005. You can have my brown body and eat it, too! *Social Text 23* (3-4), 171–191.

Perry, L. A. M., & Ballard-Reisch, D. 2004. There's a rainbow in the closet: On the importance of developing a common language for "sex" and "gender." In P. M. Backlund & M. R. Williams (Eds.), *Readings in gender communication* (pp. 17–34). Belmont, CA: Thomson/Wadsworth.

Phelan, P. 1993. *Unmarked: The politics of performance.* New York: Routledge.

Phellas, C. N. 2005. Cypriot gay men's accounts of negotiating cultural and sexual identity: A qualitative study, *Qualitative Sociology Review 1*(2), 65–83.

Philipsen, G. 1975. Speaking "like a man" in Teamsterville: Culture patterns of role enactment in an urban neighborhood, *Quarterly Journal of Speech 61*(1), 13–22.

———. 1976. Places for speaking in Teamsterville, *Quarterly Journal of Speech 62*(1), 15–25.

Phillips, C. 1996. Sea level. In P. Merla (Ed.), *Boys like us: Gay writers tell their coming out stories* (pp. 328–338). New York: Avon.

Pierce, C. 2007. Anti-homosexual and gay: Rereading Sartre, *Hypatia 22*(1), 10–23.

Pineau, E. 2000. *Nursing Mother* and articulating absence, *Text and Performance Quarterly 20*(1), 1–19.

Plummer, K. 1995. *Telling sexual stories: Power, change and social worlds.* New York: Routledge.

Poulos, C. N. 2008. *Accidental ethnography: An inquiry into family secrecy.* Walnut Creek, CA: Left Coast Press.

Pozycki, T. 2006. The lives and deaths of buffalo butt. In T. Gideonse & R. Williams (Eds.), *From boys to men: Gay men write about growing up* (pp. 89–101). New York: Carroll & Graf.

Prell, B. 2006, March 7. Untitled [obituary guestbook entry]. Accessed September 1, 2007, www.legacy.com/TulsaWorld/GB/GuestbookView.asp x?PersonId = 16918149&PageNo = 4.

Preston, J. (Ed.). 1992. *A member of the family: Gay men write about their families.* New York: Dutton.

Proulx, A. 1999. Brokeback mountain. In *Close range: Wyoming stories* (pp. 253–283). New York: Scribner.

Puente, M. 2010, August 24. Hollywood now opening arms to gay characters, families. *USA Today.* Accessed August 26, 2010, www.usatoday.com/life/ movies/news/2010-08-24-gayshollywood23_CV_N.htm?csp = usat.me.

Queers. 1990. Queers read this. Accessed June 20, 2007, www.qrd.org/qrd/ misc/text/queers.read.this.

Rao, R. R., & Sarma, D. 2009. *Whistling in the dark: Twenty-one queer interviews.* Thousand Oaks, CA: Sage.

Rasmussen, M. L. 2004. The problem of coming out, *Theory into Practice 43*(2), 144–150.

Rawlins, W. K. 1983. Openness as problematic in ongoing friendships: Two conversational dilemmas, *Communication Monographs 50*(1), 1–13.

Rees, J. T., & Usill, H. V. 1955. Introduction. In J. T. Rees & H. V. Usill (Eds.), *They stand apart: A critical survey of the problems of homosexuality* (pp. vii–xii). London: William Heinemann.

Richardson, L. 1992. Trash on the corner: Ethics and technography, *Journal of Contemporary Ethnography 19*, 103–119.

———. 2009. Tales from the crypt, *International Review of Qualitative Research 2*(3), 345–350.

Ronai, C. R. 1992. The reflexive self through narrative: A night in the life of an erotic dancer/researcher. In C. Ellis & M. G. Flaherty (Eds.), *Investigating subjectivity: Research on lived experience* (pp. 102–124). Newbury Park, CA: Sage.

———. 1995. Multiple reflections of child sex abuse, *Journal of Contemporary Ethnography 23*(4), 395.

———. 1996. My mother is mentally retarded. In C. Ellis & A. P. Bochner (Eds.), *Composing ethnography: Alternative forms of qualitative writing* (pp. 109–131). Walnut Creek, CA: AltaMira Press.

Rooke, A. 2010. Queer in the field: On emotions, temporality and performativity in ethnography. In K. Browne & C. J. Nash (Eds.), *Queer methods and methodologies: Intersecting queer theory and social science* (pp. 25–39). Burlington, VT: Ashgate.

Rosenhan, D. L. 1984. On being sane in insane places. In P. Watzlawick (Ed.), *The invented reality: How do we know what we believe to know?* (pp. 117–144). New York: W. W. Norton.

Ross, M. B. 2005. Beyond the closet as raceless paradigm. In E. P. Johnson & M. G. Henderson (Eds.), *Black queer studies: A critical anthology* (pp. 161–189). Durham, NC: Duke University Press.

Rüling, A. 2006 [1904]. What interest does the women's movement have in solving the homosexual problem? In M. A. Lomardi-Nash (Ed.), *Sodomites and Urnings: Homosexual representations in classic German journals* (pp. 25–40). New York: Haworth.

Russell, G. M., & Bohan, J. S. 2006. The case of internalized homophobia: Theory and/as practice, *Theory & Psychology 16*(3), 343–366.

Rust, P. C. 1993. "Coming out" in the age of social constructionism: Sexual identity formation among lesbian and bisexual women, *Gender & Society 7*(1), 50–77.

Savage, D. 2007, November 6, Episode 55. *Savage love podcast.* Accessed December 1, 2007, http://podcasts.thestranger.com/savagelove/.

Saylor, S. 1992. My mother's ghost. In J. Preston (Ed.), *A member of the family: Gay men write about their families* (pp. 61–74). New York: Dutton.

Schrock, D., & Boyd, E. M. 2006. Reflexive transembodiment. In D. Waskul & P. Vannini (Eds.), *Body/embodiment* (pp. 51–66). Burlington, VT: Ashgate.

Scott, D. 1994. Jungle Fever? Black gay identity politics, white dick, and the utopian bedroom, *GLQ 1*(3), 299–321.

Scott, M. B., & Lyman, S. M. 1968. Accounts, *American Sociological Review 33*(1), 46–62.

Sedgwick, E. K. 1990. *Epistemology of the closet.* Berkeley and Los Angeles: University of California Press.

———. 1993. *Tendencies.* Durham, NC: Duke University Press.

——— (Ed.). 1996. *Gary in your pocket: Stories and notebooks of Gary Fisher.* Durham, NC: University of North Carolina Press.

———. 2003. *Touching feeling: Affect, pedagogy, performativity.* Durham, NC: Duke University Press.

Seidman, S. 2002. *Beyond the closet: The transformation of gay and lesbian life.* New York: Routledge.

Seidman, S., Meeks, C., & Traschen, F. 1999. Beyond the closet? The changing social meaning of homosexuality in the United States, *Sexualities* 2(1), 9–34.

Sela, N. 2006, July 11. Prize offerred [*sic*] to whoever kills gay person. *Ynet News.* Accessed July 11, 2006, www.ynetnews.com/articles/0,7340,L3273891,00. html#n.

Shakespeare, T. 1999. Coming out and coming home, *Journal of Gay, Lesbian, and Bisexual Identity* 4(1), 39–51.

Shallenberger, D. 1991. Invisible minorities: Coming out of the classroom closet, *Journal of Management Education* 15(3), 325–334.

Sharlet, J. 2010, September. Straight man's burden: The American roots of Uganda's anti-gay persecutions, *Harper's Magazine,* 36–48.

Shelburne, C. 2010, June 4. Chely Wright discusses coming out and hitting the road. *CMT.com.* Accessed June 30, 2010, www.cmt.com/news/country-music/1640798/chely-wright-discusses-coming-out-and-hitting-the-road. jhtml.

Shitole, M. 2009. [Untitled interview]. In R. R. Rao & D. Sarma (Eds.), *Whistling in the dark: Twenty-one queer interviews* (pp. 74–84). Thousand Oaks, CA: Sage.

Shores, D. (Director). 2000. *Sordid lives* [Motion picture]. United States: Daly-Harris Productions.

Shugart, H. A. 2005. On misfits and margins: Narrative, resistance, and the poster child politics of Rosie O'Donnell, *Communication and Critical/Cultural Studies* 2(1), 52–76.

Shweder, R. A. 1986. Divergent rationalities. In D. W. Fiske & R. A. Shweder (Eds.), *Metatheory in social science: Pluralisms and subjectivities* (pp. 163–196). Chicago: University of Chicago Press.

Signorile, M. 1990, May 16. Outing seizes America, *Outweek 46,* 40.

———. 2007, January 16. Goodbye to the closet, *The Advocate* 42.

Simmel, G. 1964. *The sociology of Georg Simmel* (K. H. Wolff, Trans.). New York: The Free Press.

Skelton, T. 1997. Issues of sexuality in the teaching space, *Journal of Geography in Higher Education* 21(3), 424–431.

Slavin, S. 2004. Drugs, space, and sociality in a gay nightclub in Sydney, *Journal of Contemporary Ethnography* 33(3), 265–295.

Sloop, J. M. 2004. *Disciplining gender: Rhetorics of sex identity in contemporary U.S. culture.* Amherst: University of Massachusetts Press.

Smith, G. 2010, May 3. . . . the only openly gay male athlete, *Sports Illustrated* 54–62.

Solis, S. 2007. Snow White and the Seven "Dwarfs"—Queercripped, *Hypatia* 22(1), 114–131.

Somerville, S. 1994. Scientific racism and the emergence of the homosexual body, *Journal of the History of Sexuality* 5(2), 243–266.

Sontag, S. 1964. Notes on "Camp," *Partisan Review* 31(4), 515–530.

Soukup, P. 1992. Interpersonal communication, *Communication Research Trends* 12(3).

Stein, A. 2010. The incredible shrinking lesbian world and other queer conundra, *Sexualities* 13(1), 21–32.

Stern, H. (Executive Producer). 2006, May 3. *Howard Stern on demand* [Internet broadcast]. Accessed December 1, 2006, www.indemand.com/HSOD/index.jsp.

Stewart, C. O. 2005. A rhetorical approach to news discourse: Media representations of a controversial study on "reparative therapy," *Western Journal of Communication* 69(2), 147–166.

Stryker, S. 2008. *Transgender history*. Berkeley, CA: Seal Press.

Styles, J. 1979. Outsider/insider: Researching gay baths, *Urban Life* 8(2), 135–152.

Sublette, N. 1981. Cowboys are frequently secretly (fond of each other) [recorded by W. Nelson]. On *Cowboys Are Frequently Secretly (Fond of Each Other)* [CD]. Nashville, TN: Dreamworks Records (2006).

Sullivan, N. 2008. The role of medicine in the (trans)formation of "wrong" bodies, *Body & Society* 14(1), 105–116.

Supel, N. J. 2008, May 27. The real evil in our world? Intolerance [letter to the editor], *Tampa Bay Times,* p. 20.

Tam, J., & Heinz, F. 2010, August 24. Child of married lesbians denied enrollment into school. *NBCDFW.com.* Accessed August 27, 2010, www.msnbc.msn.com/id/38787661.

Taylor, J. 2000. On being an exemplary lesbian: My life as a role model, *Text and Performance Quarterly* 20(1), 58–73.

Thompson, R. L. 2006, August 20. I'm human. Accessed March 1, 2008, http://blog.myspace.com/index.cfm?fuseaction=blog.view&friendID=52 226707&blogID=158206522.

Tillmann, L. M. 2009a. The state of unions: Politics and poetics of performance, *Qualitative Inquiry* 15(3), 545–560.

———. 2009b. Body and bulimia revisited: Reflections on "A Secret Life," *Journal of Applied Communication Research* 37(1), 98–112.

———. 2009c. Don't ask, don't tell: Coming out in an alcoholic family, *Journal of Contemporary Ethnography* 38(6), 677–712.

Tillmann-Healy, L. M. 2001. *Between gay and straight: Understanding friendship across sexual orientation*. Walnut Creek, CA: AltaMira Press.

Trachtenberg, R. (Ed.). 2005. *When I knew*. New York: HarperCollins.

Tullis Owen, J. A., McRae, C., Adams, T. E., & Vitale, A. 2009. Truth troubles, *Qualitative Inquiry 15*(2), 178–200.

Ulrichs, K. H. 2006 [1862]. Four letters to his kinsfolk (M. A. Lombardi-Nash, Trans.). In M. A. Lomardi-Nash (Ed.), *Sodomites and urnings: Homosexual representations in class German journals* (pp. 1–20). New York: Haworth.

Urbach, H. 1996. Closets, clothes, disClosure, *Assemblage 30*, 62–73.

Van Gelder, L. 1998 [1984]. Marriage as a restricted club. In P. J. Annas & R. C. Rosen (Eds.), *Against the current* (pp. 294–297). Upper Saddle River, NJ: Prentice Hall.

Van Maanen, J. 1988. *Tales of the field: On writing ethnography*. Chicago: University of Chicago Press.

Walker, L. M. 1993. How to recognize a lesbian: The cultural politics of looking like what you are, *Signs: Journal of Women in Culture and Society 18*(4), 866–890.

Watzlawick, P., Beavin, J. H., & Jackson, D. D. 1967. *Pragmatics of human communication*. New York: W.W. Norton & Company.

Watzlawick, P., Weakland, J. H., & Fisch, R. 1974. *Change: Principles of problem formation and problem resolution*. New York: W. W. Norton & Company.

Waugh, T. 2009. [Untitled interview]. In R. R. Rao & D. Sarma (Eds.), *Whistling in the dark: Twenty-one queer interviews* (pp. 85–96). Thousand Oaks, CA: Sage.

West, C., & Zimmerman, D. H. 1987. Doing gender, *Gender & Society 1*(2), 125–151.

Whitesel, J. 2010. Gay men's use of online pictures in fat-affirming groups. In C. Pullen & M. Cooper (Eds.), *LGBT identity and online new media* (pp. 215–229). New York: Routledge.

Whitney, E. 2006. Capitalizing on camp: Greed and the Queer marketplace, *Text and Performance Quarterly 26*(1), 36–46.

Wilkinson, S., & Kitzinger, C. 1994. The social construction of heterosexuality, *Journal of Gender Studies 3*(3), 307–316.

Williams, R., & Gideonse, T. 2006. Introduction. In T. Gideonse & R. Williams (Eds.), *From boys to men: Gay men write about growing up* (pp. vii–xi). New York: Carroll & Graf.

Willman, R. K. 2009. Coming out when you're not really in: Coming out as a teachable moment, *Feminism & Psychology 19*(2), 205–209.

Winderman, I. 2007, February 15. "I hate gay people," former Heat star Tim Hardaway declares. *Sun-Sentinel*. Accessed March 9, 2007, www.sun-sentinel.com/sports/sfl-215hardaway,0,2415610.story?coll = sfla-sports-front.

Yep, G. A. 1998. My three cultures: Navigating the multicultural identity landscape. In J. N. Martin, T. K. Nakayama, & L. A. Flores (Eds.), *Readings in cultural contexts* (pp. 79–85). Mountain View, CA: Mayfield.

———. 2003. The violence of heteronormativity in communication studies: Notes on injury, healing, and queer world-making, *Journal of Homosexuality 45*(2/3/4), 11–60.

Yep, G. A., & Elia, J. P. 2007. Queering/Quaring blackness in *Noah's Arc*. In T. Peele (Ed.), *Queer popular culture: Literature, media, film, and television* (pp. 27–40). New York: Palgrave Macmillan.

Yep, G. A., Lovaas, K. E., & Ho, P. C. 2001. Communication in "Asian American" families with queer members: A relational dialectics perspective. In M. Bernstein & R. Reimann (Eds.), *Queer families, queer politics* (pp. 152–172). New York: Columbia University Press.

Yoshino, K. 2006. *Covering: The hidden assault on our civil rights*. New York: Random House.

INDEX

ABOUT THE AUTHOR

Tony E. Adams is an assistant professor in the Department of Communication, Media, and Theatre at Northeastern Illinois University. He received an Associate's degree from Danville Area Community College (Danville, IL), Bachelor's and Master's degrees from Southern Illinois University (Carbondale), and a Doctorate from the University of South Florida (Tampa). He studies and teaches about interpersonal and family communication, sex, gender, and sexuality, qualitative research, and communication theory. He has published in journals such as *Qualitative Inquiry, Soundings, Cultural Studies↔Critical Methodologies, Symbolic Interaction, Communication Teacher,* and *The Review of Communication* and books such as *The Handbook of Critical and Interpretive Methodologies* (Sage) and *Qualitative Inquiry and Human Rights* (Left Coast Press). He lives in Chicago with his partner, Gerardo Moreno.

5'6"